CULTURE, LEARNING, AND TECHNOLOGY

Culture, Learning, and Technology: Research and Practice provides readers with an overview of the research on culture, learning, and technology (CLT) and introduces the concept of culture-related theoretical frameworks. In 13 chapters, the book explores the theoretical and philosophical views of CLT, presents research studies that examine various aspects of CLT, and showcases projects that employ best practices in CLT. Written for researchers and students in the fields of Educational Technology, Instructional Design, and the Learning Sciences, this volume represents a broad conceptualization of CLT and encompasses a variety of settings. As the first significant collection of research in this emerging field of study, *Culture, Learning, and Technology* overflows with new insights into the increasing role of technology use across all levels of education.

Angela D. Benson is Associate Professor of Instructional Technology at the University of Alabama, USA.

Roberto Joseph is Associate Professor of Educational Technology and Graduate Director of Educational Technology programs at Hofstra University, USA.

Joi L. Moore is a Professor in the School of Information Science & Learning Technologies at the University of Missouri, USA.

CULTURE, LEARNING, AND TECHNOLOGY

Research and Practice

Edited by Angela D. Benson,
Roberto Joseph and Joi L. Moore

NEW YORK AND LONDON

First published 2017
by Routledge
711 Third Avenue, New York, NY 10017

and by Routledge
2 Park Square, Milton Park, Abingdon, Oxon, OX14 4RN

Routledge is an imprint of the Taylor & Francis Group, an informa business

© 2017 Taylor & Francis

The right of Angela D. Benson, Roberto Joseph, and Joi L. Moore to be identified as the authors of the editorial material, and of the authors for their individual chapters, has been asserted in accordance with sections 77 and 78 of the Copyright, Designs and Patents Act 1988.

All rights reserved. No part of this book may be reprinted or reproduced or utilised in any form or by any electronic, mechanical, or other means, now known or hereafter invented, including photocopying and recording, or in any information storage or retrieval system, without permission in writing from the publishers.

Trademark notice: Product or corporate names may be trademarks or registered trademarks, and are used only for identification and explanation without intent to infringe.

Library of Congress Cataloging-in-Publication Data
A catalog record for this book has been requested

ISBN: 978-1-138-92852-7 (hbk)
ISBN: 978-1-138-92853-4 (pbk)
ISBN: 978-1-315-68168-9 (ebk)

Typeset in Bembo
by Apex CoVantage, LLC

CONTENTS

1 Introduction to Culture, Learning, and Technology:
   Research and Practice 1
   Angela D. Benson, Roberto Joseph, and Joi L. Moore

2 Critical Pedagogy and Educational Technology 8
   Amy C. Bradshaw

3 Revisiting Instructional Technologists' Inattention to
   Issues of Cultural Diversity among Stakeholders 28
   Deepak Prem Subramony

4 Globalization, Ironic Binaries, and Instructional
   Technology: Toward the Emergence of a Robust
   Critical Theory of Technology 44
   Michael K. Thomas

5 Hip-Hop Music as a Pedagogical Tool: Teaching
   with Hip-Hop in Global Contexts 58
   Akesha M. Horton, Erik J. Byker, and Keith Heggart

6 Examining the Use of an Online Cultural Module to
   Increase Learners' Intercultural Sensitivity 75
   Joseph M. Terantino

7 How Cultural Factors Influence the Use of Social
Constructivist-Based Pedagogical Models of Distance Learning:
Examining Japanese Online Collaborative Behaviors   91
Bodi Anderson

8 Culture and Computational Thinking: A Pilot Study of
Operationalizing Culturally Responsive Teaching (CRT)
in Computer Science Education   109
*Leshell Hatley, Cynthia E. Winston-Proctor,
Gina M. Paige, and Kevin Clark*

9 Foundational Theories of Social Media Tools and Cultural
Competency: A Systematic Literature Review   127
*Sandra G. Nunn, Lequisha Brown-Joseph,
and Michelle Susberry Hill*

10 iDESIGN: Designing and Implementing a Culturally
Relevant Game-Based Curriculum   151
Roberto Joseph and James Diamond

11 Boys and Video Game Play: Re-engaging Boys
in the Classroom   165
*Shulong Yan, Yelim Mun, Jason A. Engerman,
and Alison Carr-Chellman*

12 Exploring Chinese International Students' Acceptance
of Mobile Learning   180
Zhetao Guo and Angela D. Benson

13 Students Making Science Games: The Design Process of
Students Incorporating Science Content into Video Games   196
Neda Khalili Blackburn and Kevin Clark

14 How the Cultural Clash of Essentialism and Progressivism
Shaped Technology Adoption: A Case Study of Culture,
Learning, and Technology   212
Steven Watkins and Mansureh Kebritchi

Contributors   *225*
Index   *231*

1

INTRODUCTION TO CULTURE, LEARNING, AND TECHNOLOGY

Research and Practice

Angela D. Benson, Roberto Joseph, and Joi L. Moore

Research over the past two decades has found that students who are allowed to identify with their home languages and cultures in their schools and communities can improve their learning (Banks, 1993; Ladson-Billings, 1994; Lee, 2007; Nieto, 2010). As our schools become more diverse, our learning environments and instructional products must meet the needs of the increasingly diverse student population. In order to promote student engagement among these learners and provide meaningful learning experiences for them, scholars in the field of instructional design and technology (e.g., Young, 2009; Richey, Klein, & Tracey, 2011) have begun to provide guidelines and models to incorporate cultural values in the design and development of learning environments that utilize technology.

Other scholars, as represented in the Culture, Learning and Technology (CLT) division of the Association for Educational Communications and Technology (AECT), are focused more broadly on the

> intersections and syntheses of culture, learning, and technology with particular emphases on championing inclusiveness and equity for the entire spectrum of human identification from individual, organizational, and behavioral contexts. These contexts include self-identification as well as societal identification that may influence one's experience with technology and learning.
>
> (Culture, Learning and Technology Division, 2016)

This book brings together in a single collection a series of 13 chapters that represent the spectrum of work being done at the intersection of CLT. The chapters present 1) theoretical and philosophical views of CLT; 2) research studies that examine various implementations of CLT; and 3) projects that employ best practices in CLT. The chapters represent a broad conceptualization of CLT and encompass a variety of settings. In this introduction, we present the definitions of culture, learning, and technology that bind these chapters followed by an overview of each chapter.

What is Culture?

While there are many definitions of culture, the concept remains difficult to define (Spencer-Oatey, 2012). In this volume, we embrace the broad view put forth by Spencer-Oatey (2008):

> Culture is a fuzzy set of basic assumptions and values, orientations to life, beliefs, policies, procedures and behavioural conventions that are shared by a group of people, and that influence (but do not determine) each member's behaviour and his/her interpretations of the 'meaning' of other people's behaviour.
>
> (p. 8)

Using the mathematics term "fuzzy set" to define culture is instructive and important. In mathematics, a set clearly indicates what is a member of the set and what is not. A fuzzy set, on the other hand, has boundaries that may be considered flexible. Membership in a fuzzy set is not "in" or "out," but to what degree. The fuzzy set approach to culture positions us to view individual members of a culture as sharing the characteristics of that culture to a certain degree. The definition allows for multiple types of cultures, including race-based cultures, gender-based cultures, ethnic cultures, national cultures, social class-based cultures, organizational cultures, group cultures, learning space cultures, etc. Further, the definition allows for individuals to belong to multiple cultures, sharing the characteristics of each culture to a certain degree.

What is Learning?

Learning can also be characterized in different ways. In this book, we adopt the broad definition of learning as a change in knowledge, skills or attitudes as a result "of experience, study or being taught." As such, we recognize that learning is a cultural process: a variety of ideas, life experiences, traditions, and beliefs of a learner integrated within activities at home, school, church, sports, and communities (Nasir, Rosebery, Warren, & Lee, 2006).

Learning may be formal or informal. "Informal learning is any activity involving the pursuit of understanding, knowledge or skill which occurs without the presence of externally imposed curricular criteria" (Livingstone, 2001, p. 4); while formal learning is the activity that occurs in virtual and physical classrooms around established curricula. Some examples of formal learning are K-12 courses and professional development courses within organizations. Informal learning does not include prescribed activities, but allows exploration of interesting topics in different settings. Learning may also be intentional wherein activities are focused on specific concepts and topics, while incidental learning can be unintentional and spontaneous.

Jonassen, Howland, Moore, and Marra (2003) emphasize the importance of creating meaningful learning activities with the instructor serving more as a facilitator to guide and engage learners. Characteristics of meaningful learning include:

- Active (Manipulative/Observant): Within natural environments, learners manipulate objects, observe intervention effects, and create their own explanations when interacting with objects and concepts.
- Constructive (Articulative/Reflective): Learners are able to reflect and describe their observations and activities to build their own mental models.
- Intentional (Reflective/Regulatory): Learners are able to deliberate and discover more when they are actively pursuing a cognitive goal.
- Authentic (Complex/Contextualized): Learning activities are designed within natural contexts, which can improve understanding and transference to new and real-world problems.
- Cooperative (Collaborative/Conversational): Conversations, group experiences, and social negotiation of ideas fit the knowledge building communities that learners confront within non-formal learning environments.

What is Technology?

While many think of technology as tools and artifacts, we define technology to include both process and product technology (Reiser, 2001a; 2001b). Product technologies include the tools and artifacts, or media, which most people readily recognize as technologies. These tools are often used for the design, delivery, and mediation of learning and communications. Some examples of product technologies are learning management systems for virtual learning delivery, whiteboards for in-class instruction, and ebooks and tablets for homework assignments. Process technologies, on the other hand, are the models and methods that guide the design and development of curriculum and instruction. These include curriculum and instructional design process, teaching methods, and instructional strategies.

The traditional learning technologies described above provide one dimension of technology that supports learning. With the pervasive use of tools in our everyday lives, many types of technologies impact how people learn. A quick "Google search" on our mobile devices provide "just in time" learning experiences for topics and ideas without the need for a formal and structured learning environment. However, the quick and easy access to content within different types of environments can lead to a false sense of comprehension and knowledge when users do not realize the content may be misinformation.

Another important component of technology that supports learning is the pedagogical usability. The entire technology-supported learning environment, which includes the interface, content, and tasks, must support different types of learners in various learning contexts (Silius & Tervakari, 2003). Although technology usage should be intuitive and simple for interactions with instructional materials, people will sometimes learn and adopt inefficient processes based on the technology design. These inefficiencies become the "de facto standard" for certain designs, which can eventually impact the overall learning experience. Therefore, the technology can unintentionally affect attitudes and interactions that impact the culture of a group of users.

What is in this Book?

The chapters in this book are representative of the breadth of work being done at the intersection of CLT. They reflect many different perspectives of culture, types of learning, and applications of technology.

In Chapter 2, **Critical Pedagogy and Educational Technology**, *Amy C. Bradshaw* defines critical pedagogy, introduces its key concepts and premises, explores tensions and resonance between the priorities of critical pedagogy and educational technology, and suggests an initial approach toward reconciling the fields.

In Chapter 3, **Revisiting Instructional Technologists' Inattention to Issues of Cultural Diversity among Stakeholders**, *Deepak Prem Subramony* presents a sequel to his thought-provoking 2004 position paper calling attention to the mainstream instructional technology (IT) research and development community's continued disregard for important issues related to cultural diversity among learners. This chapter explores the progress made by the IT community over the past decade in acknowledging and responding to issues connected to cultural diversity among those impacted by its research and practice.

In Chapter 4, **Globalization, Ironic Binaries, and Instructional Technology: Toward the Emergence of a Robust Critical Theory of Technology**, *Michael K. Thomas* argues that the context of globalization and the central role of technology in contemporary life oblige instructional designers to work toward the development of a robust critical theory of educational technology that use the interrelated notions of the technological sublime, neoliberalism, and performative implementation for the analysis of technology-rich innovations for learning and to provide a solid foundation for practice in the field.

In Chapter 5, **Hip-Hop Music as A Pedagogical Tool: Teaching with Hip-Hop in Global Contexts**, *Akesha M. Horton, Erik J. Byker, and Keith Heggart* present a case study of the design and delivery of a global hip-hop music course for secondary students. This chapter uses Critical Cosmopolitan Theory to examine the design and delivery of a global hip-hop music course (*Hip Hop for Global Justice*) for secondary students in Australia.

In Chapter 6, **Examining the Use of an Online Cultural Module to Increase Learners' Intercultural Sensitivity**, *Joseph M. Terantino* investigates the use of an online cultural learning module that was designed according to Merrill's (2002) First Principles of Instruction. The research explores the inclusion of native speaker perspectives in the module and its ability to aid in developing intercultural sensitivity among university students.

In Chapter 7, **How Cultural Factors Influence the Use of Social Constructivist-Based Pedagogical Models of Distance Learning: Examining Japanese Online Collaborative Behaviors**, *Bodi Anderson* examines distance learning in Japan using a coding scheme that analyzes *collaborative learning*. Findings from the study provide empirical evidence that cultural factors have a significant impact on how learners perceive, experience, and interact in distance learning environments in a manner that contradicts many core social constructivist principles.

In Chapter 8, **Culture and Computational Thinking: A Pilot Study of Operationalizing Culturally Responsive Teaching (CRT) in Computer Science Education**, *Leshell Hatley, Cynthia E. Winston-Proctor, Gina M. Paige, and Kevin Clark* report on an investigation that used a design-based research approach to build a culturally responsive model for teaching computational thinking and computer programming skills to African-American middle school students in an informal learning environment.

In Chapter 9, **Foundational Theories of Social Media Tools and Cultural Competency: A Systematic Literature Review**, *Sandra G. Nunn, Lequisha Brown-Joseph, and Michelle Susberry Hill* provide a comprehensive overview and analysis of 10 different theoretical constructs that support the integration of cultural competency with social media tools to help support users in education, business, and other situational contexts. By establishing and using these theoretical constructs, educators, students, and practitioners can serve to improve the ability of users to communicate through social media to transcend cultural considerations, facilitate information exchange, and promote greater learning outcomes.

In Chapter 10, **iDESIGN: Designing and Implementing a Culturally Relevant Game-Based Curriculum**, *Roberto Joseph and James Diamond* describe a three-year, National Science Foundation project to create a game design curriculum in after-school computer clubs. The project engages 150 6th-9th grade students and 14 of their teachers in information technology experiences that move them beyond technological literacy (computer use) to technological fluency (creating with computers). iDesign integrates culturally relevant pedagogy and game-based learning as a strategy to help underrepresented students gain skills that will enable them to master content that they might not otherwise acquire in traditional classrooms.

In Chapter 11, **Boys and Video Game Play: Re-engaging Boys in the Classroom**, *Shulong Yan, Yelim Mun, Jason Engerman, and Alison Carr-Chellman* argue that video games have the potential to play a significant part in alleviating conflicts between boys and school cultures to re-engage boys back in schools. In this chapter, the authors use a cultural lens to investigate a current crisis in education; namely, boys are underperforming and dropping out rapidly from formal educational institutions.

In Chapter 12, **Exploring Chinese International Students' Acceptance of Mobile Learning**, *Zhetao Guo and Angela D. Benson* summarize the results of a research study that used the Unified Theory of Technology Acceptance and Use (UTAUT) model to explore Chinese international students' use of mobile learning. To improve the educational use of mobile devices, it is important to investigate students' acceptance of mobile learning. As one of the largest groups of international students in U.S. universities, Chinese international students were the major focus of this study.

In Chapter 13, **Students Making Science Games: The Design Process of Students Incorporating Science Content into Video Games**, *Neda Khalili Blackburn and Kevin Clark* present the results of a project that put students in charge of creating their own video games based on science topics with which they were previously unfamiliar. The purpose of this study was to follow the design process students undertook when placed in a constructivist and constructionist learning environment with available tools and support to complete their games.

In Chapter 14, **How the Cultural Clash of Essentialism and Progressivism Shaped Technology Adoption: A Case Study of Culture, Learning, and Technology**, *Steven Watkins and Mansureh Kebritchi* describe the cultural clash between essentialist educational theory and progressive educational theory and its consequences for learning and technological adoption practices in the public education process in the United States. Technology adoption and usage in schools exists in a cultural context that people associated with the public educational process often overlook.

References

Banks, J.A. (1993). The Canon debate, knowledge contruction, and multicultural education. *Educational Researcher, 22*(5), 4–14.
Culture, Learning and Technology Division (2016). Vision Statement. Association for Educational Communications and Technology.
Gay, G. (2000). *Culturally Responsive Teaching: Theory, Research, and Practice*. New York: Teachers College Press.
Jonassen, D.H., Howland, J., Moore, J., & Marra, R.M. (2003). *Learning to Solve Problems with Technology: A Constructivist Perspective* (2nd ed.). Upper Saddle River, NJ: Merrill/Prentice Hall.
Ladson-Billings, G. (1994). *The Dreamkeepers: Successful Teachers of African American Children*. San Francisco, CA: Jossey-Bass.

Lee, C. D. (2007). *Culture, Literacy and Learning: Taking Blooming in the Midst of the Whirlwind*. New York, NY: Teachers College Press.
Livingstone, D. W. (2001). Adults' informal learning: Definitions, findings, gaps and future research. New Approaches to Lifelong Learning (NALL) Working Paper #21–2001. Ontario Institute for Studies in Education, Toronto. Retrieved from https://tspace.library.utoronto.ca/retrieve/4484/21adultsinformallearning.pdf and http://files.eric.ed.gov/fulltext/ED452390.pdf
Merrill, M. D. (2002). First principles of instruction. *Educational Technology Research and Development, 50*(3), 43–59.
Nasir, N. S., Rosebery, A. S., Warren, B., & Lee, C. D. (2006). Learning as a cultural process: Achieving equity through diversity. In R. K. Sawyer (Ed.), *The Cambridge Handbook of the Learning Sciences* (pp. 489–504). New York, NY: Cambridge University Press.
Nieto, Sonia (2010). *Language, Culture, and Teaching: Critical Perspectives*. New York, NY: Routledge.
Reiser, R. A. (2001a). A history of instructional design and technology: Part I: A history of instructional media. *Educational Technology, Research and Development, 49*(1), 53–64.
Reiser, R. A. (2001b). A history of instructional design and technology: Part II: A history of instructional design. *Educational Technology, Research and Development, 49*(2), 57–67.
Richey, R. C., Klein, J. D., & Tracey, M. W. (2011). *The Instructional Design Knowledge Base: Theory, Research, and Practice*. New York, NY: Routledge.
Silius, K., & Tervakari, A.M. (2003). An Evaluation of the Usefulness of Web-based Learning Environments. The Evaluation Tool into the Portal of Finnish Virtual University. Proceedings of mENU, 8–9.
Spencer-Oatey, H. (2008) *Culturally Speaking: Culture, Communication and Politeness Theory* (2nd ed.). London, UK: Bloomsbury Publishing.
Spencer-Oatey, H. (2012) What is culture? A compilation of quotations. GlobalPAD Core Concepts. Retrieved from http://go.warwick.ac.uk/globalpadintercultural
Young, P. A. (2009). *Instructional Design Frameworks and Intercultural Models*. Hershey, PA: IGI Global/Information Science Publishing.

2

CRITICAL PEDAGOGY AND EDUCATIONAL TECHNOLOGY

Amy C. Bradshaw

Overview

Educational technology is a human endeavor, and humans are not neutral. Our professional work reflects our positionalities and priorities, both individually and collectively. Individuals and educational technology professional organizations are increasingly recognizing the urgent need to understand complex interactions between culture, learning, and technology. With this growing realization, merely replicating what and how educational technology has been practiced in the past is not sufficient. Nor is it adequate to assess the value and appropriateness of current and future efforts according to only our own experiences, perceptions, and perspectives.

Educational technology is "the study and ethical practice of facilitating learning and improving performance by creating, using, and managing appropriate technological processes and resources" (Januszewski & Molenda, 2008). Definitional emphasis on ethical practice requires that educational technologists keep culture-related issues such as relevance, access, equity, and inclusion foregrounded in our work. However, our professional and academic training in the past has tended largely to ignore or neglect the ways issues of culture interact with learning and technology. This hinders our abilities to engage our professional work ethically. For the field of educational technology to be dynamic, adaptive, culturally relevant, and ethically responsible, we must reassess our practices and needs for further learning at individual and collective levels in terms of the nexus of culture, learning, and technology.

Critical pedagogy offers a powerful and ethical means for considering our practices and perspectives as educational technologists, particularly as we grapple with how to better synthesize culture with learning and technology. This chapter provides an introduction to key concepts and premises of critical pedagogy, considers some tensions and resonances between the fields of critical pedagogy and educational technology, and offers some initial practical suggestions toward making our individual and collective practices in educational technology more responsive and responsible at the intersections of culture, learning, and technology.

Critical Pedagogy

Introduction

The term critical pedagogy encompasses educational approaches that are focused on empowering learners to be full participants in democratic society through educational practices that are connected to learners' own experiences, address issues directly and immediately relevant to learners and their communities, and seek to transform systems and structures that contribute to oppression and marginalization. Grounded in concerns for social justice, fairness, and equity, critical pedagogy brings together critical theory, liberation ethics, and progressive education. Critical pedagogues view learning and educational work as inseparable from the rest of life. Education happens in broader social contexts and, thus, must be considered in light of, and as expressions, consequences, and replicators of issues and dynamics in the broader society.

The *critical* component of critical pedagogy relates to paying close attention to the day-to-day experiences, struggles, and realities of learners. Critical pedagogues seek to understand what works and what does not work, as the learners themselves see, experience, and express their reality, and co-create with learners the knowledge, awareness, and dispositions to break through imposed barriers to full citizenship and self-actualization. Criticality involves looking beyond surfaces and stereotypes, seeking deeper and fuller understanding of issues and circumstances in order to make visible the hidden structures and systems of domination and inequality that reinforce and increase benefits to some members of society, while reducing and blocking access to benefits for others. Criticality is not engaged for its own sake, and should not be misunderstood (as it frequently is) as simple negativity or opposition. Rather, criticality is a commitment to digging deeper in order to understand broader connections, roots, and ramifications, for the specific purpose of allowing for the full participation and humanity of all. Therefore, criticality requires attention to the struggles of those at the margins of society, and also requires continual self-examination, self-interrogation, and learning regarding one's own positionalities and perspectives, as well as reflection and action regarding how benefits and harms related to positionalities are established, influenced, and maintained.

Key Concepts and Premises of Critical Pedagogy

Conscientização. Although the term "critical pedagogy" formally emerged in the book, *Theory and Resistance in Education* (Giroux, 1983), Giroux points to the historical legacy of progressive educators and educational movements that came before him, and credits Paulo Freire for providing a language for engaging what has come to be known collectively as critical pedagogy. Freire's (1970) *Pedagogy of the Oppressed* is considered the seminal work of critical pedagogy. A foundational critical pedagogy concept that was popularized through his work, and that has become central to critical pedagogy practice worldwide, is the awakening and development of *conscientização*, or *critical consciousness*. Educating for critical consciousness is a sociopolitical educative approach that engages learners in questioning the nature of their historical and social situation, which Freire described as "reading the world." Developing critical perception is an ongoing process that cannot be imposed. In developing critical consciousness, a person will "gradually perceive personal and social reality as well as the contradictions in it, become conscious of his or her own perception of that reality, and deal critically with it" (p. 32). Educating for critical consciousness empowers learners to analyze, evaluate, and address elements in their world that manipulate, coerce, and oppress (Freire, 1970, 1973; Shor, 1992). With awakened and developing critical consciousness, people are harder to control; people will resist the dominant culture's actions that go against their own interests. Through processes of cultural hegemony, the dominant elites of society are engaged in persuading people that the elites' interests are the interests of the individual, supplanting what individual people want and need, with what the dominant elites want. Critical consciousness allows learners to recognize hegemony and differentiate between their own interests and the interests of the dominant elites, and thus is seen by those in power as a threat that must be controlled. Critical in the sense used here should not be confused with critical thinking. "Critical thinking" is a domesticated form of criticality that can be appropriated by the dominant elite to control people's creativity, and channel it to support the goals of those in power.

Praxis. Ongoing development of critical consciousness is a necessary part of engaging Freire's conception of praxis—"reflection and action upon the world in order to transform it" (1970, p. 51). Beyond the common definition of praxis as simply a blending of theory and practice, Freirean praxis includes three vital components. The first is naming, which involves clearly and accurately identifying and articulating—making visible—the issue or dynamic at hand, from the perspective of those most at risk of being harmed. The second element of praxis is critically reflecting, which includes considering the issue in its full human and historic context, from multiple perspectives, and through engaged dialogue with others, especially with individuals most at risk. The third element of praxis is taking meaningful action to transform or disrupt unjust practices, systems, or structures. All three elements are necessary: If a problem is not accurately named before reflection and action are engaged, there is high risk of an issue being misperceived and subsequently being inadequately addressed. If an oppressive dynamic is accurately named but action is taken without critical reflection, wrong action may be taken and harmful dynamics may be exacerbated, or additional harms may be created. If a harmful dynamic is accurately named and critically reflected upon, but no action to transform or disrupt is engaged, the status quo perpetuates.

Dialogue, trust, critical humility, and radical love. Critical consciousness and praxis are not strategies that a person, as the subject of a narrative, imposes on others, as objects in a narrative, in order to educate or liberate them. Rather, they are processes through which people develop understanding of their condition and by which they can liberate the oppressed *and themselves* along with them. Recognition of this co-liberatory process and outcome is crucial. "While no one liberates himself by his own efforts alone, neither is he liberated by others" (Freire, 1970, p. 53). Educating for critical consciousness requires self-awareness and self-interrogation, and the humility to recognize and adjust our perceptions about ourselves in relation to others, as well as opening ourselves to learn from others through dialogue. Sincere dialogue requires a profound love for the world and its people, humility to step out of authoritarian models of educational communication, and belief in learners as knowledge co-creators and partners in collective action toward freedom. On these premises, "dialogue becomes a horizontal relationship of which mutual trust between the dialoguers is a logical consequence" (pp. 77–78). "Through dialogue, the teacher-of-the-students and the students-of-the-teacher cease to exist and a new term emerges: teacher-student with students-teachers" (Freire, 1970, p. 67). Teachers must have humility, coupled with love and respect for their students.

> Humility helps us to understand this obvious truth: No one knows it all; no one is ignorant of everything. We all know something; we are all ignorant of something. Without humility, one can hardly listen with respect to those one judges to be too far below one's own level of competence. But the humility that enables one to listen even to those considered less competent should not be an act of condescension or resemble the behavior of those fulfilling a vow...
>
> (p. 39)

By practicing humility to listen to and learn to talk with learners authentically and dialectically, democratic teachers also teach learners to listen to them as well (Freire, 1970, p. 65). Through dialectical engagement, learners develop skills and abilities to listen to and understand multiple differing perspectives, and explore possibilities for reconciling diverse claims and experiences (their own as well as others') through logic and reason, rather than reacting primarily through and from emotion. They learn to question and be questioned regarding underlying premises of positions, to help identify unrecognized errors and oversights. Unlike debate, dialectic is not a competition with winners and losers, but a search for rich and deep understanding that acknowledges multiple experiences of reality.

Freire viewed "an enormous capacity to love" as necessary for "the arduous and often difficult task of denouncing the cruel and obscene assaults against human beings who have the least, when it is so much easier and comfortable to accommodate to the power structure from which we can reap benefits" (Macedo, 2006). Those who commit themselves to teaching must develop love not only for others, but of the very process implied in teaching. "It is impossible to teach without the courage to love, without the courage to try a thousand times before giving up. In short, it is impossible to teach without a forged, invented, and well-thought-out capacity to love" (Freire, 2005, p. 5). Intentionally cultivated practices of dialogue, trust, critical humility, and love are necessary to make oppressive structures and dynamics visible so they can be transformed. These means and purposes reveal critical pedagogy to be based, at its core, on compassion, hope, and optimism.

Educational spaces are inherently political. A necessary part of both critical consciousness development and engagement with praxis is learning to recognize harmful dynamics we are socially conditioned (through processes of *normalization* and *mystification*) not to see. As long as oppressive structures, systems, and dynamics remain invisible, they cannot be transformed or dismantled. "Education as the exercise of domination stimulates the credulity of students, with the ideological intent (often not perceived by educators) of indoctrinating them to adapt to the world of oppression" (Freire, 1970, p. 253). Anything that differs from or seeks remedy from oppression and harms imposed by standard practices of the dominant culture tends to be labeled *radical*, *dangerous*, or *political*. In contrast, a myth of neutrality protects abusive and dehumanizing dynamics and structures that align closely with and support the dominant culture from recognition. Unrecognized or misperceived, abusive and dehumanizing systems replicate (see Collins, 2009) and the myth of neutrality is reinforced. The myth of neutrality is a political tool reinforced in many settings by various forms of punishment (or withdrawal of benefits) for nonconformity. Negative consequences for raising awareness of oppressive dynamics or questioning dominant practices contributes to cultures of silence. Without societal questions raised and social inequities considered, educational practices reflect, perpetuate, and amplify inequities in the broader society. Education may operate in the name of democracy and justice, and yet in practice be authoritarian and oppressive (Kincheloe, 2005, p. 2). In such settings, demoralized or disengaged silence is not neutrality. In such settings, "washing one's hands of the conflict between the powerful and the powerless means to side with the powerful, not to be neutral" (Freire, 1985, p. 122). Critical pedagogues acknowledge that cultural politics are always in operation, even—perhaps especially—when the damper of neutrality is imposed, and are committed to transforming educational spaces to be empowering of students who are culturally marginalized and economically disenfranchised from full democratic citizenship. "Citizenship is not obtained by chance: It is a construction that, never finished, demands we fight for it. It demands commitment, political clarity, coherence, decision" (Freire, 2005, p. 161).

From childhood, we are taught hierarchies, and made to believe someone is in charge, and knows better than we do. Thus, people tend to accommodate to power structures, and especially so when they benefit from them in some way—or at least are not directly or immediately harmed by them. If we are not very mindful and intentional in our efforts and awareness, gaining some benefit from systems and structures that are harmful to others can blind us to those harms to others. The gains we receive are strong motivators for us to maintain that blindness and denial, even if we have difficulty recognizing the benefits received. A potential counter motivator we can tap into is desire to see *reality* as it is for others who do not benefit in the same ways we or others do, and through which we can gain a fuller—and therefore more authentic—understanding of the systems in which we operate. Understanding others' realities requires listening to and learning from other voices, particularly those at the margins.

Education as the practice of freedom. Engaging critical pedagogy is a commitment to freedom in multiple forms—freedom *from* oppressive practices and limiting perspectives and *from* mythologies and manipulations that facilitate oppression and hegemony, as well as freedom *to* engage issues and concerns that are immediately relevant to learners' lives, and freedom *to* trust learners to be co-creators of knowledge (rather than mere receptacles for knowledge). "Education as the practice of freedom does not begin when the teacher-student meets with the students-teachers in pedagogical situation, but rather when the former first asks herself or himself *what* she or he will dialogue with the latter *about*" (Freire, 1970/1990, p. 93).

> The classroom, with all its limitations, remains a location of possibility. In that field of possibility we have the opportunity to labor for freedom, to demand of ourselves and our comrades, an openness of mind and heart that allows us to face reality even as we collectively imagine ways to move beyond boundaries, to transgress. This is education as the practice of freedom.
> (hooks, 1994, p. 207)

The meaning of freedom warrants considerable reflection and Greene's (1988) unpacking of the term is especially helpful in articulating clear distinctions between negative and positive forms of freedom: *Negative freedom* is "the right not to be interfered with or coerced or compelled to do what [one] did not choose to do" (p. 16). In contrast, *positive freedom* "shows itself or comes in to being when individuals come together in a particular way, when they are authentically present to one another (without masks, pretenses, badges of office), when they have a project they can mutually pursue" (p. 16). Positive freedom is the freedom to exist as a full human being; one's authentic self.

Freedom of authentic being is limited or precluded through discrimination on the basis of age, color, ethnicity, gender identity, sexual orientation, physical ability, class, and cultural capital, and these aspects of identity intersect. Intersectionality (see Crenshaw, 1993; Takacs, 2003) complicates issues of unearned privilege (see McIntosh, 1988), power, and oppression. Although these factors are omitted from serious study and consideration among many educators, evidence continues to mount that equitable and inclusive environments do not only help students who are marginalized, but improve learning outcomes for all students (Milem & Hakuta, 2000; Gurin et al., 2002; Hurtado et al., 2003; Milem, 2003; Antonio et al., 2004), and also increase student engagement, enhance cognitive complexity in problem solving, and increase innovation in problem solving in team environments (Page, 2007; Page, 2010). Critical pedagogues recognize that the suffering of all marginalized people is connected, and that struggles for liberation are most effective when they are collective (see Crass, 2013). Transforming educational spaces to be empowering of students who are culturally marginalized and economically disenfranchised is a priority of critical pedagogy.

Education for transformation. Both the purpose and means of critical pedagogy are transformation—transformation of formal learning contexts from authoritative, imposing, and transactional, to dialogical, dialectical, and engaging; transformation of teacher-learner interactions into relationships of mutually supportive, engaged, knowledge co-creators; and transformation of educational spaces from what feels to many like alienating and dehumanizing status quo replicators, to humanity-affirming "locations of possibility" (hooks, 1994).

In contrast to the dynamic and evolving knowledge co-creation of transformative education, Freire refers to transmitted knowledge as a corpse—dead knowledge, disconnected from the learners, produced by others, and imposed upon learners. This is a banking model of education, wherein learners are considered vessels needing to be filled and into which teachers deposit transferred knowledge. A banking approach alienates learners from their own cultural realities and domesticates them into compliant objects.

> In their political activity, the dominant elites utilize the banking concept to encourage passivity in the oppressed, corresponding with the latter's 'submerged' state of consciousness, and take advantage of that passivity to 'fill' that consciousness with slogans which create even more fear of freedom.
> (Freire, 1990/1970, p. 95)

Critical pedagogy is not transmissive or mechanistic. "An educator cannot be viewed as a technician, a functionary carrying out the instructions of others. Educators are learned scholars, community researchers, moral agents, philosophers, cultural workers, and political insurgents" (p. 164). Moreover,

> Those truly committed to liberation must reject the banking concept in its entirety, adopting instead a concept of women and men as conscious beings, and consciousness as consciousness intent upon the world. They must abandon the educational goal of deposit-making and replace it with the posing of the problems of human beings in their relations with the world.
> (p. 79)

Table 2.1 presents some contrasts between the characteristics and outcomes of transformative educational approaches and transmissive educational approaches.

Tensions and Resonances between Critical Pedagogy and Educational Technology

Individual and collective practices in educational technology may be consistent with the premises of critical pedagogy, or might be transformed to become more so, through purposeful engagement. Some common tendencies and practices in the educational technology field may be more easily seen and understood as problematic when considered in light of the premises and purposes of critical pedagogy. Toward the goal of better understanding and honoring connections between culture, learning, and technology, we can compare critical pedagogy and educational technology in terms of philosophical orientations, priorities of the two fields, and stances regarding the major challenges of our times.

TABLE 2.1 Contrasts between transformative and transmissive education

	Transformative education	*Transmissive education*
Characteristics	Learning is grounded in learners' own directly lived contexts and experiences	Learning disregards or supplants learners' lived contexts and experiences
	"Problem Posing" model	"Banking" model, deposits knowledge as a commodity
	Knowledge as new construction, knowledge production	Knowledge as transferred corpse
	Explorative, seeks questioning and discovery	Directive, seeks compliance and conformity
	Democratic, dialogic, dialectic	Authoritarian
	More meaning based	More facts-based
	Learner and community centered	Content, teacher, or task centered
	Open ended, loosely defined, adaptable	Closed ended, well defined
Outcomes	Requires and supports higher order cognition	Engages and reinforces lower order cognition
	Supports development of internal locus of control and self-regulation	Supports development and maintenance of external locus of control
	Empowers individuals and marginalized people	Domesticates and alienates individuals and marginalized people
	Enables societal shift toward social justice	Replicates/perpetuates status quo

Philosophical Orientations

Critical pedagogy is clearly positioned on the interpretivist end of a paradigmatic continuum. Ontologically, understandings of *reality* are shaped by social, political, cultural, economic, ethnic, and gender (etc.) values. Epistemologically, what can be known is transactional and subjectivist, filtered by individual and collective values and experience. Methodologically, how we come to know is dialogical and dialectical, experiential, and hermeneutical. The purposes and priorities of critical pedagogy all logically align with critical pedagogy's philosophical orientation, practical approaches, and means of determining success of the pedagogical efforts: all can be considered critical interpretivist, or critical constructivist. In contrast, philosophical orientations within the field of educational technology fall along a much broader range. Different ontological and epistemological positions resonate for different educational technologists, who may also be drawn to a variety of instructional approaches and strategies, as well as a wide variety of methods for measuring pedagogical success, all of which might be mediated by primary setting, purpose, audience, or context. Without excusing observed confusions in educational technology practice in terms of alignment between philosophical and theoretical rationales, instructional activities and strategies, and assessment and measurement approaches, perhaps it is understandable that such misalignments are more frequently encountered in educational technology than in critical pedagogy. Critical pedagogogy's primary purposes and priorities align well with its primary philosophical orientation, and are inseparable from practice and approach. The same is not necessarily true for educational technology.

Where educational technology is practiced consistent with interpretivist philosophical orientations, there is strong potential for overlap and reconciliation between the two fields. Where educational technology is practiced with a more positivist philosophical orientation, reconciling the two fields is more challenging. Moreover, if the goal is to better understand and ethically reflect and respond to relationships between culture, learning, and technology, then the need for transformation of perspective and practice is highest in approaches that are underpinned by positivism, and in approaches that do not coherently align in terms of strategies, theoretical rationale, and philosophical grounding. For these latter groups, critical pedagogy offers a powerful opportunity for transformation.

Priorities of the Fields

Critical pedagogy's priorities include educating for liberation and empowerment of the oppressed and marginalized toward equitable and just societies. The scope and scale of problems to be addressed can range from the deeply personal to the global, but educational efforts must always be directly connected to learners' own lived contexts, and focused on issues that the learners themselves have identified as pressing. In the field of educational technology, some of the most common priorities are efficiency, efficacy, appeal, reliability, cost effectiveness, and scalability. These priorities tend to be considered neutral or positive according to the dominant culture. But what can be lost in the pursuit of these priorities? If not intentionally and mindfully considered and balanced, these common priorities can decimate possibilities for justice, equity, and inclusion. On a philosophical continuum, where do these common educational technology priorities fit? What other priorities are or could be practiced in educational technology? There is great opportunity for further inquiry into professional practice that balances priorities typically associated with educational technology with human and culture-related priorities of justice, equity, and inclusion.

Stances Regarding the Major Challenges of the Times

What do those in our field view as the major challenges of the day? Do we tend to see the world through the eyes of the dominant, or through the experiences of the oppressed? What relationships do war, famine, climate change, human migration, and species extinction have to the two fields? How are they different? Why are they different? How far removed from the major challenges of the day are our work-related efforts? In what ways do we fragment ourselves into having one set of concerns in our personal lives and a different set in our professional roles? If we keep separation between what we perceive as the core concerns of our times and the problems we are willing to recognize and approach in our professional roles, we are choosing to relegate concerns for humanity and the planet to a private concern. In doing so, we are choosing to relinquish aspects of our humanity necessary for ethical engagement in our professional roles, and are committing our professional energies to furthering the goals of the dominant elite.

Engaging critical pedagogy requires us to consider these kinds of questions, and to question our own roles, perspectives, positionalities, and epistemologies, how these have come to be, and how unreflective adherence to them may contribute to and perpetuate injustice. This is a long-term commitment toward ongoing critical consciousness development. Awakening and developing critical consciousness, and engaging in praxis are dialogical and dialectical processes that develop over time and require intentionality, critical self-interrogation, and engagement with others. As we develop critical consciousness, we become better able to selectively take advantage of technological affordances without losing sight of our own and others' humanity. If we do not keep priorities of humane practice central in our work, we risk reinforcing some frequently encountered tendencies of educational technology. Table 2.2 provides some quick contrasts between the fields along a variety of categories, and is not intended to be exhaustive, declarative, or final, but to provide a starting place to begin to engage in critical interrogation of some of the common practices and perspectives of ourselves and our field generally.

TABLE 2.2 Sample of contrasts between critical pedagogy and educational technology

	Critical pedagogy	*Educational technology*
Foundations	Critical theory	Audio visual technology
	Progressive education	Visual and museum education
	Liberation ethics	Educational psychology
	Social justice	Educational media and technology
Philosophical underpinnings, perspectives, and orientations	Critical interpretivism	Full range from positivism to critical constructivism
	There is no objectivity, only degrees of subjectivity	Claims (or goals) of objectivity are frequently encountered, subjectivity may be routed through "objective" means
	Any educational endeavor is inherently political—you cannot avoid the political	(Tendency to) avoid the "political" (unless the lesson topic is politics)
	Silence on matters of social justice is a political tool to reinforce and reproduce the status quo and dominant groups/order	
Priorities	Power relationships	Efficiency
	Equity and empowerment	Effectiveness
	Making oppressive and unjust systems visible and addressing them	Appeal
		Simplification
		Find the gap and close it
	Awareness and questioning of the larger picture	
	Complicating or "troubling" the system in order to improve conditions for all	
Frequently encountered tendencies	Complicates	Simplify
	Seek interconnections	Break things down to their component parts
	Question the dominant system	Support and reinforce the dominant system
	Seek to identify and address oppressive dynamics, therefore profoundly interested in perspectives and unmet needs of underrepresented groups	Proceduralization
		Reproducibility, reliability
		Objectification, efficiency, social neutrality, essentialist, mechanistic, technical
	Look for harmful dynamics and power differentials	
	Determine who is harmed, how, and why	
	Reflect and then engage to transform the system	

	Critical pedagogy	Educational technology
Scope, scale	Consider the entire system must engage the big questions What is the aim of the educational activity? What are the underlying assumptions?	Rarely take time or trouble to question the big picture or foundational assumptions Focus on gaps and specific pieces. Correct parts and components within existing systems that are not working well
View of education	Inherently connected and inseparable from issues in the broader society. Grounded in social, cultural, cognitive, economic, and political contexts Schooling is part of broader social structure	Largely as training? Critical thinking can apply to isolated topics and tasks Increasingly tending toward commodification and corporatization In need of grants and other funding
Purpose of education	Seek justice Dismantle oppression Transformation Empower individuals to become full human beings contributing to a just society and healthy planet	Get a job? Train workers to do the job correctly, be more efficient, make the company more money?

The goals, priorities, and means of critical pedagogy provide a powerful lens through which to view and consider our individual and collective practices in educational technology, as well as through which to bring into focus a path toward practical integration of culture, learning, and technology. Transforming our field to be more inclusive, equitable, and empowering will not happen by accident or without intentionality, commitment, and ongoing willingness to engage, struggle, make mistakes, and try again, all with a central focus on fairness, equity, and freedom to become fully actualized human beings while empowering others to do the same.

Toward a Praxis of Equitable and Inclusive Practice

Critical pedagogy is always connected to particular settings and contexts, and people directly impacted by education and training endeavors are central participants in problem identification and decision making regarding what they need. While a comprehensive guide for practically reconciling the fields of critical pedagogy and educational technology in specific settings is beyond the scope of this chapter, in the following sections some initial suggestions are provided. These are not intended as narrow procedural steps, but as suggestions for recursively engaging Freirean praxis: naming, critically reflecting, and taking appropriate action to transform harmful systems, practices, and dynamics.

Naming: Acknowledge the Need for Further Learning Regarding Culture, Equity, and Inclusion

In academic preparation for professional roles in educational technology, students typically take multiple courses in learning theory, instructional psychology, and technology tools and processes, as well as courses focused on intersections and syntheses of these domains. Such curricula are intended to prepare students to work well and confidently in the combined realm of learning and technology. As the field of educational technology has become more diverse and inter- and multinational in scope, members of the field have increasingly recognized that culture is inseparable from learning and technology. Culture interacts with educational technology both in terms of cultural influences on how educational technology is conceptualized and implemented, and in terms of how educational technology is experienced and received (see, for example, Burniske, 2003). Despite the growing awareness of important relationships between culture, learning, and technology, preparation toward professional work in educational technology does not typically include formal study of culture, cultural competence, or educating for equity and inclusion.

The absence of adequate formal focus on cultural competence and pedagogies for equity and inclusion allows for the development of fragmented and weak conceptualizations of culture, as well as inadequate understandings of why and how to address culture in our professional work. For example, although individuals and institutions are increasingly recognizing *diversity* as important in education and training contexts, focusing on diversity too frequently neglects consideration of structural and systemic issues of *equity* and *inclusion*. Understanding the relationships and differences between these terms is critically important. Without intentional grounding in equity and inclusion, emphasis on diversity can result in acknowledging culture in severely limited ways, such as merely including people of color as characters in a multimedia presentation. While visual representation of diversity is important, limiting culture, equity, and inclusion considerations to minor modifications of characters' skin color, gender, physical abilities, or age, while holding larger systemic dynamics constant, is a form of visual appropriation that reinforces systemic norms and normalization processes, and trivializes relationships between culture, learning, and technology. Primarily focusing on diversity rather than inclusion and equity also tends to invite definitional dilution that may equate minor individual differences, such as optimal time of day for studying, with cultural differences of consequence, such as indivisible identity factors used to exclude people from equal access to education or police protection. Likewise, research and practice that purportedly addresses culture by virtue of having been conducted in a country other than the U.S., or because a high proportion of participants were of a particular race or ethnicity other than white, not only does not advance our understanding of the nexus of culture, learning, and technology, it reinforces a colonizer mindset of *culture* and *diversity* as things to be objectified and collected. By focusing narrowly on diversity, it is easy to fall into categorizing, collecting, and reporting differences, while doing nothing to dismantle or transform systemic and structural inequities and increase inclusion and access for marginalized people and groups. As individuals and as a field, we need to increase and improve our understanding of these issues so that we do not allow small expressions of diversity to suffice as substitutes for structural equity and justice.

Our collective ignorance of unjust systems, issues, and dynamics operating in learning environments we design, develop, and implement must be addressed if we are serious about including "ethical practice" as part of the definition of our field. Ignorance operates as an outcome of our situatedness as knowers (Code, 1993), as a specific aspect of our group identities (Harding, 1991), and as a product of oppressive systems (Mills, 1997). Through reification and ingrained practice, individuals and whole fields can tend to operate from *epistemologies of ignorance*. Alcoff (2007) provides three types of arguments for epistemic ignorance: 1. Ignorance is contextual—"epistemic advantages and disadvantages are not the same for all" (pp. 41–43); 2. Patterns of ignorance are associated with social and group identities, focused on "specific knowing practices inculcated in a socially dominant group" (p. 47); and 3. Ignorance as "a substantive epistemic practice that differentiates the group" (p. 47). For a system of injustice to be maintained, most people (even most of the people who gain relatively more benefits as a result of the structural inequities) either remain mostly ignorant of its existence, or become convinced it is beyond their power to alter. This is accomplished through perpetuation of many myths, including myths of social neutrality, the myth of meritocracy (McNamee & Miller, 2004), and by promulgating cultures of silence. Great energy and effort are put toward maintenance of ignorance with regard to domination, oppression, inequities, injustices, privilege, and possibilities of empowerment. Dismissing any of these areas of inquiry and work serves to protect ignorance that facilitates oppression. We need to both acknowledge our ignorance and seek to correct it. We also need to be honest with ourselves about our individual dominant priorities, perspectives, practices, and tendencies, as well as those commonly encountered in our field generally, and in our broader social systems.

Critically Reflecting: Seek Deeper and Fuller Understanding with and from Other Domains

Expand your reading list. Many resources are available for increasing our understanding of critical pedagogy (e.g., Freire, 1970/1990, 1973, 2005; Shor, 1992; Kincheloe, 2008; Giroux, 2011), and other topics directly pertinent to the intersection of culture, learning, and technology. A sampling of important relevant topics includes issues such as hidden and null curricula (e.g., Anyon, 1983; Eisner, 1985), cultural competence (e.g., Goodman, 2013), systemic oppression and racism (e.g., Roediger, 2007; Kivel, 2011; Wise, 2012), intersectionality (e.g., Crenshaw, 1993; Takacs, 2003), collective liberation (Crass, 2013), microagressions (e.g., Nadal et al., 2011), unearned privilege (e.g., McIntosh, 1988; Kendall, 2013), and equity literacy (e.g., Gorski, 2014). Taking responsibility to increase our understanding of these and other issues related to culture, equity, and inclusion is necessary to improve our abilities to recognize and understand harmful systems and dynamics, in order to discern the ways we are complicit in their maintenance and perpetuation.

Seek input, engagement, and support. In working to remedy our ignorance, we need to seek support from others, including people with vastly different experiences and knowledge bases. Seeking mentoring from people with expertise in relevant specialization fields, such as sociology or ethnic and multicultural studies, can help us identify individual and collective blindspots. Potential mentors might not know the educational technology field as insiders, but they can see what appears to be most needed from the perspectives of their own primary fields. They can talk through understandings of culture-related issues with us, provide suggestions for further readings, workshops, and professional development opportunities related to equity, inclusion, and social justice, and provide input regarding efforts to transform our practices to be more inclusive and equitable.

Develop practices of self-reflection and critical self-interrogation. Critical reflection and transforming the self must remain central; always more growth and transformation are needed. In engaging critical self-reflection we also need to recognize that, although we may have been taught to emphasize what we know and to capitalize on our strengths, we also need to cultivate the humility to learn what we do not know, and seek ways to grow toward what is missing. Critical pedagogues develop habits of thought and dialogical and dialectical engagement to continually questions their own practice. The following questions support reflecting on our current practices, and can help us identify directions and opportunities for transforming our practices to be ethically responsible at the intersections of culture, learning, and technology.

1. How does our access to advanced technological products and tools influence our perceptions and expectations regarding issues of access and equity for people throughout the world?
2. Review Table 2.1: Contrasts between transformative and transmissive education.
    a. In what ways are common practices in our field consistent with transmissive educational approaches?
    b. In what ways are they—or could they be—transformative?
    c. What would we have to do individually or collectively to make our practices more consistent with transformative education?

3. How do my perspectives and practices
    a. reinforce fragmented thinking, component thinking, objectification, and reductionism?
    b. reinforce essentialism, thinking of issues and factors as separable, distinct, and unrelated?
    c. assume and perpetuate myths of social neutrality?
    d. protect me from seeing my own culpability in injustice?
    e. excuse me from responsibility to address injustice?
    f. (in whole or in any part) contribute to oppression, injustice, and inequity?
4. Critical pedagogy seeks freedom *from* oppression and marginalization, and freedom *for* emancipatory educational practice.
    a. In what ways can educational technology enhance these efforts?
    b. In what ways can educational technology undermine these efforts?
5. Think about a training session or workshop you have developed or participated in.
    a. Who is/was served by this workshop? Did the target learners have any say in whether they needed or wanted it?
    b. Does this training (in whole or in any part) contribute to oppression, injustice, inequity?
        i. If so, in what ways? How do you know?
        ii. If you think it does not, what is the basis for your dismissal? Can you find someone who disagrees? What are the bases for their perspectives?
    c. In what ways does the training assume social neutrallity?
6. How can we design instructional environments that resist, mitigate, or disrupt harmful effects of dominant power structures?
7. How might my perspectives and practices as an instructional designer change if social justice were my top priority?
8. What relationships exist between our work as educational technologists and our lives as human beings?
9. What is the impact of our work in educational technology on humanity, and on all forms of life on the planet?
10. How does our work as educational technologists contribute to mystification?
11. How does our work as educational technologists ignore or deny structural racism, sexism, homophobia, ageism, ablism, classism, etc.?
12. How does the field of educational technology afford us *negative freedom* from
    a. awareness of structural racism and other systems of oppression, both in our field and in our broader societal contexts?

b. responsibility to identify, reflect critically upon, and meaningfully address systemic injustice?
c. acknowledging the full humanity of others?
d. responsibility to claim or regain our own full humanity by working to disrupt and dismantle systems and structures of oppression and injustice for some, and unearned privilege for others?
13. How can we learn to recognize political structures that we have been conditioned not to see?
14. In considering these questions, what factors might be influencing your responses?

For these kinds of questions to become more prevalent within educational technology academic programs and professional contexts, and for us to be able to respond to them appropriately, we need to increase our understandings of both historical and current oppression, subjugation, genocide (etc.), and how injustice operates at both individual and systemic levels. We also need to become better informed about scholarly and practical work in other fields relevant to our goal of better understanding and honoring the nexus of culture, learning, and technology. Increasing our understanding of past and current injustices and inequities is necessary for ethical design, development, and implementation of technology-mediated learning environments. By reflecting on how instructional designs and implementations of educational technologies can perpetuate and exacerbate inequities and injustices, we also can begin to see how to transform our designs and practices to specifically support equity and justice.

Taking Appropriate Action: Transform Harmful Systems, Practices, and Dynamics

The following suggestions are not intended as an exhaustive list, nor as a procedural guide. Rather, these suggestions are offered as examples of practical ways to begin to engage in action toward just and equitable educational technology practice, in conjunction with the previous praxis-based suggestions in this section related to naming and critically reflecting.

1. Seek continuous, ongoing education related to issues of culture, cultural competence, equity, justice, inclusion, positionalities, and privilege.
2. Make specific and tangible changes in your practice, while working to make both overt and covert efforts align toward increased equity and justice.
3. Be open about your efforts to transform your practice, and invite others to engage with you.
4. Modify curricula and interaction styles to be more inclusive.
5. Identify underlying aims and purposes of each assignment and project. At both big-picture and practical-detail levels, reflect on whether projects, approaches, strategies, and activities align more with transmission of content,

or transformation toward empowerment and equity (review Table 2.1). If efforts and outcomes are primarily transmissive, is that approach necessary? How might specific transmissive projects or efforts be recreated to be more consistent with a transformative approach?
6. Reconsider reading materials to ensure that topics, issues, and author selections are inclusive.
7. Be more conscious of oppressive dynamics in group discussions and address issues directly.
8. Change course assignments and projects to support inquiry at the intersections of culture, learning, and technology. For example, rather than invite students to choose their own topics for particular design and development projects, assign topics that both support and require inquiry related to cultural competence, equity, and inclusion.
9. Modify syllabi to clearly communicate the kinds of respectful and inclusive social interactions you want to encourage, and be mindful that you model those in your own practice.
10. Be mindful to not address culture-related issues in positivist, mechanistic, and lower-order ways.
11. Seek opportunities to collaborate with colleagues in social justice related disciplines.

Closing Comments

This is a key moment in the field of educational technology. As we recognize that understanding and appropriately addressing the combined domain of culture, learning, and technology is required for ethical practice in educational technology, we can commit to transforming our own practice, as well as current and future professional preparation for the field, to be more equitable and inclusive. Engagement toward reconciling the aims and purposes of critical pedagogy and educational technology is a powerful approach to a needed transformation in understanding culture as inseparable from learning and technology. In accepting the challenge toward reconciliation, we reject practices and tendencies that can relegate members of our field to being mere mechanics and technical workers exercising only enough volition and imagination to effectively fill in the gaps of dominant systems, and thus reinforce them. Focusing on how our work as educational technologists can support and increase equity and justice at the intersections of culture, learning, and technology opens unlimited opportunities to engage new or continuing work with hope, optimism, and ethical purpose.

References

Alcoff, L.M. (2007). Epistemologies of ignorance. In *Race and epistemologies of ignorance*, eds. Shannon Sullivan and Nancy Tuana, 39–57. Albany, NY: SUNY Press.

Antonio, A. L., Chang, M. J., Hakuta, K., Kenny, D. A., Levin, S. L., & Milem, J. F. (2004). Effects of racial diversity on complex thinking in college students. *Psychological Science*, 15(8), 507–510. https://web.stanford.edu/~aantonio/psychsci.pdf

Anyon, J. (1983). Social class and the hidden curriculum of work. In *The hidden curriculum and moral education*, eds. Henry Giroux and David Purpel, 143–167. Berkeley, CA: McCutchan Publishing Corporation.

Burniske, R. W. (2003). Links in the chain of doing: The ethics of introducing educational technology in developing countries. *TechTrends*, 47(6) 55–61.

Code, L. (1993). Taking subjectivity into account. In *Feminist epistemologies*, eds. Linda Alcoff and Elizabeth Potter, 15–48. New York: Routledge.

Collins, J. (2009). Social reproduction in classrooms and schools. *Annual Review of Anthropology*, 38, 33–48.

Crass, C. (2013). *Towards collective liberation: Anti-racist organizing, feminist praxis, and movement building strategies*. Oakland, CA: PM Press.

Crenshaw, K. (1993). Mapping the margins: Intersectionality, identity politics, and violence against women of color. *Stanford Law Review*, 43, 1241–1297.

Eisner, E. (1985). The three curricula that all schools teach, *The Educational Imagination*. New York: Macmillan.

Freire, P. (1970). *Pedagogy of the oppressed*. New York: Continuum.

Freire, P. (1973). *Education for critical consciousness*. New York: Continuum.

Freire, P. (1985). *The politics of education: Culture, power, and liberation*. South Hadley, MA: Bergin & Garvey.

Freire, P. (1990). *Pedagogy of the oppressed*. New York: Continuum. (Original work published 1970.)

Freire, P. (2005). *Teachers as cultural workers: Letters to those who dare teach* (expanded edition). Boulder, CO: Westview Press.

Giroux, H.A. (1983). *Theory and resistance in education: A pedagogy for the opposition*. New York: Bergin & Garvey.

Giroux, H.A. (2011). *On critical pedagogy*. New York: Bloomsbury Academic.

Goodman, D. (2013). *Cultural competency for social justice: A framework for student, staff, faculty, and organizational development*. Retrieved from: http://www.dianegoodman.com/documents/CulturalCompetenceforSocialJustice.pdf

Gorski, P.C. (2014). *Reaching and teaching students in poverty: Strategies for erasing the opportunity gap*. New York: Teachers College Press.

Greene, M. (1988). *The dialectic of freedom*. New York: Teachers College Press.

Gurin, P., Dey, E. L, Hurtado, S., & Gurin, G. (2002). Diversity and higher education: Theory and impact on educational outcomes, *Harvard Educational Review*, 72(3), 330–366.

Harding, S. (1991). *Whose science? Whose knowledge? Thinking from women's lives*. Ithica, NY: Cornell University Press.

hooks, b. (1994). *Teaching to transgress: Education as the practice of freedom*. New York: Routledge.

Hurtado, S., E. L. Dey, P. Gurin, & G. Gurin. (2003). College environments, diversity, and student learning. In *Higher education: Handbook of theory and research 18*, ed. J. C. Smart, 145–190. London: Kluwer Academic Publishers.

Januszewski, A. & Moldenda, M. (Eds.) 2008. *Educational technology: A definition with commentary*. New York: Lawrence Erlbaum Associates.

Kendall, K. (2013). *Understanding white privilege: Creating pathways to authentic relationships across race*. New York: Routledge.

Kincheloe, J.L. (2005). *Critical pedagogy primer* (First Edition). New York: Peter Lang.

Kincheloe, J.L. (2008). *Critical pedagogy primer* (Second Edition). New York: Peter Lang.

Kivel, P. (2011). *Uprooting racism: How white people can work for racial justice*. New York: New Society Publishers.

Macedo, D. (2006). *Literacies of power: What Americans are not allowed to know*. Boulder, CO: Westview Press.

McIntosh, P. (1988). *White privilege: Unpacking the invisible knapsack*. Excerpted in Working Paper 189, White privilege and male privilege: A personal account of coming to see correspondences through work in women's studies. Wellesley, MA: Wellesley College Center for Research on Women.

McNamee, S.J. & Miller, R.K. (2004). The meritocracy myth. *Sociation Today*, 2(1). Retrieved February 8, 2015 from http://www.ncsociology.org/sociationtoday/v21/merit.htm

Milem, J.F. & Hakuta, K. (2000). The benefits of racial and ethnic diversity in higher education. In *Minorities in higher education: Seventeenth annual status report*, 39–67. Washington, DC: American Council on Education.

Milem, J.F. (2003). The educational benefits of diversity: Evidence from multiple sectors. In *Compelling interest: Examining the evidence on racial dynamics in higher education*, eds. M. Chang et al., pp. 126–169. Stanford, CA: Stanford University Press.

Mills, C. (1997). *The racial contract*. Ithica, NY: Cornell University Press.

Nadal, K.L., Wong, Y., Griffin, K., Sriken, J. Vargas, V. Wideman, M., & Kolawole, A. (2011). Microaggressions and the multiracial experience. *International Journal of Humanities and Social Science*, 1(7), 36–44.

Page, S.E. (2007). *The difference: How the power of diversity creates better groups, firms, schools, and societies*. Princeton, NJ: Princeton University Press.

Page, S.E. (2010). *Diversity and complexity*. Princeton, NJ: Princeton University Press.

Roediger, D.R. (2007). *The wages of whiteness: Race and the making of the American working class* (Revised Edition). New York: Verso.

Shor, I. (1992). *Empowering education: Critical teaching for social change*. Chicago, IL: The University of Chicago Press.

Sullivan, S. & Tuana, N. (2007). *Race and epistemologies of ignorance*. Albany, NY: SUNY Press.

Takacs, D. (2003). How does your positionality bias your epistemology? In *Thought & action: The NEA Higher Education Journal*, 27–38. Available: http://www.nea.org/assets/img/PubThoughtAndAction/TAA_03_04.pdf

Wise, T. (2012). *Dear White America: Letter to a new minority*. San Francisco, CA: City Lights Books.

3

REVISITING INSTRUCTIONAL TECHNOLOGISTS' INATTENTION TO ISSUES OF CULTURAL DIVERSITY AMONG STAKEHOLDERS

Deepak Prem Subramony

Introduction

A little more than a decade ago, in the summer of 2004, I published a position paper in *Educational Technology* (Subramony, 2004b) boldly critiquing the mainstream instructional technology (IT) research and development community for its continued inattention to important issues related to cultural diversity[1] among target learners. This was the first paper published since the pioneering 1997 *Educational Technology* special issue—guest-edited by Dr. Gary C. Powell—on "diversity and educational technology" (see Powell, 1997a) that was explicitly devoted to focusing attention to this specific problem. My 2004 paper—titled "Instructional technologists' inattention to issues of cultural diversity among learners"—did four things: (a) It analyzed recent IT journal issues and IT conference programs for evidence of our field's interest—or lack thereof—towards said issues; (b) It offered plausible explanations for our field's disregard for these issues; (c) It described the potential harm/damage caused to cultural minority learners as a consequence of our field's neglect of these issues; and (d) It discussed what could be and is being done by our field to better serve the needs of culturally diverse learners.

Fast forward to 2017 and we are now seeing the coming together of this full-size edited book focusing on research and practice related to culture, learning and technology. The first of its kind within our specific field, this book represents an eagerly awaited and long overdue fruit of joint efforts by a formally established group of reformist[2] scholars dedicated to righting the IT community's historic wrongs by redirecting its mainstream discourse to more appropriately respond to the realities of a rapidly globalizing and diversifying body of stakeholders. It thus makes sense to include, within such a book, a chapter dedicated to assessing the current state of our field's relationship with issues connected to cultural diversity among those impacted by its research and practice. Written as a sequel to my 2004 position paper, this chapter is organized around a consideration of the following three questions: In terms of the progress made by the IT community over the past decade or so in acknowledging and responding to said issues, (a) what has changed?; (b) what has stayed the same?; and (c) where do we go from here? Having said this, I must ask the reader to understand that the following sections represent an indicative or illustrative—rather than exhaustive—account, owing to obvious spatial/temporal constraints.

Section I: What has Changed?

Those acquainted with the arguments put forward by critical scholars[3]—such as Jamison (1992), Bromley & Apple (1998), Bowers (2000), Bowers et al. (2000), Morino (2000), Tapscott (2000), and Cuban (2001), for instance—since the initial years of the Internet-driven information age will be familiar with the idea that technology embodies economic, social, and cultural power; furthermore, recognizing that technology = power allows us to identify two distinct sets of issues—that are linked to each other like two sides of the same coin—when it comes to educational and communications technologies (ECT) and cultural diversity among stakeholders. This chapter seeks to describe the nature of our field's recognition and response over the past decade to both of the following sets of issues.

On the one hand, there is the issue of equitable access[4] to ECT—along with equitable opportunities to acquire meaningful ECT-related knowledge and skills—based on the understanding that these technologies represent the primary means of production[5] during the information age and thus possess particular power to emancipate. Consequently, inequitable access and competencies with regard to ECT lead to the Digital Divide, a persistent, pernicious and woefully under-researched socioeconomic evil of the information age whose current nature and ramifications I recently elaborated upon at the 2014 McJulien Lecture (Subramony, 2014a). On the other hand, there is the issue of the sociocultural impact of ECT on non-Western and cultural minority stakeholders. Technology that has the power to emancipate also has the power to subjugate and oppress. Critical scholars have long maintained—see Bowers (1988) for an early, pioneering argument along these lines—that (a) technologies are not culturally neutral but are in fact embedded with the perspectives and values of their creating cultures; and (b) this inconvenient truth is traditionally hidden by the vendors of said technologies in order to obscure the cultural transformations that their adoption by other societies will engender.

Overall Landscape of ECT

One of the defining trends with regard to the evolution of ECT during the current information age—including the past decade—has been their progressively increasing ubiquity and affordability. This phenomenon may be characterized as a function of the tapping of human ingenuity on an unparalleled scale as a result of the globalizing and "flattening" forces described by media commentator Thomas L. Friedman in *The World is Flat* (see Friedman, 2007). It may also be explained by invoking Dr. Everett Rogers' diffusion of innovations theory (see Rogers, 2003)—that once a product is embraced by a critical mass of adopters, economies of scale can be realized, and the stage can be set for further innovation, with increased know-how helping to simultaneously engender both superior features and reduced costs. A well-known recent example would be the Apple iPhone, which bore a price-tag of several hundred dollars when it was first released in 2007, while today more advanced versions of it are being offered by communications providers in the United States for very low prices as part of cellular contracts.

The unprecedented spread of handheld devices, low-cost netbooks/tablets/e-readers, and social media applications across multiple sections of society as a result of their growing affordability and unavoidability—along with concomitant ECT initiatives such as 1:1 laptops/tablets in schools across the nation—have served to alleviate some of the concerns specifically surrounding issues of equitable access to the emancipatory potential of ECT, going so far as to precipitate speculations in some circles regarding whether the Digital Divide even exists as an issue any more (see Subramony, 2014b). Moreover, we are also seeing a remarkable uptick in the use of ECT—in the form of camera phones and online video sharing websites—by oppressed/marginalized groups to document, publicize, and seek justice for abuses of power by trigger-happy law enforcement personnel.

Reframing the Concept

In 2007 the Definition and Terminology Committee of the Association for Educational Communications and Technology (AECT) presented a revised definition of the concept of educational technology, making alterations to AECT's preexisting definition of IT for the first time since 1994. Readers will notice that the subsequent sections of this chapter prominently and extensively detail steps taken by individuals and entities associated with AECT with regard to addressing issues of cultural diversity among stakeholders impacted by our field. This is because AECT both historically and currently has played an outsize role in impacting the evolution of theory and practice within the IT field and profession. The oldest professional home for this field, AECT has—ever since its establishment in 1923 as the National Education Association's Department of Visual Instruction—continuously maintained a preeminent position within the field, representing professionals in a broad range of occupations who have an interest in improving learning through the use of media and technology. Currently AECT is a professional association of thousands of educators and others who carry out a wide range of responsibilities in the study, planning, application, and production of communications media for instruction. AECT has grown into a major organization for those actively involved in the designing of instruction and a systematic approach to learning, providing an international forum for the exchange and dissemination of ideas within the field and serving as the international spokesperson for the improvement of instruction. (AECT, 2016a; 2016b)

AECT's revised definition—"Educational technology is the study and ethical practice of facilitating learning and improving performance by creating, using, and managing appropriate technological processes and resources" (AECT Definition and Terminology Committee, 2007, p. 1)—is noteworthy in its incorporation of the words "ethical" and "appropriate." Discussing the intended meaning of these words within the context of the reworked definition, The Committee—made up of key leaders in the field including Drs. Alan Januszewski and Michael Molenda—explained (AECT Definition and Terminology Committee, 2007) that (a) "ethical" practice necessitates understanding the power position of those designing and developing technological solutions by considering questions such as who is included, who is empowered, and who has authority during these processes; and that (b) "appropriate" technological solutions are connected with the local users and cultures. The Committee also invoked specific sections of AECT's *Code of Ethics* document to imply that such solutions must avoid content promoting gender, ethnic, racial, or religious stereotypes; emphasize social/cultural diversity; and reflect culturally and intellectually diverse viewpoints. AECT's adoption of this transformed definition represents a significant step forward in the IT community's coming to terms with the fact that in today's flat world (Friedman, 2007) our research and practice stand to impact a far more culturally diverse body of stakeholders than ever before.

Minorities in Media

Around the same time, Minorities in Media (MIM)—a historic, groundbreaking AECT affiliate organization established by Dr. Wesley J. McJulien back in the 1970s as a professional interest and support group for African-American IT scholars (see Wennberg, 2000)—started to experience a resurgence in activity with regard to publishing works addressing culturally diverse stakeholders during the late 2000s. These initiatives were in addition to MIM's usual role in showcasing research and practice in this area at AECT's annual International Conventions.

Particularly noteworthy was a 2007 special issue of Howard University's respected, peer-reviewed *Journal of Negro Education* dedicated to "Looking beyond the Digital Divide: Participation and Opportunities with Technology in Education," edited by Drs. Kevin A. Clark and Joi L. Moore and featuring contributions from a galaxy of MIM scholars and others (see Clark & Moore, 2007). In terms of cultural and geographical scope, this special issue covered K-12 and adult education contexts across the United States (including Alaska) and the Caribbean. Areas covered by this special issue included using ECT in the context of culturally diverse learners' professional development, using innovative ECT tools to serve the needs of diverse learners, integrating culture into the discourse surrounding ECT, and reviews of books and other media pertaining to culture, learning, and technology. Thus, both the fundamental sets of issues discussed earlier in this chapter—namely, equitable access to ECT tools/skills/opportunities, and the sociocultural impact of ECT—were tackled by the articles comprising this special issue.

Another significant endeavor by MIM during this period was bringing out an *Educational Technology* special issue focused on "culturally relevant technology-based learning environments" in 2009. Guest-edited by Drs. Roberto Joseph and Kevin A. Clark, and intended as a long overdue sequel to Dr. Powell's trailblazing 1997 effort, this special issue also featured works by a range of scholars—from both within and outside MIM—spanning a wide variety of cultural contexts across the United States, Asia, and Latin America (see Joseph & Clark, 2009). Topics explored in this special issue included incorporating cultural values into the instructional design process, designing and applying ECT in culturally responsive/relevant/participatory ways with a view towards closing achievement gaps, understanding culturally diverse learners and their relationships with ECT, and using ECT to preserve traditional knowledge/culture/language. Culturally cognizant ECT products/initiatives presented included *The Hispanic Math Project, Rappin' Reader, Say, Say Oh Playmate, Clover, Riding the Freedom Train, The Virtual Bead Loom*, the *African-American Distributed Multiple Learning Styles System* (Frederick et al., 2009), the *United Sugpiaq Alutiiq Video Game* (Hall & Sanderville, 2009), and *CompuGirls* (Scott et al., 2009). So once again, both of the key sets of issues mentioned earlier in this chapter were addressed here.

Besides, in addition to numerous journal articles, book chapters, and conference presentations produced by various MIM members, it is important to highlight Dr. Patricia A. Young's path-breaking efforts to promote the integration of culture throughout the instructional design process leading to the creation of ECT products (see Young, 2008a); these endeavors were crowned by her construction of a formal Culture Based Model—the first of its kind in our field—which she elaborated via multiple journal articles and book chapters (see Young, 2008b; 2008c; 2011), and exhaustively contextualized, detailed, and expanded in a seminal book that is already being acknowledged as one of the classics in our field (see Young, 2009).

Culture, Learning, and Technology

Another important development—in terms of helping cultural diversity issues gain a foothold within the mainstream IT discourse—since the publication of my 2004 article was the metamorphosis of MIM into a formal Division of AECT, namely, the Culture, Learning and Technology (CLT) Division, in 2013. Given

AECT's status as the definitive and preeminent professional organization for scholars and practitioners in our field, the establishment of a full-fledged AECT Division focusing on the cultural dimensions of learning and technology represents a significant step forward. While the erstwhile MIM's "affiliate organization" status with AECT allowed it a certain autonomy and independence, getting on board with AECT as a full-fledged Division gave this group of scholars much more visibility and recognition, and much more policy-making input—afforded the group a seat at the big table, so to speak—within the larger organization. It is worth noting that the CLT Division's establishment was unanimously supported by the entire AECT Board of Directors (AECT Executive Director Dr. Phillip Harris, personal communication, 2013). As CLT Division President for 2013–15 Dr. Camille Dickson-Deane explained (personal communication, 2014), the Division seeks to build upon the core values of MIM while adjusting for current needs by expanding its mission and vision to be inclusive to all; it focuses on adhering to MIM founder Dr. McJulien's visions while ensuring that it also addresses issues pertaining to current society as they relate to the intersection of culture, learning, and technology. This book represents a key effort by the Division in this regard.

Furthermore, with most critical IT scholars having long recognized the significant emancipatory potential of ECT—for instance, C.A. Bowers has discussed how ECT, by serving as open media for the democratization of knowledge, can be highly useful in helping oppressed/marginalized culture groups (a) maintain networks and share information over vast distances; and (b) increase their effectiveness in the political arena (see Bowers et al., 2000)—the CLT Division has been trying to harness the power of the World Wide Web, including Web 2.0, to attract the attention of wider audiences across the field. As of May 29, 2015, the Division—in collaboration with the AECT Graduate Student Assembly—had successfully convened three free informational webinars on topics related to culture, learning, and technology, with one more such webinar currently in the works. Featuring reformist IT scholars from around the world, these webinars covered a range of issues including the cultural ramifications and impact of computer games, effective ECT use within the contexts of college-level online diversity courses and K-12 level global citizenship courses, equitable access to the emancipatory potential of ECT, and the power dynamics related to the creation, diffusion, and adoption of ECT. Furthermore, the Division has been engaging key social media platforms as part of its efforts to maintain networks and share information on a global scale. Around the aforementioned date, the Division's Facebook page—accessible at https://www.facebook.com/groups/aectclt—featured 107 individual members. The Division has also been employing multiple Twitter hashtags—such as #aectconnect, #globalcitizenship, #digitaldivide, and so on—to provoke conversations focusing on issues related to culture, learning, and technology. Other Web 2.0 initiatives currently in the pipeline include a dedicated Twitter account, LinkedIn page, and podcast series, along with establishing bylaws to direct protocol for social media usage, according to Dr. Akesha Horton, the CLT Division's Vice President for Communications (personal communication, 2015).

Meanwhile, the CLT Division's establishment also appears to be having the effect of encouraging increasing interest in social/cultural issues related to IT among the wider AECT membership. One unprecedented development has been the decision by *Educational Technology Research and Development (ETR&D)*—AECT's flagship peer-reviewed journal—to launch a new "Cultural and Regional Perspectives" section, with Dr. Young as its inaugural editor. ETR&D's editorial board have established this section with a view to providing a home for scholarly articles featuring "fresh ideas and a regional slant on the latest cultural, learning, and technology issues" and situating research studies within cultural, social, political, economic, environmental, or psychological contexts. The section seeks to publish works that explore how individuals, groups, societies, and cultures affected by ECT, and, conversely, how they in turn affect ECT (Section Editor Dr. Patricia A. Young, personal communication). Another instance involves a major online reference work—commissioned by AECT in collaboration with Springer—that features substantive, original, peer-reviewed articles examining critical facets of learning theory, educational research, instructional design and development, and educational practice and policy. Entitled *Learning, Design, and Technology: An International Compendium of Theory, Research, Practice and Policy* and co-edited by AECT Past Presidents Drs. Michael Spector, Barbara Lockee, and Marcus Childress, this virtual compendium notably includes "Cultural and Regional Perspectives" as one of its 16 sections, once again with Dr. Young as Section Editor.

Section II: What has Stayed the Same?

In Section I of this chapter, I attempted to describe the progress made by reformist IT scholars to direct our field's attention to issues connected to cultural diversity among various stakeholder groups impacted by its research and practice. In this section I would like to argue that, notwithstanding the laudable efforts detailed in the preceding pages, when one looks at the bigger picture it becomes disturbingly clear that issues of social and cultural diversity continue to remain a veritable sideshow as far as the mainstream IT discourse is concerned, as opposed to being systemically incorporated across its length and breadth. Consider some of the efforts I enumerated in the previous section, such as occasional special issues, the formation of AECT's CLT Division, and the launch of the special ETR&D section. In the absence of sufficient attention being paid to issues of cultural diversity outside of these "special" initiatives, it could be argued that such endeavors represent not growing interest in these issues within the wider IT community but rather their ongoing marginalization, their continued intellectual segregation and ghettoization within sharply circumscribed forums and circles.

If every Division of AECT were to systemically incorporate the examination of cultural and power variables within their respective areas of focus, establishing a separate CLT Division would be redundant and unnecessary. If key IT journals were to feature articles addressing issues of cultural diversity on a regular basis, there would be no need to devote so-called special issues to deal with these topics. In a similar vein, why must ETR&D designate a special section to focus on cultural/regional perspectives, as opposed to ensuring the reflection of said perspectives within its regular Research and Development sections? Same goes for the virtual compendium mentioned at the end of the preceding paragraph; rather than relegate cultural/regional perspectives to one of its 16 sections, why not incorporate such perspectives across all sections?

Presentations and Articles

To get an idea of how much attention was being paid at AECT outside of the CLT Division to pertinent issues such as power, culture, equity, inclusion, privilege, hegemony, or oppression, I performed a content analysis of the titles and abstracts of sessions listed across the 108 pages of the Program of the 2014 AECT Convention recently held in Jacksonville, Fla. Not one of the ten Presidential Sessions emphasized any of the aforementioned issues, and neither did a single one of the 16 Workshops offered. Only one out of eight theory/research-based training/educational programs highlighted as part of the Design and Development Showcase reflected a culture-based focus. Meanwhile, out of hundreds of regular concurrent, roundtable, and panel presentations outside of the CLT Division, I could only discern 17 as explicitly featuring an examination of the above issues. Please note that there were additional sessions presenting research conducted among non-US populations; however, those presentations were omitted from the aforementioned count if their abstracts provided little evidence suggesting that they meaningfully addressed the germane issues enumerated above.

Along the same lines I also examined issues of ETR&D published over the second half of 2014 (v. 62, issues 4, 5, and 6) and the first half of 2015 (v. 63, issues 1, 2, and 3). During this one-year time period, only one out of 40 articles published within the Research and Development sections of ETR&D (namely, Jere-Folotiya et al., 2014) dealt with any of the issues named above. Once again, articles merely presenting research conducted among non-US populations were not counted unless they made one or more of the aforementioned key issues their major focus of interest. Out of curiosity I dug back one more year, looking at issues published over the second half of 2013 (v. 61, issues 4, 5, and 6) and the first half of 2014 (v. 62, issues 1, 2, and 3). During this time period, a similarly small fraction of articles—two out of 42—published within the journal's Research and Development sections (i.e., Russell et al., 2013, and Nistor et al., 2013) featured any significant consideration of power, culture, equity, inclusion, privilege, hegemony, or oppression. Furthermore, when I examined the 2014 edition of AECT's *Handbook of Research on Educational Communications and Technology*—which can, like ETR&D, be characterized as a concrete, representative, and influential manifestation of the mainstream discourse within our field—I found only four out of its 74 constituent chapters (viz., Moore & Ellsworth, 2014; Young, 2014; Morgan, 2014; and Kozma & Vota, 2014) making these issues their primary focus.

Textual Materials

Almost two decades ago, Dr. Powell had described how the ethnocentrism of the mainstream IT community left them predisposed to regard diversity at best as interesting, and at worst as a deficit (see Powell, 1997b). He and others have long emphasized that the problem is not just that stakeholder diversity is ignored by the mainstream IT discourse, but that it views any deviation from the ethnocentric ideal/norm with a deficit perception, whether that deviation be culturally diverse learners, learners from lower socioeconomic status (SES) groups, or differently abled learners. In other words, instead of seeing stakeholder diversity as a professional opportunity to be enthusiastically embraced and celebrated—or simply as the nature of ordinary reality in our present age of unparalleled global interconnectedness and human mobility—the mainstream IT discourse perceives it as a special need to be accommodated.

Back in 2004, when my *Educational Technology* position paper came out, the then-current (fourth) edition of the standard text *Designing Effective Instruction* (Morrison et al., 2004) clubbed "culturally diverse learners" and "learners with disabilities" under the common label "nonconventional learners;" these were described as "individuals . . . whose preparation, behavior and expectations may not be typical." Furthermore, culturally diverse learners were defined as "members of ethnic cultures with backgrounds and behaviors that differ markedly from those of the majority of learners." (p. 61). In response, one might ask what kind of preparation, behavior and expectations might be considered "typical" in the "flat world" that Friedman (2007) describes? What kind of learners might be assumed as constituting the "majority" in today's schools and workplaces?

In the subsequent (fifth) edition of the text (Morrison et al., 2007), the umbrella label "nonconventional learners" was removed, but the sections about "culturally diverse learners" and "learners with disabilities" were still placed one after the other (pp. 59–60). One noteworthy difference was the addition of the "growth of global corporations and outsourcing" as a reason for giving special attention to the characteristics of culturally diverse learners (p. 61). Finally, in the most recent (seventh) print edition of *Designing Effective Instruction* (Morrison et al., 2013) that I could get my hands on, the two sections were still placed one right after the other (pp. 56–58). Apart from the aforementioned couple of pages, the only other reference to cultural diversity in any of the editions cited was contained in a very brief paragraph addressing the issue of legal problems arising from the inclusion of discriminatory materials in training programs (found on pp. 371–372 in the 2004 edition, p. 384 in the 2007 edition, and p. 411 in the 2013 edition).

Graduate Programs

Apart from examining recent conference presentations, journal articles and textual materials, I also decided to look at four preeminent graduate programs in our field—housed at Indiana University (IU), Utah State University (USU), Pennsylvania State University (Penn State), and the University of Georgia (UGA)—to see if either of these programs offered one or more graduate-level IT courses making issues of cultural diversity among stakeholders their primary focus. I specifically examined the courses that were coded EDUC-R 5XX through EDUC-R 7XX in IU's School of Education Graduate Bulletin 2012–2014 (Indiana University, n.d.); ITLS 5XXX through ITLS 7XXX in USU's 2014–2015 General Catalog (Utah State University, n.d.); EDTEC 5XX through EDTEC 5XX 8XX and INSYS 5XX in Penn State's University Bulletin (Pennsylvania State University, n.d.); and EDIT 5XXX through EDIT 9XXX in UGA's Fall 2015 Bulletin (University of Georgia, n.d.).

Based on my scrutiny of these sources, neither IU, nor USU, nor Penn State appeared to offer a single course primarily addressing cultural diversity issues in IT research and/or practice. It is possible that elective courses targeting these issues might have been offered from time to time under the umbrella of EDUC-R 685/EDUC-R 695 topical seminars at IU, as part of ITLS 6870/ITLS 7870 current issues seminars at USU, or under the label of EDTEC 597/EDTEC 897 special topics courses at Penn State; however, the schools' respective bulletins/catalogs did not offer any information in this regard. Meanwhile, UGA's bulletin featured a single three-credit course—cross-listed as EDIT 4600/EDIT 6600 and titled "Multicultural Perspectives on Technology"—that was dedicated to helping students recognize, analyze, and benefit from diverse, global perspectives on the use and meaning of technology in educational contexts.

Section III: Where do we go from here?

Dr. Amy Bradshaw in her recent presentation at AECT (Bradshaw, 2014) skillfully correlated our field's attitudes and perspectives apropos race, ethnicity, and social justice issues over the course of its history and evolution with social, cultural, and political developments taking place concurrently within the wider world outside. By doing this she was able to clearly demonstrate how, in its collective blind spot regarding these issues and in its adherence to common fallacies of social neutrality, the IT community was basically reflecting broader societal norms and trends. Dr. Charles Reigeluth—one of our field's most celebrated reformist scholars—has long maintained that our K-12 public education system, designed to meet our educational needs during the industrial age, "is fundamentally inadequate for meeting our vastly different educational needs in the information age" (Joseph & Reigeluth, 2010, p. 97) and thus needs systemic change to help transform the current paradigm into a different one.

In my 2004 position paper in *Educational Technology*, as well as in a subsequent piece in the same publication (Subramony, 2012), I highlighted Dr. Reigeluth's tireless advocacy for systemic reform as opposed to piecemeal tinkering, and his pioneering arguments (see Reigeluth, 1999) exhorting the IT community to change the very structure of our current systems of training and education that discourage diversity and prevent diverse learners from realizing their full potential. Joseph & Reigeluth (2010) explain how we need to bring stakeholders of diverse backgrounds, experiences, and opinions together and ensure that no voices are left out[6], or else our efforts to move forward will be weakened and will be more susceptible to adverse reactions from these very same stakeholders. It is very heartening to note that this perspective is also clearly reflected in the 14 "Essential Conditions" to effectively leverage technology for learning that have been put forward by the International Society for Technology in Education (ISTE)[7]. These critical elements (ISTE, 2016)—aimed at offering educators and school leaders a research-backed framework to guide implementation of the ISTE Standards—include (a) developing a shared vision for educational technology among all relevant stakeholders; (b) empowering stakeholders at every level to be leaders in effecting change; (c) equitable access to current and emerging technologies and digital resources including robust and reliable Internet connectivity for all students, teachers, staff, and school leaders; and (d) engaging communities to support and fund the effective use of ECT.

Understanding the aforementioned perspective should make it abundantly clear that our field will not be able to adequately and appropriately respond to its rapidly globalizing and diversifying family of stakeholders as long as research and practice relating to issues of cultural diversity remain relegated to the sidelines of its mainstream discourse. Our present information age is marked by global interconnectedness and human mobility on a hitherto unimaginable scale, leading to our field's activities impacting an exponentially expanding universe of stakeholders. In order to remain relevant—and avoid perpetrating irreparable harm—in such an era, our field needs to systemically transform its research and practice to more meaningfully confront issues of power, culture, equity, inclusion, privilege, hegemony, and oppression impacting these stakeholders. The examination of these issues needs to be moved beyond sporadic special issues, isolated special sections, and segregated special interest groups and be systemically integrated across the entirety of our field's research and practice.

Operationalizing such systemic integration will not be easy or quick; it will require a united effort on all our parts towards bringing about a tectonic shift in our collective mindset that allows out field to rapidly evolve and transform into one whose:

a) Core, mainstream textbooks on instructional systems design (ISD) and educational technology integration stop espousing deficit perceptions of diversity and instead explicitly emphasize the importance of sociocultural cognizance and responsiveness throughout the ISD and technology integration processes;
b) Top academic departments/programs feature the widespread use of sociocultural and critical lenses to examine key issues within the majority of their ISD and technology integration courses at the undergraduate, Master's and doctoral levels;
c) Leading academic/professional organizations encourage every single one of their divisions/interest groups to systemically incorporate the examination of cultural and power variables within their respective areas of focus, eventually rendering separate entities like MIM and AECT's CLT Division redundant and unnecessary;
d) Highly respected journals and books feature articles confronting the aforementioned issues within their core/mainstream sections on a regular basis, thus eliminating the need to devote so-called special issues or sections to deal with these topics; and
e) Highly influential conferences emphasize the aforementioned issues across their programs, from presidential sessions through workshops to concurrent, roundtable, and poster sessions.

Only once the scenario described above becomes living reality will we as a field be able to eventually arrive at the point where *all* of our scholars, teachers, and practitioners—irrespective of their own social, cultural, economic, intellectual/academic, and ideological backgrounds—possess the necessary skills and competencies to be able to engage in the kind of socioculturally cognizant and responsive inquiry, teaching, and practice that truly meets the needs of 21st-century stakeholders across the globe.

Notes

1 As Powell (1997c) explains, culture in this context encompasses "the sum total of ways of living, including values, beliefs, aesthetic standards, linguistic expression, patterns of thinking, behavioral norms, and styles of communication" (p. 15) pertaining to a given group of people. Meanwhile, diversity as used in this chapter refers to differences based on culture, nationality, race, ethnicity, language, and religion.
2 As in belonging to a movement that advocates for the amendment or improvement of a currently unsatisfactory or inappropriate state of affairs within a given system.
3 Critical scholars interpret the acts and the symbols of society to understand how various social groups are oppressed, believing that understanding the ways human beings

are oppressed enables one to take action to change oppressive forces. These scholars align themselves with the interests of those opposed to dominant order of society, and explore how competing interests clash and how conflicts are resolved in favor of particular groups (Seiler, 2006).
4 Equitable access implies more than merely "equal" access. Ensuring fairness also demands remedies to redress injustices that have historically denied or restricted access to certain sections of society. Thus, in order to maximize opportunities for access experienced by historically underserved groups, resources must also be committed towards leveling the playing field (Kranich, 2005).
5 Means of production refer to the tools (instruments) and the raw material (subject) you use to create something (Blunden, 2008).
6 A well-known example of policy making that was imposed top-down across diverse stakeholder constituencies without first listening to their voices and facilitating their buy-in—and thus resulting in predictably fierce opposition and outrage—was the infamous No Child Left Behind; I provided a post-mortem of that socioculturally tone-deaf educational policy initiative from a change management perspective in a 2006 Educational Technology article (Subramony, 2006).
7 An influential nonprofit organization serving educators and education leaders that is renowned for its widely adopted ISTE Standards for learning, teaching, and leading in the digital age.

References

Association for Educational Communications and Technology (AECT). (2016a). *What is AECT?* Retrieved February 3, 2016 from the AECT website: http://www.aect.org/newsite

Association for Educational Communications and Technology (AECT). (2016b). *AECT in the 20th century: A brief history.* Retrieved February 3, 2016 from the AECT website: http://www.aect.org/newsite

Blunden, A. (2008). *Marxists internet archive encyclopedia.* Retrieved February 3, 2016 from https://www.marxists.org/glossary/terms/m/e.htm Jacksonville, November 2014.

Bowers, C. A. (1988). *The cultural dimensions of educational computing: Understanding the non-neutrality of technology.* New York, NY: Teachers College Press.

Bowers, C. A. (2000). *Let them eat data: How computers affect education, cultural diversity, and the prospects of ecological sustainability.* Athens, GA: University of Georgia Press.

Bowers, C. A., Vasquez, M., & Roaf, M. (2000). Native people and the challenge of computers: Reservation schools, individualism, and consumerism. *American Indian Quarterly, 24*(2), 182–199.

Bradshaw, A. C. (2014). *Field of privilege: Why instructional design and technology must engage issues of race, ethnicity, and social justice.* Paper presented at the Association for Educational Communications and Technology's 2014 International Convention in Bromley, H., & Apple, M. W. (Eds.). (1998). *Education/technology/power.* Albany, NY: State University of New York Press.

Bromley, H. & Apple, M. W. (1998). Education, technology, power: Educational computing as a social practice. Albany, NY: State University of New York Press.

Clark, K. A., & Moore, J. L. (2007). Introduction and overview. *The Journal of Negro Education, 76*(1), 1–4.

Cuban, L. (2001). *Oversold and underused*. Cambridge, MA: Harvard University Press.
Definition and Terminology Committee of the Association for Educational Communications and Technology. (2007). Definition. In A. Januszewski & M. Molenda (Eds.), *Educational technology: A definition with commentary* (pp. 1–14). New York, NY: Routledge.
Frederick, R., Donnor, J. K., & Hatley, L. (2009). Culturally responsive applications of computer technologies in education. *Educational Technology, 49*(6), 9–13.
Friedman, T. L. (2007). *The world is flat: A brief history of the twenty-first century*. New York, NY: Farrar, Straus, and Giroux.
Hall, L. D., & Sanderville, J. M. C. (2009). United Sugpiaq Alutiiq (USA) video game. *Educational Technology, 49*(6), 20–24.
Indiana University (n.d.). *School of Education graduate bulletin 2012–2014*. Retrieved June 9, 2015 from the Indiana University website: http://bulletins.iu.edu/iu/educ-grad/2012–2014/courses/instructional-systems-technology.shtml
International Society for Technology in Education (ISTE). (2016). *Essential conditions*. Retrieved February 3, 2016 from the ISTE website: http://www.iste.org/standards/essential-conditions
Jamison, P. K. (1992). *Adopting a critical stance towards technology and education: The possibility for liberatory technology in an information technology age*. Unpublished dissertation, Indiana University.
Jere-Folotiya, J., Chansa-Kabali, T., Munachaka, J. C., Sampa, F., Yalukanda, C., Westerholm, J., & Lyytinen, H. (2014). The effect of using a mobile literacy game to improve literacy levels of grade one students in Zambian schools. *Educational Technology Research and Development, 62*(4), 417–436.
Joseph, R., & Clark, K. (2009). Introduction to special issue. *Educational Technology, 49*(6), 3–4.
Joseph, R., & Reigeluth, C. M. (2010). The systemic change process in education: A conceptual framework. *Contemporary Educational Technology, 1*(2), 97–117.
Kozma, R. B., & Vota, W. S. (2014). ICT in developing countries: Policies, implementation, and impact. In J. M. Spector, M. D. Merrill, J. Elen, & M. J. Bishop (Eds.), *Handbook of research on educational communications and technology* (pp. 885–894). New York, NY: Springer Science+Business Media.
Kranich, N. (2005). *Equality and equity of access: What's the difference?* Retrieved February 3, 2016 from the American Library Association website: http://www.ala.org/offices/oif/iftoolkits/toolkitrelatedlinks/equalityequity
Moore, S. L., & Ellsworth, J. B. (2014). Ethics of educational technology. In J. M. Spector, M. D. Merrill, J. Elen, & M. J. Bishop (Eds.), *Handbook of research on educational communications and technology* (pp. 113–127). New York, NY: Springer Science+Business Media.
Morgan, K. (2014). Technology integration in multicultural settings. In J. M. Spector, M. D. Merrill, J. Elen, & M. J. Bishop (Eds.), *Handbook of research on educational communications and technology* (pp. 867–871). New York, NY: Springer Science+Business Media.
Morino, M. (2000). *Policy & philanthropy: Keys to closing the digital divide*. Reston, VA: Morino Institute.
Morrison, G. R., Ross, S. M., & Kemp, J. E. (2004). *Designing effective instruction*, 4th ed. Hoboken, NJ: John Wiley & Sons, Inc.
Morrison, G. R., Ross, S. M., & Kemp, J. E. (2007). *Designing effective instruction*, 5th ed. Hoboken, NJ: John Wiley & Sons, Inc.

Morrison, G.R., Ross, S.M., Kalman, H.K., & Kemp, J.E. (2013). *Designing effective instruction, 7th ed.* Hoboken, NJ: John Wiley & Sons, Inc.

Nistor, N., Göğüş, A., & Lerche, T. (2013). Educational technology acceptance across national and professional cultures: a European study. *Educational Technology Research and Development, 61*(4), 733–749.

Powell, G.C. (1997a). Diversity and educational technology: Introduction to special issue. *Educational Technology, 37*(2), 5.

Powell, G.C. (1997b). On being a culturally sensitive instructional designer and educator. *Educational Technology, 37*(2), 6–14.

Powell, G.C. (1997c). Understanding the language of diversity. *Educational Technology, 37*(2), 15–16.

Reigeluth, C.M. (1999). What is instructional-design theory and how is it changing? In C.M. Reigeluth (Ed.), *Instructional-design theories and models, volume II: A new paradigm of instructional theory* (pp. 5–30). Mahwah, NJ: Lawrence Erlbaum Associates.

Rogers, E.M. (2003). *Diffusion of innovations, 5th ed.* New York, NY: Free Press.

Russell, L.R., Kinuthia, W.L., Lokey-Vega, A., Tsang-Kosma, W., & Madathany, R. (2013). Identifying complex cultural interactions in the instructional design process: A case study of a cross-border, cross-sector training for innovation program. *Educational Technology Research and Development, 61*(4), 707–732.

Scott, K.A., Aist, G., & Hood, D.W. (2009). CompuGirls: Designing a culturally relevant technology program. *Educational Technology, 49*(6), 34–39.

Seiler, R.M. (2006). *Human communication in the critical theory tradition.* Retrieved February 3, 2016 from the University of Calgary website: http://people.ucalgary.ca/~rseiler/critical.htm

Subramony, D.P. (2004). Instructional technologists' inattention to issues of cultural diversity among learners. *Educational Technology, 44*(4), 19–24.

Subramony, D.P. (2006). School administrators' responses to No Child Left Behind (NCLB): Insights from the Alaskan Arctic and elsewhere. *Educational Technology, 46*(4), 28–33.

Subramony, D.P. (2012). Implementing technological solutions within K-12 contexts: A comprehensive route guide. *Educational Technology, 52*(5), 14–19.

Subramony, D.P. (2014a). *The 2014 McJulien Lecture: Reframing the Digital Divide within a 'flat world' context.* The Association for Educational Communications and Technology's 2014 International Convention in Jacksonville, November 2014.

Subramony, D.P. (2014b). Revisiting the digital divide in the context of a 'flattening' world. *Educational Technology, 54*(2), 3–9.

Tapscott, D. (2000). The digital divide. In R. Pea (Ed.), *The Jossey-Bass reader on technology and learning* (pp. 127–154). San Francisco, CA: Jossey-Bass.

University of Georgia (n.d.). *Fall 2015 UGA bulletin.* Retrieved June 9, 2015 from the University of Georgia website: http://bulletin.uga.edu/CoursesHome.aspx

Utah State University (n.d.). *2014–2015 general catalog.* Retrieved June 9, 2015 from the Utah State University website: http://catalog.usu.edu

Wennberg, H-E. (2000). Wesley Joseph McJulien: Leader, teacher, and media pioneer. In R.M. Branch & M.A. Fitzgerald (Eds.), *Educational Media and Technology Yearbook, Vol. 25* (pp. 157–159). Englewood, CO: Libraries Unlimited, Inc.

Young, P.A. (2008a). Integrating culture in the design of ICTs. *British Journal of Educational Technology, 39*(1), 6–17.

Young, P.A. (2008b). The Culture Based Model: Constructing a model of culture. *Journal of Educational, Technology & Society, 11*(2), 107–118.

Young, P. A. (2008c). The Culture Based Model: A framework for designers and visual ID languages. In L. Botturi & T. Stubbs (Eds.), *Handbook of visual languages for instructional design: Theories and practices* (pp. 52–75). Hershey, PA: IGI Global.
Young, P. A. (2009). *Instructional design frameworks and intercultural models.* Hershey, PA: IGI Global.
Young, P. A. (2011). The significance of the Culture Based Model in designing culturally-aware tutoring systems. *AI & Society, 26*(1), 35–47.
Young, P. A. (2014). The presence of culture in learning. In J. M. Spector, M. D. Merrill, J. Elen, & M. J. Bishop (Eds.), *Handbook of research on educational communications and* technology (pp. 349–361). New York, NY: Springer Science+Business Media.

4

GLOBALIZATION, IRONIC BINARIES, AND INSTRUCTIONAL TECHNOLOGY

Toward the Emergence of a Robust Critical Theory of Technology

Michael K. Thomas

Introduction

The fields of instructional design and educational technology have long been agnostic with regard to both culture and theory (e.g. Dick & Carey, 1978). Though clearly ensconced in systems theory and cognitivism, the progenitors of the field preferred to emphasize efficiency and effectiveness rather than speak back to post-structuralist voices who preferred to emphasize context. Smith and Ragan (1999) while attempting to take a balanced "pragmatist" view of instructional design as accounting for such issues while retaining a sense of sciencism state that,

> *It is our belief that most instructional designers are pragmatists. We would categorize ourselves, personally, as pragmatists, with beliefs that are also consistent with moderate constructivism. We also share with empiricists a valuing of testing knowledge through the accumulation of data, and a belief that there are some generalizable principles of learning that can be "discovered".*
>
> (p. 18)

Globalization has become a profound contextualizing factor impacting all sectors of society. But it is not only a context. It is also both a cause and a consequence. It is a context as well as an *emergent property* of contemporary society. Globalization has been made possible through new communication and transportation technologies. However, in any large-scale process such as globalization, there are winners and losers. While globalization removes some barriers, it erects others. While it emancipates some, it enslaves others. While it empowers it disempowers. And it does this with violence. Bauman (1998) puts, at the heart of this phenomenon, space/time compression. Instant communication and rapid transportation compress time and compress space. A consequence of this is the withering control of the state. Weber (1946) famously defined a state as "a human community that (successfully) claims the *monopoly of the legitimate use of physical force* within a given territory" (p. 78). Where there is less government regulation, control, or claim of authoritative jurisdiction, there is an encroaching from the private sphere. There is then an amplification of this competition between state control and corporate interests. Bauman (1998) writes,

> *Neo-tribal and fundamentalist tendencies, which reflect and articulate the experience of people on the receiving end of globalization, are as much legitimate offspring of globalization as the widely acclaimed 'hybridization' of top culture—the culture at the globalized top.*
>
> (p. 3)

If globalization is a process that weakens states founded and legitimated by way of geographic locality, it is a process that strengthens geographic free entities, such as corporations and other transnational organizations while at the same time promoting a singular triumphant culture by way of advanced technology.

Globalization has also meant that throughout the world, governments are embarking on projects to broadly implement technology in schools and institutions of higher education. There are different reasons these governments offer as to why this should happen. Invariably, there is an appeal to the related notions of progress, development, and the preparation of young people for an imagined technology-rich future. There are also concerns regarding globalization and economic self-sufficiency that, they argue, may be addressed by implementing technology-rich innovations in learning contexts. However, with these notions come others that may not be so apparent. These unofficial warrants for action may be so inextricably interwoven into the fabric of societal common sense that arguing against them would seem utterly ridiculous. Dystopian, ironic binaries may lay concealed under layers of glossy sense making ready to be revealed lurking with their more insalubrious counterparts. When we say "progress" for example, we are also necessarily also talking about a lack of progress, stagnation, or backwardness. To invoke a sense of direction is to simultaneously imagine both forwardness and backwardness and create warrants for specific actions. To talk about efficiency is to also talk about inefficiency and to talk about wealth making is to talk about the infliction of poverty.

Technology itself is not immune to the problem of unwelcome interwoven notions. Many have argued that what we think of technology today is the product of a specific set of values, cultural proclivities, lifestyles, and habits of mind. Heidegger, who explored the essence of technology, wrote,

> *Everywhere we remain unfree and chained to technology, whether we passionately affirm or deny it. But we are delivered over to it in the worst possible way when we*

> regard it as something neutral; for this conception of it, to which today we particularly like to do homage, makes us utterly blind to the essence of technology.
>
> (Heidegger, 1977, p. 4)

He clearly warned that technology was neither a benign nor even a neutral set of tools for us to use for our collective benefit. He continued,

> modern technology too is a means to an end. That is why the instrumental conception of technology conditions every attempt to bring man into the right relation to technology. Everything depends on our manipulating technology in the proper manner as a means.
>
> (Heidegger, 1977, p. 5)

But are we really trapped in a gilded or iron cage of technological rationality and its associated inevitabilities (Ritzer, 2000)? The *instrumental* conception or theory of technology Heidegger refers to here posits that technology is essentially neutral or indifferent. This suggests that technology is indifferent; a dumb tool to be wielded by the hand of an intentional agent. We accept a *substantive* theory of technology rather than an *instrumental* theory of technology (Feenberg, 1991, p. 5). This means that there is a reciprocal relationship between a tool and a user of a tool. We are made different by the tools we design and use. The common political refrain "guns don't kill people. People kill people" demonstrates an instrumentalist view of technology that asserts that it is not the technology that does the killing. Instead it is the person who possesses all agency. A *substantive* theory of technology considers that technology changes us. That technology itself contains values and judgments. Technology becomes a way of life that is not value neutral but, on the contrary, is value laden and it changes us as it remakes culture and epistemology (Feenberg, 1991). From a *substantive* standpoint, the gun changes the person in a manner reminiscent of the One Ring mystically calling out to and eventually changing those who would yield it. Sméagol was substantively changed into Gollum by the tool he used (Tolkien, 1978). Other philosophers of technology such as Horkheimer and Adorno (1972) in *Dialectic of Enlightenment* argued that rationality or "reason" is itself a product of a classed society. Marcuse critiqued the advancement of a,

> progressive transfer of power from the human individual to the technical or bureaucratic apparatus, from living to dead labor, from personal to remote control, from a machine or group of machines to a whole mechanized system.
>
> (Marcuse, 1966, p. 15)

Marcuse argued that the capitalist technical system is not neutral but reflects a particular class interest (Feenberg, 1995, p. 28). Habermas noted in his theory of communicative action that increasing spheres of human life are forced to conform to a technical rationality (Habermas, 1984). Technology is seen as being an inevitable process that unfolds like a juggernaut with obvious and not-so-obvious consequences. It is seen as a force of nature that is not subject to human agency. Of technology Apple (1988) states, "It is set apart and viewed as if it had a life of its own, independent of social intentions, power, and privilege" (p. 150). This question of the essence of technology has alarmed many other thinkers on the subject. Indeed, the science fiction genre of literature is replete with stories of "mad scientists" who cast aside their humanity in the name of progress only to create malevolent misanthropic processes that escape their control to wreak havoc on the world. However, this is unacceptable. We must ask of the changes we see taking place who the ultimate winners and losers will be, and assess the full spectrum of consequence, both intended and unintended, with equal vigor.

Educational Technology

The use of technologies in schools and other learning contexts is a story of unintended consequences. Actually it is more of a story of a general absence of consequences. Many have observed that the application of technology to learning environments comes with great promise but has very little impact on learning (Cuban, 1986; 2001; 2004; Clark, 1994). Our purpose here is not to promote romanticism that calls for a return to an imagined low-technology, natural, "noble-savage" existence nor is it to promote Luddism that seeks to cast a metaphorical wrench in the workings of educational technologies. It is to call for a collective initiative to work toward a critical theory of educational technology that will explain, predict, and inform the design, development, and implementation of technology-rich innovations in educational contexts (Feenberg, 1991). Such a theory should take into account the often competing narratives at work in this field and take a stance with respect to issues of social justice, global economic trends, and human psychological proclivities. It should consider ideology, both apparent and not so apparent (Apple, 2004). One way to approach this is to discover what concentration of discourses makes possible the patterns of thought and argument that surround the implementation of technology-rich innovations in educational contexts (Gee, 2011). Buckingham (2007) concerning the marketing of educational technologies states,

> It represents a coming together of public and private interests, and a concentration of discourses that are symptomatic of the field more broadly. Technology is presented here as a source of innovation, of empowerment and liberation, and of authentic educational practice. Yet, in much less celebratory terms, it is part of a broader move toward bureaucratization, regulation and surveillance. These discourses define the roles of the student and the teacher in diverse ways, and they also invoke much broader assumptions about the nature of learning.
>
> (p. 13)

To explore this, it is necessary to examine how people talk and think about educational technology in different parts of the world in the context of globalization. How do people of differing cultural inclinations and from different identity complexes talk about, think about, and enact technological change in learning contexts? We seek to contribute to a conversation among educators and instructional designers to work toward the emergence of a robust critical theory of educational technology that may function as a lens to examine the discourses we produce about educational technologies and a prism through which to view and to critique the products and systems we design, develop and implement. While there have been many critiques of educational technology implementation (e.g. Cuban, 1986; 2001) there is still a paucity of research that looks specifically at the implementation of educational technology systems in countries outside of North America and Europe conducted with a view to contributing to a critical theory of educational technology of the sort that Feenberg (1991; 1995; 1999) has called for and that is informed by philosophers of technology such as Horkheimer and Adorno (1972), Marcuse (1964; 1966; 1969), Habermas (1984), and Heidegger (1977).

Culture

Such a theory should also consider the notion of culture and how it plays upon instructional design processes (Thomas, Mitchell, & Joseph, 2002). If culture is at the heart of meaning making, then it functions, like theory, as a lens for viewing the world and must be thought of as the cornerstone of instructional design. Everything we see and think and learn is tied up in culture. In this way, both theory and culture are ways of seeing and coming to know the world. They are epistemic frames of reference through which we experience everything. As Young (2009) states,

> *Culture is significant to how learners learn. It is the way learners see the world and themselves in it.*
>
> (p. 13)

Elsewhere Young argues,

> *The role of culture in learning moves beyond challenging dominate ideologies or world views; it is about defining and identifying instances, methods and processes of learning that are specific to individuals and groups. Thereafter, the selection of instructional strategies begins. That is, instructional strategies cannot be applied to learners; in this sense, instructional strategies must be developed from an ethnographic evaluation of the learner. Instructional strategies are derived from versus applied to the learner.*
>
> (Young, 2014, p. 349)

But culture, like technology, cannot be thought of as an agnostic signifier. Contrary to instrumentalist views of technology, tools must be thought of as having agency. Culture must also be viewed as agentive. If technology is a tool of culture, so too is culture a tool of technology. The designer does cultural work and inherently this involves agency, politics, and the policing of thought and action.

It is also important to pursue the problem of educational technology implementation in contexts that help to explore the notion of alternative modernity. That is, can there be a culture of modernity that is not fully grounded in a Western, globalized view of technology (Feenberg, 1995)? What would such a non-Western science or technology look like?

In my own work in instructional design and research on educational technology implementation (e.g. Thomas, Barab, & Tuzun, 2009) and the discourses of educational communications and technology that underpin their design and implementation in non-Western cultural contexts (Thomas & Nayan, 2011; Thomas & Yang, 2013), I have sought to illuminate the ways that educational technology is talked about, thought about, and leveraged as warrants for design and action. The goal, again, is to work toward an instructional design *praxis* or action grounded in and guided by theory that is itself built upon solid, well-reasoned, and ethical principles. In this way, we may be able to develop a culture of design and culture work that is more in keeping with our collective lofty ambitions.

The Technological Sublime, Neoliberalism, and Performative Implementation

Based on this work examining educational technologies in Malaysia (Thomas & Nayan, 2011), Taiwan (Thomas & Yang, 2013) and more recently Turkey and Oman, it may be asserted that there are three notions that serve as impetus for the vision of technology in schools as it currently exists. Wherever I have looked, I have found these processes at work. These are the technological sublime, neoliberalism, and performative implementation. Each of these will be explored so as to illuminate their constituent parts with examples. However, all of these collectively are the drivers of technology in schools in the contemporary period.

The Technological Sublime

The technological sublime is the idea that there are no problems for which technology has no answer (Nye, 1994). Technology will solve problems even if those problems are themselves caused by technical means. This is the notion of the machine messiah. The *technological sublime* is underpinned by progressivism, futurist optimism, tool fetish, modernism, and humanist rationalism. In a progressivist conception of society, history, and technology, the future is always better than the past. There is the assumption that there are identifiable regular paths of development and that societies and technological abilities unfold in predictable stages. Just as there are stages of child development, there are stages of economic development. In this way, there can be a conception of the "developed" world and the developing world. Futurism both in serious industrial efforts and in "science" fiction carries a future imagination of a world that is populated by more "advanced" machines and even beings. In these visions of the future, present day societal ills are machined away by means of technological prowess. There is unbridled optimism about the future and the ability of technical approaches to conjure these technotopias. Tools themselves become objects of longing and their specifications and comparison become entertaining. There is delight in the tool rather than in what it does. This tool fetish is particularly apparent in discussions of weaponry.

However, this *"techno-imaginary"* is hobbled by a troublesome escort. From the very beginning of the industrial revolution it became clear that advancement comes with consequences. Surrender to nonhuman agents is dehumanizing and ensnares us in an inexorable scientific bureaucracy that is humiliating, gross, and essentially perilous. This Frankensteinesque view of technology calls into question the notion of the technological sublime but retains the suggestion that history plays out in predictable, comprehensible patterns. In this way, it is a sobering critique but does not escape its own genesis of structuralism. This is partly due to another component of modernistic structuralism and that is rationalism. Rationality is the exercise of centralizing reason, rather than faith, mysticism, emotion, or feeling. Rational choices are logically consistent but emotionally distant. We can see then that the technological sublime is at once optimistic and pessimistic in its vision of the future and therefore in its own incarnation.

Neoliberalism

The second notion that undergirds the contemporary vision of technology in schools is *neoliberalism*. Neoliberalism provides a concentration of discourses that animate a preoccupation with freedom, shrinking governmental roles, disempowering regulatory structures, and backgrounding moralistic constraints on action.

> *Neoliberalism is, in the first instance, a theory of political economic practices that proposes that human well-being can best be advanced by liberating individual entrepreneurial freedoms and skills within an institutional framework characterized by strong private property rights, free markets, and free trade.*
>
> (Harvey, 2005, p. 2)

Embedded in this notion is social Darwinism and a faith that markets can and should substitute for structures that seek to offer means for the instantiation of social justice. Markets can regulate justice, fairness, and the improvement of the human condition and should then be left to their own devices (Mirowski, 2009). Those business practices that are problematic are *naturally selected* to wither with those that result in success being confirmed for thriving. This *laissez faire* attitude taken to an extreme leads to companies generally doing what they want or at least policing themselves. Hill (2007) argues that neoliberal policies "have resulted in (a) a loss of equity, economic and social justice, (b) a loss of democracy and democratic accountability, and (c) a loss of critical thought" (p. 111). The wealth gap between rich and poor nations is profound and has been intensified rather than ameliorated (Hill, 2007).

A Practice-Based Example: Virtual Schools

What trends do we see in educational technology that are influenced by neoliberal impulses? There are many but one is the rise of *virtual* schools.

Virtual schools are schools that operate at a distance using computers and the internet. Some have face-to-face or brick and mortar components while others operate wholly online. While this has become an accepted alternate method for the delivery of instruction in higher education, or for adult learning, it is becoming increasingly commonplace for K-12 education. Advocates of virtual schooling make arguments that champion its cost effectiveness, its liberating influence, its preparation for economic conditions, and its function as an alternative to the bureaucratic, inefficient and arguably ineffective structure of traditional schools. However, there is skepticism regarding the appropriateness of the virtual approach for younger children.

Barbour and Reeves (2009) state,

> Over the past decade, there have been numerous studies that have shown that the only students that are typically successful in online learning environments are those who have independent orientations towards learning, who are highly motivated by intrinsic sources, and who have strong time management, literacy, and technology skills. These characteristics are ones that are typically associated with adult learners.
>
> (p. 413)

One reading of the rise of virtual schools is that they are an attack on public schooling and that by weakening public schools, local communities have become weaker making it easier for dominant groups to marginalize weaker ones. Indeed, one criticism of educational technology generally is that it erodes traditional local knowledge and local autonomy (Postman, 1992). Apple (2001) writes about the related trend of home schooling,

> In many ways the movement toward home schooling mirrors the growth of privatized consciousness in other areas of society. It is an extension of the "suburbanization" of everyday life that is so evident all around us. In essence, it is the equivalent of gated communities and of the privatization of neighborhoods, recreation, parks, and so many other things. It provides a "security zone" both physically and ideologically . . . Cultural and intellectual diversity, complexity, ambiguity, uncertainty, and proximity to the Other, all these are to be shunned.
>
> (pp. 175–176)

Virtual schooling could also mean that education could increasingly be turned over to private entities further commodifying education. A major trend in virtual schooling is outsourcing professional development to private entities (Lowes, 2007). Florida Virtual Schools actually licenses its courses to schools in other states.

Common devices for advertising educational technology tools leverage the powerful symbol of the student, teacher, family, or school that is "left behind." This pitiable wretch failed to purchase the newest tool and thereby is left out of the party, forced to peer longingly through a transparent but impenetrable barrier between tech-rich and tech-poor. The rhetoric also centers on "21st Century Skills." These arguments emphasize that there should be an alignment between what is done in schools and how the business sector operates in this imagined 21st century. The Partnership for 21st Century Skills (2015) states,

> *The Partnership for 21st Century Skills is a national organization that advocates for 21st century readiness for every student. As the United States continues to compete in a global economy that demands innovation, P21 and its members provide tools and resources to help the U.S. education system keep up by fusing the three Rs and four Cs (critical thinking and problem solving, communication, collaboration, and creativity and innovation). While leading districts and schools are already doing this, P21 advocates for local, state and federal policies that support this approach for every school.*

Embedded in this mission is a sense of competition, a focus on economic interest, and a top down model for curricular change and the implementation of technology-rich solutions. Not surprisingly, this organization partners with private corporations such as Microsoft, Apple, Adobe, Educational Testing Service, Lego, Crayola, Disney, Verizon, and others. It is clear that 21st Century Skills and educational technology is big business and preparing children for "competing" in this imagined future.

Performative Implementation

The technological sublime and neoliberalism have conspired to create a style of educational technology implementation that I term *performative implementation*. That is, technology appears in schools so that it may play the theatrical role of a 21st Century tool of innovation. There is a show of technology for learning and the guise of using technology to make creative, problem solving children ready to compete in the "new economy." However, as we have seen, the actual uses of technology in schools tend to be for control, scientific management, objective assessment, and making people uncritical. The implementation of the *Smart Schools* project in Malaysia is a profound example of a government going to great lengths to talk about or to perform a broad scale implementation of educational technology but very little impact on pedagogy (Thomas & Nayan, 2011).

I wish here to call for a *critical* view of educational technology that might interrupt the largely celebratory claims coming from industry, the government,

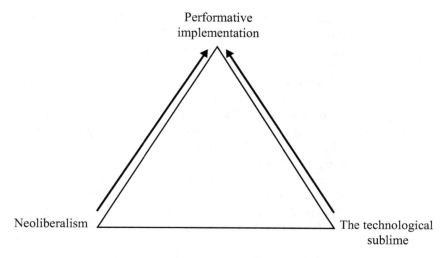

FIGURE 4.1 The mutually affirming principles of neoliberalism and the technological sublime give rise to performative implementation

from some sectors in academia, and organizations such as the Partnership for 21st Century schools (see Figure 4.1). The goal of this is *not* to show that technology in schools is a bad thing but rather to open up a space for asking these questions in the first place. Who are the winners and losers in this enterprise? To what extent are claims of its appropriateness inflated by vendors? What is the future likely to be for children today? I believe that this can be accomplished by way of research. But this must be a research approach that focuses on culture and concepts. An approach that is not *essentially* ideological but is able to leverage theory to highlight the problems in data-driven ways. We must look not only to the validity of the celebratory claims of the technology proponents but also of what Messick would call *consequential validity* of educational technology innovations (Messick, 1989). My purpose here is to disrupt the celebratory and uncritical adoptions of technology in schools and interrogate them from a standpoint of skepticism and a general cynicism and thus illuminate the discourses that animate the drive for technology in schools. This should not be read as a *Luddite* project. On the contrary, the goal here is to find visions of *appropriate* uses of technology rather than uses *per se*.

Toward an Ideal of Analytic Understanding of Technology for Learning

To summarize, there are driving forces that animate contemporary educational technology. In Table 4.1, an attempt is made to summarize these and then propose how these might be rethought so as to ameliorate the problems that come about because of these driving forces. The column on the left points to existing habits of mind and patterns of action related to educational technology. These properties are represented as normalized, current conditions. The column on the right presents questions or perturbations for these habits of mind and patterns of action with a view to achieving the induction of more robust, sensitizing, *critical* theories of educational technology.

As we have seen, globalization has been made possible by advanced technologies that have compressed space and time leading to deterritorialization and the withering of state and local control. This has meant the rise of neoliberal, free-market corporate proponents who coercively reassert the project of the commodification of both people and inanimate resources. This has also meant the promotion of a particular homogenizing culture grounded in consumerism. In education, this has meant the application of educational technologies to promote this commodification with an emphasis on efficiency and privatization. The patterns of discourse surrounding the implementation of educational technologies have been dominated by the technological sublime, neoliberalism, and performative implementation.

Postmodernism offered the world a coherent critique of grand theoretical narratives and pointed to the haughtiness of enlightenment pronouncements.

TABLE 4.1

Current Condition of Educational Technologies	*Questioning Educational Technologies*
The performance of progress – We have to be seen as progressive or we are no good. There must always be "forward movement" in the form of relative advantage (Rogers, 1995).	What is the *relative advantage* of this technology-rich tool, approach, or policy? What are its advantages and disadvantages? Who are the winners and losers? What can be said of its *consequential validity*?
Cheap hope – Technology is the easiest thing to offer hope without much thought. There does not need to be change of schools or even teachers. Just put the machines there and that's enough (Cuban, 1986).	What should be reformed in reform efforts? Instruction? Mechanisms of control? What do reform efforts reform?
Technological sublime – Educational technologies are brought forward with the assumption that there are no problems worth solving for which there isn't a technical solution (Nye, 1994).	Are technologies being used as solutions in search of problems?
Overselling – Business interests want to sell things to schools. This is because there is big money in it. What can you sell to schools? Books, services, furniture, machines (Cuban, 2001)?	Is this innovation being oversold? Technology should use what people already have for what people already do to solve problems they already experience. What technologies do children already use? What problems do they already have? What are they continually doing to resolve these problems?

Current Condition of Educational Technologies	Questioning Educational Technologies
Controlling – Educational technologies are used for control rather than instruction. Evaluation is a control technology for sorting (Apple, 1988).	Is this a *controlling* technology? Is this an *instructional* technology?
Cultural neutrality – Educational technologies are treated as culture neutral (Thomas, Mitchell, & Joseph, 2002).	What is the cultural impact of this innovation?
Erasing local knowledge – Technology wipes away local knowledge (Postman, 1992).	In what ways does this innovation realign existing power structures? To what extent and in what ways does this innovation align with the culture of the people for whom it was designed? To what extent were the voices of members of this culture incorporated into the design process?
Parallel paths – Educational technologies assume parallel or predictable paths of development (Feenberg, 1991).	To what extent does it assume static or parallel development paths?
West worship – The West is worth following. Educational technologies from the U.S. or U.K. carry an assumption of superiority.	To what extent does this innovation assume the superiority of a particular place, people, or perspective?
Validity of presence – The mere presence of educational technologies is treated as unquestionably a good thing.	To what extent is this performative implementation?
Cost effectiveness – Educational technologies are introduced because of cost effectiveness rather than for instructional effectiveness. Efficiency is the central concern.	To what extent is this innovation market driven? Who are the winners and losers?
Punishing spirals – There is an amplifying causal loop at work. There is evaluation based on technology that then punishes schools for not having a lot of technology. The result is a spiral downwards (Thomas & Yang, 2013).	To what extent are evaluation measures supportive or punitive? What might be said of their consequential validity?

It called into question the notion of the dispassionate scientist free from cultural contestations and mysticism (Layton, 1997; Latour, 1987). It offered the world a vocabulary for critique. Critical theory (e.g. Horkheimer, 1982) offered the world a set of hypotheses and lenses through which to not only describe conditions but also find ways to change them. Critical Race Theory (CRT) (Ladson-Billings, 1995; Ladson-Billings & Tate, 1995) offered the world a set of assumptions that could be used to foreground some ideas and background others for the purpose of illuminating injustices, deconstructing oppressive legislation, and leveraging convergent interests to further the cause of social justice. Instructional designers and educational technologists must also work toward the development of a robust critical theory of educational technology that may tentatively use the interrelated notions of the technological sublime, neoliberalism, and performative implementation in the analysis of technology-rich innovations for learning in the complex context of globalization.

References

Apple, M.W. (1988). *Teachers and texts: A political economy of class and gender relations in education*. New York, NY: Routledge.
Apple, M.W. (2001). *Educating the "right" way: Markets, standards, God, and inequality*. New York, NY: RoutledgeFalmer.
Apple, M.W. (2004). *Ideology and curriculum: Third edition*. New York, NY: RoutledgeFalmer.
Barbour, M.K., & Reeves, T.C. (2009). The reality of virtual schools: A review of the literature. *Computers and Education*, 52(2), 402–416.
Bauman, Z. (1998). *Globalization: The human consequences*. New York, NY: Columbia University Press.
Buckingham, D. (2007). *Beyond technology: Children's learning in the age of digital culture*. Cambridge, UK: Polity.
Clark, R.E. (1994). Media will never influence learning. *Educational Technology Research & Development*, 42(1), 21–29.
Cuban, L. (1986). *Teachers and machines: The classroom use of technology since 1920*. New York, NY: Teachers College Press.
Cuban, L. (2001). *Oversold and underused: Computers in the classroom*. Cambridge, MA: Harvard University Press.
Cuban, L. (2004). *The blackboard and the bottom line: Why schools can't be businesses*. Cambridge, MA: Harvard University Press.
Dick, W., & Carey, L. (1978). *The systematic design of instruction*. Glenview, IL: Scott, Foresman and Company.
Feenberg, A. (1991). *Critical theory of technology*. New York, NY: Oxford University Press.
Feenberg, A. (1995). *Alternative modernity*. Berkeley, CA: University of California Press.
Feenberg, A. (1999). *Questioning technology*. London, UK: Routledge.
Gee, J.P. (2011). *An introduction to discourse analysis theory and method: Third edition*. New York, NY: Routledge.
Habermas, J. (1984). *The theory of communicative action: Lifeworld and system: A critique of functionalist reason*. Boston, MA: Beacon.
Harvey, D. (2005). *A brief history of neoliberalism*. Oxford, UK: Oxford University Press.
Heidegger, M. (1977). *The question concerning technology and other essays*. New York, NY: Harper & Row, Publishers, Inc.
Hill, D. (2007). Educational perversion and global neoliberalism. In E. Wayne Ross & R. Gibson (Eds.), *Neoliberalism and education reform* (pp. 107–144). Cresskill, NJ: Hampton Press, Inc.
Horkheimer, M. (1982). *Critical theory: Selected essays*. New York, NY: Continuum.
Horkheimer, M., & Adorno, T.W. (1972). *Dialectic of enlightenment*. New York, NY: Herder and Herder.

Ladson-Billings, G., (1995). Toward a theory of culturally relevant pedagogy. *American Educational Research Journal*, *32*(3), 465–491.
Ladson-Billings, G., & Tate, W. (1995). Toward a critical race theory of education. *Teachers College Record*, *97*(1): 47–68.
Latour, B. (1987). *Science in action*. Cambridge, MA: Harvard University Press.
Layton, R. (1997). *An introduction to theory in anthropology*. Cambridge, UK: Cambridge University Press.
Lowes, S. (2007). Professional development for online teachers. In C. Cavanaugh & R. Blomeyer (Eds.), *What works in K-12 online learning* (pp. 161–178). Eugene, OR: International Society for Technology in Education.
Marcuse, H. (1964). *One-dimensional man: Studies in the ideology of advanced industrial society*. Boston, MA: Beacon.
Marcuse, H. (1966, March-April). The individual in the "great society": Part I: Rhetoric and Reality. *Alternatives Magazine*, pp. 14–16, 20.
Marcuse, H. (1969). *An essay on liberation*. Harmondsworth, UK: Penguin.
Messick, S. (1989). Validity. In R. L. Linn (Ed.), *Educational measurement: Third Edition* (pp. 13–103). New York, NY: Macmillan.
Mirowski, P. (2009). Postface: Defining neoliberalism. In P. Mirowski & D. Plehwe (Eds.), *The road from Mont Pelerin: The making of the neoliberal thought collective* (pp. 417–455). Cambridge, MA: Harvard University Press.
Nye, D. E. (1994). *American technological sublime*. Cambridge, MA: The MIT Press.
Partnership for 21st Century Learning. (2015). About the Partnership for 21st Century skills. Retrieved from http://www.p21.org/news-events/press-releases/906-read-the-p21-statement-on-the-us-department-of-educations-national-educational-technology-plan/ September 4, 2015.
Postman, N. (1992). *Technopoly: The surrender of culture to technology*. New York, NY: Vintage Books.
Ritzer, G. (2000). *The McDonaldization of society: New century edition*. Thousand Oaks, CA: Pine Forge Press.
Smith, P. L., & Ragan, T. J. (1999). *Instructional design: Second edition*. Upper Saddle River, NJ: Merrill.
Thomas, M. K., & Nayan, R. (2011). Smart Schools for saving the soul: A juxtaposition of neofundamentalist and neoliberal discourse concentrations in contemporary Malaysia. *Discourse: Studies in the Cultural Politics of Education*, *32*(4), 513–529.
Thomas, M., Mitchell, M., & Joseph, R. (2002). The third dimension of ADDIE: A cultural embrace. *Tech Trends*, *46*, 40–45.
Thomas, M. K., Barab, S. A., & Tuzun, H. (2009). Developing critical implementations of technology-rich innovations. *Journal of Educational Computing Research*, *41*(2), 125–154.
Thomas, M. K., & Yang, W. L. (2013). Neoliberalism, globalization, and creative educational destruction in Taiwan. *Educational Technology Research and Development*, *61*(1), 107–129.
Tolkien, J. R. R. (1978). *The hobbit*. London, UK: George Allen & Unwin.
Weber, M. (1946). Politics as a vocation. In H. H. Gerth & C. Wright Mills (Eds.), *From Max Weber: Essays in sociology* (pp. 77–128). New York, NY: Oxford University Press.
Young, P. A. (2009). *Instructional design frameworks and intercultural models*. Hershey, PA: IGI Global/Information Science Publishing.
Young, P. A. (2014). The presence of culture in learning. In J. M. Spector, M. D. Merrill, J. Elen, & M. J. Bishop (Eds.), *Handbook of research on educational communications and technology: Fourth edition* (pp. 349–361). New York, NY: Springer Academics.

5

HIP-HOP MUSIC AS A PEDAGOGICAL TOOL

Teaching with Hip-Hop in Global Contexts

Akesha M. Horton, Erik J. Byker, and Keith Heggart

Introduction

The literature tells us that youth, particularly those who live in urban settings, are becoming engaged as active global citizens primarily through out-of-school practices (Abe, 2010; Aldridge & Stewart, 2005; Horton, 2012). One such practice, which has been constant for decades, is pop-culture. This chapter examines how hip-hop—a global form of pop-culture—is at the nexus of culture, learning and technology. Hip-hop is a new literacy practice that represents a convergence of culture and identity through artistic expression. The chapter presents a case study of the design and delivery of a global hip-hop music course (*Hip-Hop for Global Justice*) for secondary students. The course was designed to engage students in topics of critical cosmopolitanism and global citizenship via the use of digital social media tools. Using a principled assemblage of qualitative research methods, the chapter describes and explains the events that took place in a global hip-hop mini-course based in an Australian high school. It analyzes the developments in students' understandings of their role as global citizens, exploring how this role was enacted through the use of technology and hip-hop, and maps this understanding of global citizenship against the critical cosmopolitan theory framework, before concluding with some comments about the implications for education and avenues for future research.

Defining Hip-Hop Culture

This chapter necessarily engages with notions of culture, learning, and technology, as they are central to the lives of the young people in the project described. However, it is also necessary to explain what is meant by the term "culture" and how it relates to our work. By culture, we follow John Miller Chernoff's (1981) assertion that culture is the "dynamic style with which people organize and orient themselves to act through various mediators" (p. 36). In this chapter, we examine how musical expression is a way that people orient themselves and identify who they are in social and cultural ways. In particular, we investigate hip-hop as a dynamic mediator of culture.

So what is hip-hop culture? We draw upon the work of Malone and Martinez (2014) in defining hip-hop culture. In particular they examine the dynamic nature of hip-hop culture through three stages. The first stage is that hip-hop culture raises awareness about societal issues. The second stage is that hip-hop culture has the potential to orient people toward justice in changing social and economic circumstances. The third stage of hip-hop culture builds on the justice orientation to focus on political engagement and social action. Hip-hop culture can be expressed in many ways. For example, the Portland Youth Summit (2012) shares that the five elements of hip-hop have their roots in the ancient Khemit traditions of Africa. Specifically they describe the elements in the following ways:

- Graffiti is the writing of language or the scribe that documents the history
- Emcee is the oral griot, the conveyer of the Message
- DJing is the heartbeat, the drum, of the art or movement; DJ comes from the Djembe drum
- B-Boys and B-Girls are those who perform exercise and provide human expression through dance or body movement to keep the body in proper health
- Knowledge of Self, which is the fifth element, is defined by the Zulu Nation as "'overstanding' (deeper and more critical than understanding)" (Samy Alim & Pennycook, 2007, p. 90).

In this chapter, we also employ the term "global hip-hop culture." By adding the term "global," we are acknowledging that hip-hop culture has a global application in that it allows young people with different cultural backgrounds to connect and interact in aesthetic activities in the multicultural suburbs. It even provides a global kinship and represents an alternative counter narrative to more mainstream cultures. Some hip-hop intellectuals thus refer to a counter citizenship in the fictitious, alternative, and global hip-hop nation. Further, global hip-hop culture, as Malone and Martinez (2014) describe, "unlike all other genres, . . . hip hop in both its core and its elements contains a unique movement culture, which carries with it certain cultural, social, and political possibilities other musical genres rooted in specific traditions do not" (Kindle Locations 178–180). By defining hip-hop as an "organic globalizer" they posit that the multicultural roots of hip-hop make it a cultural phenomenon and institutionalized social reality on the global scale that provides a form of expression to marginalized communities in its ability to produce "a network of grassroots social institutions built around issues of social justice" (Kindle Locations 238–240). Scholars such as Samy Alim and Pennycook (2007) and Mitchell (2001) explore the role language has had in defining hip-hop culture as a global phenomenon. Specifically, Samy Alim and Pennycook view "language from within the multiethnic, multilingual global [hip-hop nation] HHN, a postmodern 'nation' with an international reach, a fluid capacity to cross borders, and a reluctance to adhere to the geopolitical givens of the present" (p. 90).

Theoretical Framework

This chapter is framed by Critical Cosmopolitan Theory (Byker, 2013). Critical Cosmopolitan Theory provides a conceptual model, which explicates the development of critically conscious global competencies. Paulo Freire, the Brazilian educationist, wrote that conscientization or critical consciousness was the higher purpose of education (Freire, 1970). From a Freirean perspective, education goes beyond just acquiring the skills of learning how to read and write and compute numbers; education is about emancipation (Freire, 1970). Freire (2001) believed that emancipation included becoming critically conscious of global issues in order to work toward the liberation of people from social injustices. Freire asserted that critical consciousness means being able to "read the world" and "rewrite the world" (Freire, 1970). In this chapter, we argue that hip-hop connects to both reading and rewriting the world. By reading the world, Freire (1998) means the reflective act of analyzing society's systems of power as well as examining one's position within those systems of power. Reading the world also means having one's eyes opened to the implications of socio-historically constructed ideas used to organize and, often, segregate members of society. For example, the socio-historical construct of race has led to the exploitation and marginalization of people groups in society (Coates, 2015).

When eyes are opened to society's injustices, then Freire argues that people are ready to begin rewriting the world. By rewriting the world, Freire (1994) means the transformation of how people engage in creative endeavors and social activities in order to address the systems of power and transform societal injustices. Reading and rewriting the world are critical acts of consciousness. They are the hallmarks of an education for emancipation and form one part of the foundation of Critical Cosmopolitan Theory. The other part of the foundation is being cosmopolitan (Appiah, 2010).

Cosmopolitan is a term that is synonymous with global competency and global citizenship. The term "global citizen" has its etymological roots in the Greek word *kosmopolitês* or cosmopolitan, which means a citizen of the world. Kwame Appiah, a cultural theorist, argues that the word, cosmopolitan, captures the notions of what being a global citizen entails. Appiah (2010) explains that cosmopolitan is wrapped up in two big ideas about what it means to be human, "One idea is that as humans we have obligations to one another . . . the other idea is that we take value in human lives, which means taking an interest in practices and beliefs that give our lives significance" (p. xv). Critical Cosmopolitan Theory adopts Appiah's definition for cosmopolitan and adds it to the Asia Society's definition for what it means to be a globally competent person.

Founded in 1956, the Asia Society has a strong vision for helping to prepare young people to be global citizens. The Asia Society website includes many resources including a free, electronic book called *Educating for Global Competency* (Mansilla & Jackson, 2011). In that text, Mansilla and Jackson (2011) define global competency as "the capacity to understand and act on issues of global significance" (p. 2). The definition is illustrated in greater depth through the development of a Global Competency Matrix, which outlines four specific global competencies that are part of global citizenship. The four global competencies include: 1) Investigate the world; 2) Recognize perspectives; 3) Communicate ideas; and 4) Take action. The competencies build upon each other and have a certain scope and sequence to their order. Investigate the world is the interest in and exploration of one's larger world beyond just an immediate community. Recognizing perspectives is the appreciation for diversity and the recognition of multiple perspectives and points of view. Communicating ideas is the ability to communicate about global issues with diverse audiences. Taking action is about doing something to raise awareness in order to improve a situation or improve the lives of people around the globe (Mansilla & Jackson, 2011).

Figure 5.1 provides a graphic representation of Critical Cosmopolitan Theory by drawing parallels between global competencies in the Asia Society's Global Competency Matrix and Paulo Freire's tenets about critical consciousness. The main presupposition of Critical Cosmopolitan Theory is that being a global citizen requires maturation toward critical consciousness. Such maturation includes the integration of global competencies with Freirean skills like reading and rewriting the world.

As Figure 5.1 depicts, there is congruence among the Asia Society's global competencies and Freire's conceptual understanding of an emancipatory education. Figure 5.1 is not meant to dichotomize the competencies and concepts into categorical steps; rather, each competency blends and builds on the other. The same is true for Freire's concepts. Taken together, Critical Cosmopolitan Theory

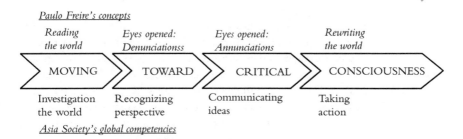

FIGURE 5.1 A graphic representation of Critical Cosmopolitan Theory

is about the development of an active global consciousness where the outcome is a person who is equipped to take action and rewrite the world. Indeed, an active, critical consciousness represents the maturation of the four global competencies in a person who is compelled to make a difference by rewriting the world.

Literature Review

Born in the late 1960s and early 1970s in the African American, Latino, and urban communities as a dynamic form of expression, hip-hop is an important lens for sociopolitical analysis and representation of marginalized communities (Aldridge & Stewart, 2005). Samy Alim, Ibahim, and Pennycook (2009) explain that hip-hop should be understood as a "second orality" (p. 2) bound up in electronically mediated reality that is . . . embedded in relations of power and politics. Scholars across a wide range of disciplines, including sociology, cultural studies, literacy studies, history, and education highlight the centrality of hip-hop to today's youth and its potential as a source for academic learning and political engagement (Samy Alim, 2007; Ibrahim, 2004; Pardue, 2007; Rose, 1994; Sarkar & Allen, 2007; Stovall, 2006).

According to Abe (2010), hip-hop's emergence as a global presence has risen from a group of educators working to connect the inner-workings of the culture to formal academic curriculum. Duncan-Andrade and Morrell (2008) point out that many rappers also view themselves as people who, to some degree, take on the responsibility within their community of promoting social consciousness. This links with Andrzejewski and Alessio's (1999) ideas about the way that hip-hop can be linked to global citizenship. They write "Following the advice of John Dewey, education for global citizenship should be grounded in the personal experiences of the student and her/his community" (online). As a result, hip-hop music has become the dynamic voice of global youth culture with enormous potential for social and political change. Though scholars have documented the global spread of hip-hop, there is an absence of research that explores the intersection of hip-hop and global citizenship education.

Researcher Terkourafi (2010) observed an absence of and need for sufficient academic research connected to hip-hop-related empirical studies. Fostering a critical understanding in students who regularly consume hip-hop texts and the competing ideologies they incorporate serves a dual purpose. It prepares students for addressing the more subtle yet similar conflicting messages present in discussions around global citizenship education. Ibrahim (2009) suggests that this type of multiplicity (between danger and possibility, i.e. hardcore (gangsta') rap and knowledge (conscious) rap) is interwoven in the essence of hip-hop pedagogy, and can provide deep learning experiences when engaged with correctly. Also, Loflin and Evans (2015) propose that "urban students, who may have particularly been subjected to years of social, cultural, political, and intellectual alienation, are ready for a new kind of pedagogical experience in their classrooms and schools" (p. 2360) that hip-hop can offer.

These points illuminate one of the many ways hip-hop can be used to help urban youth develop global citizenship competencies. Hip-hop education also asks students to analyze the implicit underpinning shared by both global citizenship education and socially conscious hip-hop, which is social justice. Examining how issues of social justice are constructed in global hip-hop can also foster the development of youths' global citizenship competencies.

Research Questions

The last 15 years have seen an increase in hip-hop pedagogy in academic and political arenas, where hip-hop is commonly defined as a new literacy (Mahiri, 2006; Richardson, 2006; Morrell, 2002). New literacies are key tools necessary for operating in the new millennium and in an increasingly globalized world. In his research study, Nat Turner (2012) points to the multimodal composition of each of the elements of hip-hop and how they are used by urban youth to produce multimodal media such as songs and video that display a "critical engagement with issues uncovered through the community research project" (p. 500).

In their studies around hip-hop pedagogy and aesthetic learning practices, Söderman and Sernhede (2015) share how hip-hop scholars believe that "hip-hop culture can serve as a pedagogy on its own" (p. 5). Further, in the Bridges (2011) study of how hip-hop culture has influenced the teaching identities of Black male urban educators, Bridge describes how elements from hip-hop culture such as "a call to service, a commitment to self-awareness, and a resistance to social injustice" (p. 328) have intersected with critical pedagogies to inform definitions of hip-hop pedagogy.

It was these themes that we sought to explore through the *Hip-Hop for Global Justice* course. Having identified the features of technology, hip-hop and global citizenship, and determined that it was important to hear students' voices about these matters; we distilled these ideas into two research questions:

1. How does participating in a technology course that engages urban youth in researching global issues and creating hip-hop digital texts in response to them shape how the youth define and enact the practices of global citizenship?
2. In what ways can a technology course that engages urban youth in researching global issues and creating hip-hop digital texts in response to them be adapted to different contexts?

Method

Course and Context

Australia boasts racially and ethnically diverse populations. According to the Australian Bureau of Statistics as of June 30, 2015, over 1 in 4 of Australia's citizens were born outside of the nation's borders (online). Almost half were born overseas or had at least one parent who was born overseas, and 20 percent speak a language other than English. In response to this increasing diversity, Australia has developed a multicultural policy, which seeks to foster cultural inclusiveness and be supportive of the needs of its globalized society (Bowen & Lundy, 2011). Samy Alim (2011) explains, "there is scarcely a county in the world that does not feature some form of mutation of rap music" (p. 4). Some populations are specifically targeted for hip-hop initiatives. For example, Stavrias (2005) shares, "The popularity of hip-hop culture in general in Indigenous communities throughout Australia can be taken as a given" (p. 53).

The *Hip-Hop for Global Justice* course was delivered at a Catholic secondary school in Australia with more than 800 students in Years 7–12. Despite having a rating on the Index of Community Socio-Economic Advantage of better than average, the school produces more students in the bottom two quartiles of achievement than the Australian national average, and significantly fewer students in the top quartile (11 percent versus 25 percent) than would be expected of this school (Myschool, 2016).

One of the core objectives of the course was to help participants become more digitally literate. The course was delivered in the school at a time when it had just implemented Google Apps for Education (GAFE). GAFE is a collection of cloud-based software that is free for schools to use inside and outside of the classroom. The course was delivered through a mix of face-to-face discussion and online activities. The course site was developed on Google Sites and incorporated Google Docs, Maps, Blogger, and YouTube, tools that students could access freely inside and outside of school. Australian hip-hop artist, L-Fresh, visited and provided lyrical workshops on the final day of the course.

In a session following the course, students were taken to a recording studio where they met with a professional sound engineer and created a final version of their song. L-Fresh provided a review:

> *These guys know how to write rhymes and they focused in on the topic really well. They articulated their thoughts really well. And they flowed nicely on the beat. I would encourage them to keep exploring the art of rap, and to keep writing songs that allow them to express how they feel on certain issues that they are passionate about.*
>
> (Personal interview with L-Fresh, 2012)

Data Collection and Analysis

We examined the *Hip-Hop for Global Justice* course as a case study. The flexibility of case studies allowed for the collection and analysis of a wide variety of data. Merriam (1998) states case studies are, "useful in presenting basic information about areas of education where little research has been conducted" (p. 27). Due to the absence of research analyzing the intersection of the three domains explored in this study (i.e., global citizenship, digital literacies, and hip-hop), a single case study afforded us the ability to gather a depth of knowledge (Kohn, 1997) in how these disciplines interacted with each other in separate contexts. This approach necessitates multiple sources of data be collected, including interviews, surveys and artifacts, in an effort to increase validity and reliability of the case study. The artifacts produced in the course were the result of participants' decision of what should be appropriate deliverables for the course. The students decided to create a song as well as participate in reflections on the materials they viewed and read via blog posts. These texts then became central data for this study.

Our case study investigated the artifacts created during the *Hip-Hop for Global Justice* course by a class of 13 students (n=13). All the students were in Grade 7 and were identified by their school teachers based on their diversity, their interest in hip-hop and/or because they were at-risk. Of the 13 students, 12 were boys. Two identified as Zimbabwean immigrants, two as Maltese immigrants, two as Indigenous Australians, and one as a Pacific Islander. Four were white Australians. Two declined to provide demographic information.

In the middle of the course and after the course concluded, participants agreed to a series of interviews. The interviews—comprised of semi-structured, open ended questions—allowed the researchers to identify how students made sense of global citizenship, their experiences with hip-hop and how they think it relates to global citizenship. Additionally, they allowed an understanding of how participants used digital technology and how they relate it to both hip-hop and global citizenship. Since students have participated in a class that focuses on all three of these areas of interest, it was also possible to draw upon artifacts produced from the class (i.e. the song and blog posts) during the interviews to help understand how the students think about and experience ideas of global citizenship and digital technologies.

As part of the study, students also completed online polls using Polls Everywhere.com. On the course's first day, the participants completed an anonymous poll about their perceptions of hip-hop and the storytelling within hip-hop. At the end of the course, students completed an exit poll in which they responded to questions about the relationship of hip-hop to global citizenship.

Findings

This section provides a discussion of the practices of global citizenship that students were able to enact over the course of the class. Using qualitative content analysis from the interviews conducted with the students, as well as a review of the digital products students completed in the class for evidence of global citizenship markers, we examined how students used hip-hop and digital tools demonstrate two markers: compassion and creativity (Alger & Harf, 1986; Banks, 2004; Heilman, 2008; Schattle, 2008).

Compassion

Contemporary conversations have explored the idea of openness toward "other" cultures, people and environments that promotes compassion. Heilman (2008) defines compassion as, "the sympathetic awareness of others' situations, together with a desire to realize universal human rights in today's world" (p. 30). Davies and Pike (2009) discuss the concept of "plural and parallel allegiances of global citizenship" (Kindle, Chapter 5). This idea explores the ability of one to "stretch" allegiances past local and national boundaries in the sense that one develops true empathy or compassion for those located outside of one's own geographical and cultural context.

One of the goals of the course was to help students increase their awareness of commonalities that exist between them and people situated across the globe. Since hip-hop culture is a global phenomenon, this course aimed to help "hip-hop heads" or true hip-hop aficionados find a sense of "plural and parallel allegiances of global citizenship," which they could use as a foundation to develop a sense of compassion for one another.

The students discussed several big ideas as possible topics for their songs, including drugs use, domestic violence, and immigration issues, but ultimately decided to go with another topic, one which they felt that they could actually play a role in enacting some sort of substantive change about: school backpacks. While the student-lyricist disliked carrying heavy backpacks, they were able to manage the task. They, however, expressed concern for students younger than them who they observed struggling with the task. They also saw the act of being forced to carry a specific type of backpack throughout their day as a commentary on the lack of voice students in general have in how their day unfolds. These student-artists saw hip-hop as a vehicle of free expression that could get the word out to other students to think about the fairness of this policy. The student-artists explained on their blog, "[We] wrote about the thing we hated the most and we wanted to change in our school which was the horrible school bags."

Via an interview after recording the song, the students shared:

Student 1: Well, you go to school for six hours and I just thought six hours of pain. Cuz, you know, wearing the bag is like hell. It's painful. Carrying the school bag, from one point to another. Yeah
S2: Yes, exactly.
S1: It's kinda unfair because it seems like . . .
S2: It's like the little kids, the bag is walking.
S1: It's like kindergarten kids carrying that big bag.
S1: Well, we didn't write it about us. Me, I can carry it but . . .
S2: Just public service.
S1: I'm pretty sure no one wants his or her bag.

The students drew on their compassion toward the younger students in the school in their song and contrasted it with what they felt was injustice and a lack of concern among the school's administration about the pain that the backpacks inflicted on students. The song states:

> *They tell us integrity, justice, and peace*
> *Well that's a load of . . .*
> *How is this justice when we have no say*
> *Our voices are not being heard*
> *They can't get it through they heads . . . Coz what they tell you is just so whack*
> *You heard me right/*
> *It's just so whack.*

This excerpt highlights what students view as the administration's hypocrisy. Specifically challenged is the sincerity of the administration's promotion of "integrity, justice, peace," against the silencing of students' voices in making even a simple choice like selecting a backpack. They state, "Our voices are not been held," noting complaints about the backpacks are not acknowledged by the school administrators or teachers who "can't get it through their heads." This lack of recognition leads the students to view the administration's attempt to teach them justice and integrity as bogus, writing, "It's just so whack."

Later in the song, the students write about how the backpacks cause them pain.

> *School bags are heavy*
> *Everyday I'm sufferin*
> *Can't even dance, coz I'm never shuffling*
> *They're big, black, and just plain old ugly*
> *Don't wanna carry, coz they get all bulky*
> *When I take it off, I'm gonna relax*
> *They are really hurting me,*
> *Kill 'em with our raps.*
> *I have to carry my bag*
> *Like Jesus walking with a cross*
> *There ain't no turning back.*

On face value the backpacks are a small issue for the older students. Requiring young students to use the heavy backpacks was significant because it caused physical pain for the younger students in their everyday lives. The students were not seeking "justice" for themselves, but rather for students younger than them who suffered under the weight of the backpacks, and, as the song indicates, ultimately under the weight of the school administration's refusal to hear the students' complaints or to have compassion for the students.

Creativity

Heilman (2008) defines creativity as "the ability to use one's unique talents to synthesize ideas and values to make something new that serves the common good" (p. 30) Creativity is an important attribute of global citizenship. It helps young people who are exposed to global media and cultures through physical and virtual interactions learn to fuse aspects of the "other" with which they identify, without choosing between cultures. Instead they can explore ways of creatively incorporating traits of each culture (Arnett, 2002; Suárez-Orozco, 2004).

The course provided students a forum to enact this type of creativity. The students stated they expressly aimed at using wordplay, humor, and religious faith in their hip-hop song to attract the interest of fellow students. Their hope was to rally students behind the idea that a change was needed by creating songs students would initially laugh about and later think about. Once this idea had been processed by their classmates, the student-artists were interested in the idea of organizing a protest in order to make the school faculty take note of their concerns.

The song, *6 Hours of Pain*, provides an example of how the student-lyricists attempted to use humor to get their point across:

> *I have to carry my bag, like Jesus walking with a cross;*
> *There ain't no turning back:*
> *Let's all protest and get rid of these bags;*
> *Either Pimp them or cut us some slack;*
> *Cause they so black;*
> *And they ain't coming back;*
> *Causing asthma attacks;*
> *They're so whack!*

The bags are obviously not as torturous as Jesus' trip to the cross nor do they cause asthma attacks, but these lyrics added the impact needed for the intended audience—their classmates in the Catholic school they attend. Using the term *Jesus walking* also invokes ideas of one of Kanye West's most popular songs, *Jesus Walks*:

> *(Jesus Walks)*
> *God show me the way because the devil trying to break me down*
> *(Jesus Walks)*
> *The only thing that that I pray is that my feet don't fail me now*
> *(Jesus Walks)*

The student-lyricists are implying that the bags are heavy enough to break them down. *Either Pimp them or cut us some slack;* the artist is requesting an artistic license to decorate the bags as illustrated in the television show *Pimp my Ride*. The show takes a "ride" or vehicle that is in poor condition and fixes it up so the vehicle is not only drivable, but also aesthetically pleasing; customized to the personality of the car owner.

The students-lyricists worked collaboratively to create the song. While one focused on the functionality of the bags, (i.e. too heavy for smaller students to carry and "causing asthma attacks"), the other student-lyricist was focused on the outer appearance of a bag he was forced to carry throughout the day;

> *They're big, they're black*
> *They're just plain old ugly*
> *Don't want to crack*
> *Because they're just so bulky*

By using rhetorical devices common to hip-hop as well as sampling a small but pertinent line from West's lyrics, the students are pulling in several covert messages a hip-hop "head" or fan would understand to reiterate the points they are making about the bags. They are demonstrating a command of hip-hop language and culture. The students in this study are participating in emceeing or rapping, one of the four elements of hip-hop culture (Portland Youth Summit, (2012). Samy Alim (2011) provides evidence of youth exercising creativity in order to engage in global ill-literacy practices that "not only challenge dominant constructs of static, one-dimensional relationships between language and culture" (p. 123), but also promote social transformation. The term ill-literacy is an example of this point, where ill is an abbreviated version of skilled, but also represents Intimate, Lived, and Liberatory. This is the type of language illustrated in *6 Hours of Pain*. Another connection hip-hop has to creativity has been highlighted in the research around the possibility that there is a connection between improvisational hip-hop (e.g., freestyling) and Csíkszentmiháyli's concept of flow (López-González & Limb, 2012).

Discussion

We return now to the chapter's theoretical framework, Critical Cosmopolitan Theory. How were the case study participants moving toward a critical consciousness? In addressing that question, we start by acknowledging the contextualization of the hip-hop music that the students created. First, the participants who composed the hip-hop were mostly in Grade 7. Their composition was situated in the issues that are important to 12 or 13-year-olds. In this way, the students' age and experience contextualized their hip-hop composition. Even though the students discussed a range of topic choices for their songs, school backpacks was the topic that was important and pressing to the students. It was also an issue around which they believed they had some power to enact change.

Religious expression was a second form of contextualization. In the case study, the participants attended Catholic school. Their lyrics included Christian terminology and themes about sacrifice, redemption, and forgiveness. The participants' religious beliefs were deeply connected to the lyrics that they composed. Hip-hop, as an art form, is about expression. The students expressed their faith and beliefs through hip-hop, which shows the adaptability of the hip-hop form.

A third way that the hip-hop was contextualized was relevance. At first glance, rapping about backpacks seems to be a little naive when there are much more pressing global issues like racism or global warming or the refugee crisis. Yet, the backpacks were deeply authentic and relevant to the participants' day-to-day world in the school. The hip-hop that the students composed was rooted in an issue that was relevant to the students' lives and localized to the school community. It was an issue that mattered a great deal to the students. The forms of contextualization are part of Freire's two prongs of critical consciousness: reading the world and rewriting the world.

How the participants contextualized their hip-hop lyrics was an example of "reading the world." The students identified that heavy backpacks were an issue that they deemed as unjust within the school community. The act of the reading the world was demonstrated as they confronted the unequal power structure through their lyrics. Rather than sitting back and taking it, the students stood up for what they believe to be true about the backpacks as a symbol of that power dynamic. Reading the world, for instance, is captured in following lyrical lines: *They tell us integrity, justice, and peace. Well that's a load of . . . How is this justice when we have no say.* The participants were moving toward critical consciousness as they read their immediate world and spoke out about systems of power in the school that seemed hypocritical.

The students also demonstrated critical consciousness by engaging in the act of rewriting the world. Perhaps more than other lyrical genres, hip-hop allows for the fluid and authentic means of rewriting the world. Students rapping out *"Kill 'em with our raps"* is a demonstration of the students' understanding of hip-hop as a powerful text for agitating for change. Examining the entire rap shows how the students are communicating a deeper consciousness about an issue that is important in their lives and one that affects the younger kids. In this way, the students demonstrated how the act of rewriting the world is translated into the hip-hop form at a Catholic school in Australia.

As stated earlier, Critical Cosmopolitan Theory is about the development of an active global consciousness where people are equipped to take action and rewrite the world. The development of critical consciousness through hip-hop is also situated and defined by context. Rewriting the world, as a critical consciousness act, is much different when situated outside of Detroit, Michigan. For example, in a separate study that is still being conducted, high school students from Detroit created their own hip-hop music based on their experiences growing up in inner-city Detroit. Rather than rapping about backpacks, the Detroit area student rapped about how experiences in their communities paralleled other communities they learned about via hip-hop from international artists such as the Japanese based group Duty Free Shopp and Australian artist Maya Jupiter. The development of critical consciousness is a political act, but it also highly contextual. This chapter just told of one case study. More research is needed into the effects of hip-hop within school communities. The scope of this research agenda should be comparative and international.

Conclusion

The hip-hop project described in this chapter is a small project involving a limited number of students who took part in the process that lasted for a few weeks. It would be shortsighted to generalize too much from their experience. However, the project itself, and the students' responses to the project, does much to identify possible avenues for future research, and it is worth briefly highlighting a number of these.

Principally, this project took place in the interstitial spaces between hip-hop, citizenship, and technology. Although each of these areas has been examined by researchers, the nexus of all three areas and the way that they fit together remains only vaguely mapped out. This research project suggests that this nexus is worthy of future research. Specifically, it suggests that here lies fertile ground for defining exactly what "active citizenship" means to youth in Australia in the 21st century. By approaching a definition through the actions of students, we are offered a new perspective on what it means to be a young person, and what it means for a young person to take action about social justice issues in their local communities. In a departure from other definitions that are often developed by academics or governmental policy makers, it would appear that youth culture (in this case expressed through hip-hop), technology (and especially its ubiquitous nature and ease of use) and global perspectives are central to the perspective of active citizenship held by young people.

Linked to this idea are new ways that young people might enact citizenship. Often, debate about active citizenship is limited to either civic knowledge about government institutions, voting participation rates, or charity events. While none of these are necessarily bad, it would be foolish to limit our understanding of enacted citizenship to just these; rather, we must look for other ways that young people behave as citizens—and for this chapter, global citizens. Perhaps unsurprisingly, young people themselves have much to say on this topic.

References

3412.0—Migration, Australia, 2014–15. (2016, March 30). Retrieved January 04, 2017, from http://www.abs.gov.au/ausstats/abs@.nsf/mf/3412.0

Abe, D. (2010). Hip-hop and the academic canon. *Education, Citizenship, and Social Justice, 4*(3), 263–272.

Alger, C.F., & Harf, J.E. (1986). Global education: Why? For whom? About what? In R.E. Freeman (Ed.), *Promising Practices in Global Education: Handbook with Case Studies* (pp. 1–13). New York: National Council on Foreign Language and International Studies.

Alridge, D.P., & Stewart, J.B. (2005). Hip-hop in history: Past, present, and future. *Journal of African American History* (formerly the *Journal of Negro History*), *90*(2), 190–195.

Andrzejewski, J., & Alessio, J. (1999). Education for global citizenship and social responsibility. Retrieved from the Progressive Perspectives Monograph Series Educause Website: http://80www.uvm.edu/~dewey/monographs/glomono.html#Education%20for%20Global%20Citizenship%20and%20Social http://www.uvm.edu/~dewey/monographs/glomono.html#Education%20for%20Global%20Citizenship%20and%20 Social

Appiah, K.A. (2010). *Cosmopolitanism: Ethics in a world of strangers*. New York: W.W. Norton & Company.

Arnett, J.J. (2002). The psychology of globalization. *American Psychologist, 57*(10), 774–783.

Banks, J.A. (Ed.) (2004). *Diversity and citizenship education: Global perspectives*. San Francisco, CA: Jossey-Bass.

Bowen, C., & Lundy, K. (2011). The people of Australia: Australia's multicultural policy. Parliament of Australia. Retrieved from: http://www.immi.gov.au/media/publications/multicultural/pdf_doc/people-of-australia-multicultural-policy-booklet.pdfhttp://www./

Bridges, T. (2011). Towards a pedagogy of hip hop in urban teacher education. *Journal of Negro Education*, 325–338.

Byker, E.J. (2013). Critical cosmopolitanism: Engaging students in global citizenship competencies. *English in Texas Journal, 43*(2), 18–26.

Chernoff, J.M. (1981). *African rhythm and African sensibility*. Chicago, IL: University of Chicago Press.

Coates, T.N. (2015). *Between the world and me*. New York: Spiegel and Grau Publishing.

Davies, I., & Pike, G. (2009). Global citizenship education: Challenges and possibilities. In R. Lewin (Ed.), *The Handbook of Practice and Research in Study Abroad: Higher Education and the Quest for Global Citizenship*. New York: Routledge.

Duncan-Andrade, J.M.R., & Morrell, E. (2008). *The art of critical pedagogy: Possibilities for moving from theory ton practice in urban schools* (vol. 285). New York: Peter Lang.

Freire, P. (1970). *Pedagogy of the oppressed*. New York: Continuum.

Freire, P. (1994). *Pedagogy of hope*. New York: Continuum.

Freire, P. (1998). *Teachers as cultural workers*. Boulder, CO: Westview Press.

Freire, P. (2001). *Pedagogy of freedom: Ethics, democracy, and civic courage*. Lanham, MD: Rowman & Littlefield Publishers.

Heilman, E.E. (2008). Including voices from the world through global citizenship education. *Social Studies and the Young Learner, 20*(3), 30–32.

Horton, A. (2012). Hip-hop as global passport: Examining digital citizenship and digital literacies through hip-hop culture. In B.J. Porfilio & M.J. Viola (Eds.), *Hip-Hop (e): The Cultural Practice and Critical Pedagogy of International Hip-Hop. Adolescent Cultures, School, and Society*. New York: Peter Lang.

Ibrahim, A. (2004). Operating under erasure: Hip-hop and the pedagogy of affective. *Journal of Curriculum Theorizing, 20*(1), 113–133.

Ibrahim A. (2009). Taking hip-hop to a whole nother level: Métissage, affect, and pedagogy in a global hip-hop nation. In H. Samy Alim, A. Ibrahim, & A.D. Pennycook (Eds.), *Global Linguistic Flows: Hip Hop Cultures, Youth Identities and the Politics of Language*. New York: Routledge.

Kohn, L.T. (1997). Methods in the case study analysis. Technical Pub. No. 2. Washington, DC: Center for Studying Health System Change.

Loflin, J.H., & Evans, J.M. (2015). They say that we are prone to violence, but it's home sweet home: The praxis of hip hop, self-actualization, and democratic education for addressing the roots of violence. *International Journal for Cross-Disciplinary Subjects in Education, 6*(4), 2358–2367.

López-González, M., & Limb, C.J. (2012, January). Musical creativity and the brain. In *Cerebrum: The dana forum on brain science* (vol. 2012). Dana Foundation.

Mahiri, J. (2006). Digital DJ-ing: Rhythms of learning in an urban school. *Language Arts, 84*(1), 55–62.

Malone, C., & Martinez Jr, G. (Eds.). (2014). *The organic globalizer: Hip hop, political development, and movement culture*. New York: Bloomsbury Publishing USA.

Mansilla, V.B., & Jackson, A. (2011). *Educating for global competency*. New York: Asia Society. Retrieved from: http://asiasociety.org/files/book-globalcompetence.pdf

Merriam, S.B. (1998). *Qualitative research and case study applications in education*. San Francisco, CA: Jossey-Bass.

Mitchell, T. (2001). *Global noise: Rap and hip hop outside the USA*. Middleton, CT: Wesleyan University Press.

Morrell, E. (2002).Toward a critical pedagogy of popular culture: Literacy development among urban youth. *Journal of Adolescent & Adult Literacy, 46*(1): 72–77.

Myschool.edu.au. (2016). Home. Retrieved from: http://www.myschool.edu.au/School Profile/Index/46891/McCarthyCatholicCollege/43220/2010

Nat Turner, K.C. (2012, October). Multimodal hip hop productions as media literacies. *The Educational Forum, 76*(4), 497–509.

Pardue, D. (2007). Hip hop as pedagogy: A look into "heaven" and "soul" in São Paulo, Brazil. *Anthropological Quarterly*, (3), 673–708.

Portland Youth Summit (2012). The 5 elements of hip-hop music. Retrieved from: http://portlandyouthsummit.org/about-us-2/

Richardson, E. (2006). *Hip hop literacies*. [Kindle for iPad]. Retrieved from Amazon.com

Rose, T. (1994). *Black noise: Rap music and black culture in contemporary America*. Hanover, NH. Wesleyan University Press.

Sammy Alim, H. (2007). Critical hip-hop language pedagogies: Combat, consciousness, and the cultural politics of communication. *Journal of Language, Identity, and Education, 6*(2), 161–176.

Samy Alim, H. (2011). Global ill-literacies hip hop cultures, youth identities, and the politics of literacy. *Review of Research in Education, 35*(1), 120–146.

Samy Alim H., Ibrahim A., & Pennycook, A.D. (Eds.) (2009). *Global linguistic flows: Hip hop cultures, youth identities and the politics of language*. New York: Routledge.

Samy Alim, H., & Pennycook, A. (2007). Glocal linguistic flows: Hip-hop culture (s), identities, and the politics of language education. *Journal of Language, Identity, and Education, 6*(2), 89–100.

Sarkar, M., & Allen, D. (2007). Hybrid identities in Quebec hip-hop: Language, territory and ethnicity in the mix. *Journal of Language, Identity and Education, 6*(2), 117–130.

Schattle, H. (2008). *The practices of global citizenship*. Lanham, MD: Rowman & Littlefield Publishing Group, Inc.

Söderman, J., & Sernhede, O. (2015). Hip-hop–what's in it for the academy? Self-understanding, pedagogy and aesthetical learning processes in everyday cultural praxis. *Music Education Research*, 1–14.

Stavrias, G. (2005). Droppin' conscious beats and flows: Aboriginal hip-hop and youth identity. *Australian Aboriginal Studies*, *5*(2), 44–54.

Stovall, D. (2006). We can relate: Hip-hop culture, critical pedagogy and the secondary classroom. *Urban Education*, *41*(6), 585–602.

Suaréz-Orozco, M., & Qin-Hilliard, D.B. (eds.) (2004). *Globalization: Culture and education in the new millennium*. Berkley and Los Angeles, CA: University of California Press.

Terkourafi, M. (Ed.). (2010). *The languages of global hip hop*. Chicago, IL: A&C Black.

6
EXAMINING THE USE OF AN ONLINE CULTURAL MODULE TO INCREASE LEARNERS' INTERCULTURAL SENSITIVITY

Joseph M. Terantino

Introduction

The world is becoming increasingly more globally minded and it is imperative that university students develop intercultural skills, including intercultural sensitivity, which will enable them to communicate and interact successfully with people from other cultures. The integration of culture components into coursework has been achieved via multiple avenues. For example, many foreign language educators have experimented with different approaches to connect students with target cultural informants, natives of the target culture, including, but not limited to, guest speakers (Albirini, 2009), ethnographic interviews (Hoyt, 2012; Lee, 2012), online discussion boards (Garrett-Rucks, 2013; Liaw, 2006; McBride & Wildner-Bassett, 2008), instant messaging (Jin & Erben, 2007), and virtual exchanges (Furstenberg, Levet, English, & Maillet, 2001; Lomicka, 2006). All of the aforementioned approaches highlight the importance of integrating the native speaker's perspective of the target culture; several utilize technology to make this connection or virtual connection possible.

The purpose of the study presented in this chapter is to examine the inclusion of native speaker perspectives in an online cultural learning module and its ability to aid in developing intercultural sensitivity. This research builds on such studies that integrate cultural informants and draws on Bennett's (1993) model for intercultural sensitivity, a scale for the range of attitudes toward cultural differences, as a theoretical framework, and examines how intercultural sensitivity may apply as a mechanism for evaluating intercultural education via online learning modules. Specifically, this research explores the impact that completing an online cultural module, containing native speakers' perspectives of a controversial issue, has on the intercultural sensitivity of Spanish language learners. Utilizing short video clips, text materials, and reflective prompts embedded in an online module, the participants of this study, university level students in a Spanish practical conversation course, explore Puerto Rico's political status in relation to the U.S.

Literature Review

Global Competence and Intercultural Sensitivity

Within language teaching and learning, global competence, or intercultural competence, is particularly significant, because it transforms the speaker of the second language from a "fluent fool" (Bennett, 1997) to a culturally competent interlocutor. As such, in its 2014 position statement, the American Council on Teaching Foreign Languages (ACTFL) describes global competence as the ability to communicate in the target language, in addition to other skills that highlight one's ability to successfully navigate another culture. These skills include the ability to:

- Interact with awareness, sensitivity, empathy, and knowledge of the perspectives of others;
- Withhold judgment, examining one's own perspectives as similar to or different from the perspectives of people with whom one is interacting;
- Be alert to cultural differences in situations outside of one's culture, including noticing cues indicating miscommunication or causing an inappropriate action or response in a situation;
- Act respectfully according to what is appropriate in the culture and the situation where everyone is not of the same culture or language background, including gestures, expressions, and behaviors; and
- Increase knowledge about the products, practices, and perspectives of other cultures (ACTFL, 2014).

ACTFL's statement on global competence rightfully portrays language and culture as interrelated entities. This distinction supports the previous work of others in the field. Kramsch (1993), for example, does not distinguish between language and culture. Thus, from her perspective teaching a language inherently includes teaching culture and vice versa. Risager expands on this inherent connection by exploring the terms *linguaculture* and *languaculture* to refer to culture in language or the cultural dimensions of language (2006; 2007; 2012). Last, Davis, Cho, and Hagenson (2005) reinforce the point when they state that, "Achieving intercultural competence through intercultural learning is a major goal that complements the development of the students' language competence" (p. 2).

Therefore, as we teach language we must also teach culture and intercultural skills, including intercultural sensitivity. Bennett (2004), from a non-linguistic perspective, offers the following description of *intercultural sensitivity*:

The crux of intercultural adaptation is the ability to have an alternative cultural experience. Individuals who have received largely monocultural socialization normally have access only to their own *cultural worldview,* so they are unable to experience the difference between their own perception and that of people who are culturally different. The development of intercultural sensitivity describes how we gain the ability to create an alternative experience that more or less matches that of people in another culture. People who can do this are considered to have an *intercultural worldview.*

(p. 74)

It is this cultural worldview and the development of intercultural sensitivity that are the primary focus of the study presented in this chapter. It is, therefore, imperative that online cultural modules provide an opportunity for students to examine the cultural worldviews of others and then determine how to relate to this alternative viewpoint—the essence of having an intercultural worldview. The intercultural point of view is the central factor used to indicate the students' levels of intercultural sensitivity according to Bennett's Developmental Model of Intercultural Sensitivity (1993).

Bennett's model consists of six individual stages (see Table 6.1), which are used to identify key characteristics of an individual's ability to understand cultural difference. The first three phases (Denial, Defense, and Minimization) are considered to be ethnocentric in nature. This means that the individual evaluates other cultures according to the standards of one's own culture. As one moves up the scale, the remaining three phases (Acceptance, Adaptation, and Integration) are considered to be ethnorelative in nature, signifying that the individual is able to adapt his or her behavior in many cultural contexts. Table 6.1 also provides specific descriptions for each of the six stages.

TABLE 6.1 Overview of Bennett's Developmental Model of Intercultural Sensitivity

Stages	*Bennett's (1993) descriptions*
Denial	Unaware of the existence of cultural differences
Defense	Acknowledge cultural differences but feel threatened by them
Minimization	Minimize cultural differences in order to protect one's own cultural identify
Acceptance	Recognize and value cultural differences without judging them as positive or negative
Adaptation	Adapt cognitively and behaviorally to cultural differences. Operate successfully within another culture
Integration	Interact comfortably with a variety of cultures. Integration of cultural awareness into everyday interactions

Developing Intercultural Sensitivity

As mentioned at the onset of this chapter, a variety of teaching methods have been developed to address culture and develop students' global competence or intercultural competence. More traditional approaches include lectures, personal interviews, guest speakers (Albirini, 2009), and ethnographic interviews (Hoyt, 2012), which require that students interact with target cultural informants. However, with the advent of technology-based tools, additional approaches now include a wide variety of Web 2.0 tools, including the use of online discussion boards (Garrett-Rucks, 2013; Liaw, 2006; McBride & Wildner-Bassett, 2008), mobile technologies (Botha, Vosloo, Kuner, & Van de Berg (2009), and virtual exchanges (Furstenberg, Levet, English, & Maillet, 2001; Lomicka, 2006). Collectively, the approaches examined in these previous studies demonstrate the capacity of technology to "promote the kind of sociality, criticality, and co-construction that lead to important shifts of perspective" (McBride & Wildner-Bassett, 2008), especially where opportunities for intercultural connections would not have been possible otherwise.

Furthermore, to help develop cultural awareness and intercultural sensitivity, this study builds on recent research that highlights the value of integrating the perspectives and participation of native speakers in explicit cultural instruction (Garrett-Rucks, 2013; Hoyt, 2012). Respectively, these studies employed videos of "French informants" relaying their opinions of French cultural practices and ethnographic interviews with "native Francophones." Both studies found that by interacting with cultural informants, students were able to better explore culture and make significant gains in cultural awareness and intercultural sensitivity. In Garrett-Rucks' (2013) research, technology, via online discussion boards, afforded the opportunity for university French students to connect and discuss culturally relevant topics with French cultural informants. Specifically, her findings indicated that participants experienced "sizeable growth" in intercultural sensitivity in response to the online instructional materials. Garrett-Rucks' study is also significant because it demonstrates the value of using Bennett's Model of Intercultural Sensitivity as a means to categorize self-reported data for research purposes such as that presented here.

The Study

This study employed a mixed-method approach to examine the impact of using an online cultural module to increase language learners' intercultural sensitivity. As Creswell (2013) notes, the mixed-method approach enables researchers to address research questions through collecting and interpreting a variety of data sets. The following sections of this chapter outline the procedures implemented for participant selection, data collection, and data analysis.

The Course and Online Cultural Module

The study took place at a large, southeastern university in a Spanish practical conversation course, which spanned 15 weeks over the academic semester. The practical conversation course stressed expansion of effective listening comprehension and speaking skills through culturally and linguistically appropriate activities. It was also based on six thematic units: striking up a conversation, describing people and things, expressing opinions, expressing wants and needs, arguing a point, and narrating a story.

The online cultural module, "A Multimedia Module for Raising Cultural Awareness: Examining Perspectives of Puerto Rico in Relation to the U.S.," was a standalone, one-week lesson designed to engage Spanish students in a critical evaluation of the issue regarding Puerto Rico's political status. The module, created with SoftChalk, was designed based on the First Principles of Instruction as defined by Merrill (2002). In particular, this problem-based approach to instruction allows students to progress through four distinct phases of learning: activation of prior experience, demonstration of skills, application of skills, and integration of these skills into real world activities. Table 6.2

TABLE 6.2 Overview of online cultural module content

Page#	Content of the page	First principle of instruction
1	Title page	
2	Technical requirements	
3	Introduction to the module	Activation
4	Purpose of the module	Activation
5	Learning objectives	Activation
6	Defining cultural worldview and impression of Puerto Rican culture	Activation
7	Assessment of prior knowledge related to Puerto Rico	Activation
8	A comical introduction to the issue: video clip from The Daily Show	Demonstration
9	Historical overview of Puerto Rico's political status	Demonstration
10	Reflection prompt: what does it mean to be a country?	Activation
11	Overview of current options for Puerto Rico's political status	Demonstration
12	2012 plebiscite	Demonstration
13	A Puerto Rican politician's perspective of the issue	Demonstration
14	Native Puerto Rican students' perspectives of the issue	Demonstration
15	Native Puerto Rican faculty members' perspectives of the issue	Demonstration
16	Post-module reflection prompt	Application
17	Redefining worldview and impression of Puerto Rican culture	Application
18	Finishing up	
19	Note of completion	

presents a page-by-page overview of the module including how each page corresponds with the First Principles of Instruction (Merrill, 2002). To aid the students in developing intercultural sensitivity, the module provided opportunities for them to explore intercultural worldviews, including divergent views on the same issue, and to consider a shift of cultural perspective (McBride & Wildner-Bassett, 2008).

The module comprised 19 slides or pages that included an overview for the purpose of the module (pages 3–5), major content related to the issue (pages 8–15), and components for expressing worldview statements (pages 6 and 17). The content of the module presented various points of view relating to Puerto Rico's political status. For this purpose, two native Puerto Rican faculty members and two native Puerto Rican students recorded their thoughts and feelings in English and Spanish to share with the Spanish language learners.

The political status of Puerto Rico was chosen as the central *problem* for the cultural module, because it remains a highly debated issue within Puerto Rico and the U.S. Currently, Puerto Rico is a Commonwealth with access to certain, but not all, rights or responsibilities afforded to U.S. citizens. Over the last 60 years, Puerto Rico has struggled to define its identity. As shown in Table 6.3, there are several options for the future of Puerto Rico: to keep its current Commonwealth status, shift toward becoming an official state within the U.S., seek complete independence from the U.S., or adopt a relationship of free association with the U.S. Plebiscites in 1967, 1993, 1998, and 2012 have all posed variations of this question of status to the citizens of Puerto Rico, and yet no overwhelming favor has been shown for any option (Pantojas-Garcia, 2013).

TABLE 6.3 Options for political status of Puerto Rico

Option	What the option includes
Statehood	This option involves incorporating Puerto Rico into the U.S. as the 51st state.
Independence	This option would sever ties between the U.S. and Puerto Rico and would allow for complete autonomy for Puerto Rico.
Commonwealth	This is Puerto Rico's current status. This status affords citizens limited rights, and obliges them to certain responsibilities as part of the U.S.
Free Association	This option is very similar to the Commonwealth status, but provides more decision-making power to Puerto Rico in its own affairs. The U.S. would have a reduced ability to impose decisions and regulations on Puerto Rico.

The Participants

The participants for this study were 15 students who were participating in the Spanish conversation course. Although completing the online module was a required component of the face-to-face course, the students gave their informed consent to participate in the study. Most students enrolled in the course directly after completing the second-year courses. The vast majority of the students were Spanish majors or minors, or they were majors in International Affairs or International Business, which require a third-year language course. All of the students were in their 20s; 13 were Caucasians, one was African-American, and one was Hispanic.

Data Collection

This mixed-method study employed multiple methods of data collection including student reflective statements and a student focus group. First, the students completed the online cultural module outside of class. The instructional delivery of content in the online module was preceded and followed by open-ended questions designed to summon worldview and cultural viewpoints of Puerto Rico from the participants. At the beginning of the module (page six), responses were solicited for the following prompts:

1. Write a statement about how you view the world and its array of cultures (cultural worldview).
2. Write a statement in which you define what you think of Puerto Rican culture based on what you know before completing this module (cultural viewpoint of Puerto Rico).

At the close of the module (page 17), responses were solicited to the same questions to determine if any changes came after completing the module. Throughout the module these student responses were tracked anonymously using student ID numbers. Second, a face-to-face focus group was conducted with the entire class after the students had completed the online module. The focus group was employed to allow further opportunities for student reflection about this method of online cultural learning and its inclusion of native speakers' perspectives.

Data Analysis

Similar to Garrett-Rucks (2013), in which Bennett's Developmental Model of Intercultural Sensitivity was utilized to categorize students' discussion board posts related to cultural issues, the students' in-module statements, their cultural worldviews, and cultural viewpoints of Puerto Rico, were reviewed via discourse analysis methods and classified according to the six stages of intercultural sensitivity. See Table 6.4 for a more comprehensive description of the coding scale.

TABLE 6.4 Overview of the coding scale based on Bennett's (1993) model

Stages and coding	
Stage 1 - Denial	1
Stage 2 - Defense	2
Stage 3 - Minimization	3
Stage 4 - Acceptance	4
Stage 5 - Adaptation	5
Stage 6 - Integration	6

Three raters, published authors in the field of intercultural competence, scored each statement according to the scale of one to six presented in Table 6.4. Adopting Garrett-Rucks' (2013) scoring approach, when a single statement contained contradictory elements, the statement was assessed as an average of the two scores. For example, indicators of Stage 4 and Stage 2 equal a Stage 3 classification. Initially, inter-rater reliability was 85%. After discussing how to treat contradictory indicators within a statement, the raters achieved 100% inter-rater reliability.

Paired sample t-tests were then implemented to determine the degree of change related to intercultural sensitivity as reflected in each participant's worldview and cultural viewpoint statements, pre- and post-module. Additionally, the constant comparison method (Glaser & Strauss, 2009) was employed to systematically code the focus group transcript. Emerging themes were identified using three recursive processes: category construction, data verification, and testing and confirming (Merriam, 2009). However, utilizing the role of technology and native speakers' perspectives as a priori categories, the primary purpose of this stage of analysis was to determine how the participants perceived the value of these items in relation to cultural learning.

Results

Pre-Module Statements

Each of the 15 students contributed pre-module statements pertaining to worldview and cultural viewpoint of Puerto Rico. Each statement ranged from 12 to 121 words and from one to six sentences. As depicted in Table 6.5, the pre-module responses contained an equal number of ethnocentric statements (15 with 10 minimization and five defense) and ethnorelative statements (15 with 11 acceptance and 4 adaptation) that were recorded for the two prompts. Interestingly, more pre-module cultural viewpoint statements related to Puerto Rico were classified as ethnocentric (nine) than were the worldview statements (six).

TABLE 6.5 Overview of pre-module ethnocentric and ethnorelative scoring

	I feel the world is:	I think Puerto Rican culture is:
Ethnocentric	6	9
Ethnorelative	9	6

The ethnocentric worldview statements were characterized by a tendency to describe world cultures as being essentially the same, a clear indicator of the minimization stage, which is predicated on minimizing the differences between cultures. The following two statements are representative of this tendency:

- *I feel the world is* . . . made of a bunch of different cultures, but ultimately we are all pretty similar. Most of us have the same wants and needs. We only act differently to fit in with the people surrounding us.
- *I feel the world is* . . . made of cultures that are pretty much the same, just appear different on the surface. The problem is that most people don't really know that much about other cultures so we assume they are very different.

Similarly, the ethnocentric statements regarding Puerto Rico also tended to minimize the differences between the cultures of the U.S. and Puerto Rico:

- *I think the Puerto Rican culture is* . . . not really that different from the U.S. I have never been there, but many Puerto Ricans live here, so I don't see how they could be that different.
- *I think the Puerto Rican culture is* . . . a lot like the U.S. because it is really a part of the U.S. anyway. I think they do many of the same things we do like watch TV, play sports, and other things. Maybe it is only different in the language and some customs.
- *I think the Puerto Rican culture is* . . . I don't know much about Puerto Rico, but I bet it is a lot like the U.S. because of the relationship that we have had with it.

On the contrary, the ethnorelative worldview statements were characterized by a tendency to accept, even appreciate, that differences do exist between cultures, an indicator of the acceptance stage. The following statements display this form of acceptance:

- *I feel the world is* . . . a very different place depending on where you are, but that is also what makes the world so special.
- *I feel the world is* . . . has a lot of different cultures, people, and languages. These differences are what make the world so unique.
- *I feel the world is*[. . .]a remarkably diverse place. There are so many cultures around the world and each brings something new and interesting to learn.

With regard to Puerto Rico, the ethnorelative statements also tended toward the acceptance stage. Each of the following statements clearly describes the Puerto Rican culture as having unique characteristics and the latter two statements express a desire to learn more about Puerto Rico:

- *I think the Puerto Rican culture is* . . . a unique part of the United States and that it could have a much bigger influence in the United States than it already does. Puerto Rico has a lot of different aspects of their culture that could be introduced in the U.S.
- *I think the Puerto Rican culture is* . . . something I would like to experience. Maybe I will be able to travel there before I graduate. I am sure it is different and interesting, but right now, I don't know much.
- *I think the Puerto Rican culture is* . . . something I would like to learn more about because they have their own way of doing things that would be nice to see.

Post-Module Statements

The 15 students also contributed individual post-module statements pertaining to worldview and cultural viewpoint of Puerto Rico. Each statement ranged from 15 to 118 words and from one to seven sentences. As indicated in Table 6.6, post-module responses contained 12 ethnocentric statements (eight minimization and four defense) and 18 ethnorelative statements (eight acceptance and 10 adaptation). Again, more cultural viewpoint statements related to Puerto Rico were classified as ethnocentric (seven) than were the worldview statements (five).

Overall, the same distinguishing characteristics of each stage were identified in the participants' responses. However, the most prominent difference between the pre- and post-module responses was that the post-module responses contained more statements classified in the adaptation stage (10). The following examples of adaptation emphasize the importance of considering where you are as you approach culture and cultural interactions:

- *I feel the world is* . . . I guess your perspective of the world depends on where you are. It seems like Puerto Ricans view the world differently than I would because of their experiences.
- *I feel the world is* . . . a place where you have to be flexible to adapt according to where you are or where you live. You can't be the same person everywhere you go because things may be different. You have to be a different version of you depending on where you are at the time.

TABLE 6.6 Overview of post-module ethnocentric and ethnorelative scoring

	I feel the world is:	*I think Puerto Rican culture is:*
Ethnocentric	5	7
Ethnorelative	10	8

With regard to Puerto Rico, the ethnorelative statements also tended toward the acceptance stage. The following statements express the students' perception of Puerto Rico's uniqueness:

- *I think the Puerto Rican culture is* . . . a very unique place. It has a long history with the U.S. and that makes it a part of our country, but it also maintains its own sense of being, of what it is independent of the U.S.
- *I think the Puerto Rican culture is* . . . evolving. Puerto Rico is a special case because it's not a country; it's part of our country. Yet, they have a lot of customs that we don't have. A lot of what I learned about Puerto Rico was really interesting and I would love to experience some of this firsthand.

Development in Intercultural Sensitivity

Three paired sample t-tests were conducted with the data coded according to Bennett's (1993) model, as depicted in Table 6.7, for cultural worldview, cultural viewpoint of Puerto Rico, and both combined. With regard to the first question, cultural worldview, there was not a significant difference in the pre-module scores (M = 3.8, SD = 1.01) and the post-module scores (M = 4.23, SD = 0.98); t(14) = 1.26, **p** = 0.23. For the second question, cultural viewpoint of Puerto Rico, there also was not a significant difference in the pre-module scores (M = 3.37, SD = 0.88) and the post-module scores (M = 3.8, SD = 1.05); t(14) = 1.11,

TABLE 6.7 Options for political status of Puerto Rico

Student	I feel the world is:	I think the Puerto Rican culture is:	Participant's pre-module average	I feel the world is:	I think the Puerto Rican culture is:	Participant's post-module average
1	5	3.5	4.25	5	5	5
2	3	3	3	3	5	4
3	2	2	2	4	4.5	4.25
4	4	5	4.5	4.5	3	3.75
5	3	3	3	3.5	3.5	3.5
6	3.5	4	3.75	5	2.5	3.75
7	2	2	2	5	5	5
8	3.5	3.5	3.5	5	4.5	4.75
9	5.5	3.5	4.5	3.5	4.5	4
10	4	3	3.5	3.5	3.5	3.5
11	4.5	4	4.25	5	4	4.5
12	5	2	3.5	5.5	4.5	5
13	4	4	4	5	3.5	4.25
14	4	4	4	4	2	3
15	4	4	4	2	2	2
Average	3.80	3.37	3.58	4.23	3.80	4.02

p = 0.29. Last, for the combined scores there was not a significant difference in the pre-module scores (M = 3.58, SD = 0.79) and the post-module scores (M = 4.02, SD = 0.83); **t**(14) = 1.31, **p** = 0.21.

Although the differences between pre-module statements and post-module statements were not found to be statistically significant, the raw scores in Table 6.7 indicate that collectively the participants experienced average increases of roughly 0.43 for cultural worldview, cultural view of Puerto Rico, and for both combined. Therefore, the raw scores provide some evidence of a moderate transition from minimization toward acceptance when considering the group of students as a whole. Perhaps more importantly, analysis of the individual participant's scores also showed substantial variability in intercultural sensitivity, both within and between the pre- and post-module statements. For example, 9 of the 15 participants experienced moderate gains in average score, four experienced decreases, and two remained in the same stage of intercultural sensitivity. Of the most notable examples of this variability, participant #7 experienced a three-point gain, moving from defense to adaptation (ethnocentric to ethnorelative), and participant #15 experienced a two-point drop in classification, moving from acceptance to defense (ethnorelative to ethnocentric).

Reactions to the Online Cultural Module

Findings from the focus group revealed that the students considered the online cultural module to be valuable because it provided easy access to an organized collection of multimedia resources, including texts and videos from cultural informants. Several students referenced variety as an important component of the module:

- I really liked how the module had so many different videos and they were from different people: comedians, politicians, professors, students, etc. Being that they were all online and organized in the same place really helped to find the information easily and to go back and forth between the different parts.
- I had never seen or done an online assignment like this. I liked the way everything was so clear and organized. It was very easy to follow from one page to the next and it was easy to understand where we were going with the information. I also liked that there were a lot of different things like videos and short quizzes and short responses. That helped to keep my attention. Most of the time when a professor gives us an online assignment, you just have to read a lot and then write a reflection.

Participants also described the value of the online module in terms of providing additional information that students could access on a voluntary basis. In particular, one student indicated, "I liked the extra stuff that was provided. I was able to look at a lot of optional things because they were right there." In addition, the students appeared to appreciate having control over navigating the online module and the pace by which they completed the module:

- The best part of the module was being able to do it outside of class and whenever I wanted to. Because I work and have other responsibilities, being able to just open it and do it when I choose is really important.
- This was a good assignment because you could do it as slow or as quickly as you wanted to. I liked being able to just click back and forth and open some things and not others. Picking and choosing what to do within the module was neat.

Reactions to the Inclusion of Native Speakers' Perspectives

Throughout the focus group the students indicated that the inclusion of native speakers' perspectives of the issue supported an increase in intercultural understanding and retention of module content that would not have been possible otherwise. The videos in which Puerto Rican faculty and students presented their candid thoughts were often cited as the "most valuable" component of the online module. Two participants explained this in the focus group:

- The video clips from people at our university were the best part of this project, because it helped to bring the issue home for me. Otherwise, it would have been just another theoretical discussion of an issue that may or not have had any meaning for me personally.
- Watching the video clips from Puerto Rican students and faculty members, one that I even know personally, was a really cool way to help introduce the topic. I felt like I connected very easily with the topic after seeing these because it felt more personalized for me.

In addition to making the online cultural module personal and relevant, the participants described the potential for the video clips to present multiple and authentic perspectives of the target culture being studied:

- I honestly never considered what the Puerto Rican people think about being connected to the U.S. I always assumed they were happy with the situation. Seeing different people talk about it made me think more about the different sides of the issue.
- Where else would I get to see and hear what someone from Puerto Rico thinks about their status? Without these videos I would be limited to what I know or what I could read. It was even neat to see that even they didn't completely agree on what should be done for their island.

Another important element expressed by the participants, as indicated in the statement above, is that of being able to access authentic perspectives of the target culture, perhaps where it would not have been possible otherwise. Overall, based on the participants' focus group statements and the evaluation of their in-module responses, it appeared that the native speakers' perspectives presented in the module supported the students' ability to understand and empathize with perspectives different than their own, key characteristics of intercultural sensitivity.

Limitations

When considering the overall impact of this research, there are several limitations to keep in mind. Most importantly, based on the small sample size (n = 15) and the limited duration of the study, the findings are not readily generalizable to other contexts. Similarly, the cultural issue identified and presented in the online cultural module was very specific to the Puerto Rican culture. Therefore, the results are also not generalizable to other cultures or content. Last, all of the data examined in this study, including the in-module responses and focus group transcript, were self-reported by the participants. It is possible that the Hawthorne effect (Parsons, 1974) may apply if the students felt compelled to provide responses they felt the instructor would deem favorable; however, self-reported data have been widely used in studies of intercultural competence and sensitivity (Albirini, 2009; Garrett-Rucks, 2013; Hoyt, 2012, Lee, 2012). It is also reasonable to argue that deducing one's level of intercultural sensitivity from in-module statements may be problematic based on the limited scope and number of statements provided.

Conclusion

Through the use of the online module the students were able to make moderate gains in intercultural sensitivity, as evaluated in their pre- and post-module statements. Although the differences were not found to be statistically significant, the moderate gains in the raw scores appear to be congruent with previous research such as Garrett-Rucks (2013), which also documented gains in intercultural sensitivity after participating in explicit, online cultural instruction. However, the nature of these gains was not uniform. Several students experienced gains and/or reductions in their intercultural sensitivity scores within and across the pre- and post-module statements.

Overall, the study was successful in determining that students appreciated the value of explicit cultural instruction via an online module. The study also helped to identify the importance of online instruction. In particular, the students enjoyed having independent access to a wide variety of online materials, including video statements from the target cultural informants. Without the online module and the participation of the cultural informants, the students would not have been exposed to the insider's perspective of the issue. Last, this research further supports the inclusion of cultural informants as a valuable component of instruction, as previously indicated by others (Albirini, 2009; Garrett-Rucks, 2013; Hoyt, 2012).

This study also provides direction for future applications of a similar online cultural module. For example, such online cultural instruction could be further improved if it included an explicit experiential activity, which includes opportunities for interacting with native speakers of the target culture. A shortfall of this study was that it did not include any such experiential activity, even though the students were exposed to the cultural informants' perspectives. With regard to future research, it is important to focus on evidence of intercultural learning that can be triangulated through a variety of sources. Being able to document intercultural sensitivity through the participants' in-module statements was valuable, but would also be bolstered if combined with another data source to support any findings.

References

Albirini, A. (2009). Using technology, literature and guest speakers to raise cultural awareness of Arabic language learners. *The International Journal of Language Society and Culture, 28*, 1–15.

American Council on Teaching Foreign Languages (ACTFL) (2014). Global Competence Position Statement. Alexandria, VA.

Bennett, M.J. (1993). Toward ethnorelativism: A developmental model of intercultural sensitivity. In R.M. Paige (Ed.), *Education for the intercultural experience* (pp. 21–71). Yarmouth, ME: Intercultural.

Bennett, M.J. (1997). How not to be a fluent fool: Understanding the cultural dimensions of language. In A.E. Fantini (Vol. Ed.) & J.C. Richards (Series Ed.), *New ways in teaching culture. New ways in TESOL series II: Innovative classroom techniques* (pp. 16–21). Alexandria, VA: TESOL.

Bennett, M.J. (2004). Becoming interculturally competent. In J.S. Wurzel (Ed.), *Toward multiculturalism: A reader in multicultural education* (62–77). Newton, MA: Intercultural Resource Corporation.

Botha, A., Vosloo, S., Kuner, J., Van de Berg, M. (2009). Improving cross-cultural awareness and communication through mobile technologies. *International Journal of Mobile and Blended Learning, 1*(2), 39–53.

Creswell, J.W. (2013). *Research design: Qualitative, quantitative, and mixed methods approaches.* Thousand Oaks, CA: Sage Publications.

Davis, N., Cho, M.O., & Hagenson, L. (2005). Intercultural competence and the role of technology in teacher education. *Contemporary Issues in Technology and Teacher Education* (CITE), *4*(4), 384–394.

Furstenberg, G., Levet, S., English, K., & Maillet, K. (2001). Giving a virtual voice to the silent language of culture: The CULTURA project. *Language Learning and Technology, 5*, 55–102.

Garrett-Rucks, P. (2013). A discussion-based online approach to fostering deep cultural inquiry in an introductory language course. *Foreign Language Annals, 46*(2), 191–212.

Glaser, B. G., & Strauss, A. L. (2009). *The discovery of grounded theory: Strategies for qualitative research*. Piscataway, NJ: Transaction Books.

Hoyt, K. (2012). Developing intercultural competence via semi-directed cross-cultural interviews. *NECTFL, 93*.

Jin, L., & Erben, T. (2007). Intercultural learning via instant messenger interaction. *Calico Journal, 24*(2), 291–312.

Kramsch, C. (1993). *Context and culture in language teaching*. New York, NY: Oxford University Press.

Lee, L. (2012). Engaging study abroad students in intercultural learning through blogging and ethnographic interviews. *Foreign Language Annals, 45*(1), 7–21.

Liaw, M. L. (2006). E-learning and the development of intercultural competence. *Language Learning & Technology, 10*(3), 49–64.

Lomicka, L. (2006). Understanding the other: Intercultural exchange and CMC. In L. Ducate & N. Arnold (Eds.), *Calling on CALL: From theory and research to new directions in foreign language teaching* (pp. 211–236). San Marcos, TX: CALICO.

McBride, K., & Wildner-Bassett, M. (2008). Interpersonal and intercultural understanding in a blended second culture classroom. In S. Sieloff Magnan (Ed.), *Mediating discourse online* (pp. 93–124). Philadelphia, PA: Benjamins.

Merriam, S. B. (2009). *Qualitative research: A guide to design and implementation*. San Francisco, CA: John Wiley & Sons.

Merrill, M. D. (2002). First Principles of Instruction. *Educational Technology Research and Development, 50*(3), 43–59.

Pantojas-Garcia, E. (2013). The Puerto Rico status question: Can the stalemate be broken? *Caribbean Journal of International Relations and Diplomacy, 1*(2).

Parsons, H. M. (1974). What happened at Hawthorne? New evidence suggests the Hawthorne effect resulted from operant reinforcement contingencies. *Science, 183*(4128), 922–932.

Risager, K. (2006). *Language and culture: Global flows and local complexity*. Clevedon, UK: Multilingual Matters.

Risager, K. (2007). *Language and culture pedagogy: From a national to a transnational paradigm*. Clevedon, UK: Multilingual Matters.

Risager, K. (2012). Linguaculture and transnationality: The cultural dimensions of language. In J. Jackson (ed.), *Routledge Handbook of Language and Intercultural Communication*, London and New York: Routledge.

7

HOW CULTURAL FACTORS INFLUENCE THE USE OF SOCIAL CONSTRUCTIVIST-BASED PEDAGOGICAL MODELS OF DISTANCE LEARNING

Examining Japanese Online Collaborative Behaviors

Bodi Anderson

As research into cultural issues and distance learning evolves, some have questioned the cultural appropriateness of current social constructivist-based pedagogical models that often drive distance learning. Research has hinted that in the Middle East and Asia, where cultural values and student and teacher roles are quite different than in the Western world, learners may not always be able to successfully function in traditional distance learning settings (Andersson, 2008; Chen, Mashhadi, Ang, & Harkrider, 1999; Shattuk, 2005; Wong & Trinidad, 2004). In a case study of international graduate students living in the United States, Shattuk (2005) states: "Social constructivist-based pedagogy couched in the highly interactive communication world can be a lonely place for an international online learner whose cultural experiences are different than the dominant educational cultures" (p. 186). Further, studies of distance learning programs in Middle Eastern and Asian countries have noted that when social constructivist-based models of distance learning are exported as is, students and instructors of non-Western cultures have problems adapting to and implementing them (Andersson, 2008; Al-Oteawi, 2002; Fang, 2007; Wong & Trinidad, 2004). Though the aforementioned studies have suggested that there may be problems with the current model of distance learning, there is still a conclusive lack of empirical support for this idea and a further examination into cultural factors and dimensions and the role they play in distance learning is needed.

The primary purpose of the present study is to explore how cultural factors influence the use of social constructivist-based pedagogical models of distance learning in international settings, namely Japan. In order to do so, the study will first operationalize both the concepts of distance learning and culture. Distance learning will be operationalized with reference to guiding theory, specifically social constructivism and *collaborative learning*. Culture will be operationalized primarily with use of Geert Hofstede's (1980; 1991) model of cultural dimensions. Using Hofstede's (1980; 1991) cultural dimensions as a lens for interpretation, the present study aims to examine the role of culture in the distance learning classroom by focusing on the key distance education concept of *collaborative learning* and empirically examining any potential contrast with ideals key to current social constructivist pedagogical models.

An Operational Definition of Distance Learning

A conceptual view of distance learning can often be seen as consisting of two symbiotic components: technology and theory. In order to establish an operational definition for distance learning, these two components will be briefly examined with emphasis on the latter. A key point, as noted by Garrison and Akyol (2009), is that teachers, researchers, and theorists should not be seduced by the technology aspects of distance learning alone, in that theory in distance learning must embrace both the technological side and the theoretical in order to create a sustainable and successful model. In distance learning, the technology is not simply a tool but an integrated part of theory.

While the technological side of distance learning can be seen in the use of Computer-Mediated Communication (CMC), the primary pedagogical foundations of distance learning lie in social constructivist theory, which is tied closely with Vygotsky's (1978) Zone of Proximal Development model. This model states that a learner's cognitive development is highly correlated with their social interaction and collaboration, and thusly knowledge is created by negotiating meaning with others. Social constructivist theory in distance learning is noted as having a student-centered, as opposed to teacher-centered, approach in the classroom and focuses on social construction of knowledge through negotiated meanings (Gunawardena & McIssac, 2003). Woo and Reeves (2007) add that key characteristics and applications of social constructivism in distance learning also include an emphasis on the intersubjective construction of knowledge, including multiple interpretations of knowledge, a focus on the critical role of peers in learning, the need for collaboration in learning and the opportunity for students to publicly share and then revise their work based on social critiques, and to reflect on what they have learned with others.

Collaborative learning

The concept of *collaborative learning* predates the current CMC-based paradigm of distance learning and was originally described by Vygotsky (1978) as learning among students and/or between students and an instructor; the instructor assists students in the gap between what they could accomplish alone and what they could accomplish in cooperation with others. Garrison (2000) argues that distance education theories in the twenty-first century need to reflect a collaborative approach to education. Garrison and Archer (2000) note that since the turn of the century, face-to-face learning and particularly online learning in higher education has undergone a shift into initiatives that focus on collaborative and socially constructed knowledge, which they also call a collaborative constructivist approach. Regarding the current paradigm of distance learning, So and Brush (2007) note that in distance learning research there have been increasing interests toward *collaborative learning* approaches. This phenomenon can be explained by two impetuses: social constructivism and CMC. Thus *collaborative learning* can be seen as a key theoretical and pedagogical construct sharing a symbiotic relationship with social constructivism and CMC in progressing current distance learning theory. In analyzing collaborative interaction, it is believed this current study will contextualize culture in distance learning settings.

An Operational Definition of Culture

Perhaps the most frequently cited and used operational definition of culture in social science research on culture is Hofstede's (1980; 1991) cultural dimensions model. Hofstede (1980; 1991) argues that nationality and ethnic origin are significantly related to cultural values and perspectives. Furthermore, Hofstede (1980; 1991) argues that culture is not only who we are, how we think, and how we respond to our environment, but more so, how we learn. This model identifies four distinct cultural dimensions based on value orientations that are considered salient and shared across cultures worldwide: individualism-collectivism, power-distance, uncertainty avoidance, and masculinity-femininity.

Building on these four dimensions, researchers have added further defining components to Hofstede's model. One such component is Hall's (1976) *communication context* dimension, which examines linguistic factors, namely the amount of information that is implied versus stated directly in a message. Hall's *communication context* dimension is frequently used in studies that incorporate Hofstede's original four dimensions (Gunawardena, Wilson, & Nolla, 2003).

From 1980 to 1999, Hofstede's (1980; 1991; 1994) model has been cited nearly 1700 times in the Social Sciences Citation Index, and has been validated in more than 150 empirical studies making it the most frequently cited model with regard to culture analyzed in the social sciences (Ford, Connelly, & Meister, 2003). One of the reasons for the frequent use of Hofstede's model of cultural dimensions is because it offers an empirically measurable and well-validated means for operationalizing culture. Moreover, in studies of cultural issues in distance learning settings, Hofstede's model is the most used in operationalizing culture (Gunawardena, Wilson, & Nolla, 2003; Gunawardena & Zittle, 1997;

Kim & Bonk, 2002; Lowry, Zhang, Zho, & Fu, 2010; Zhang, Lowry, Zhou, & Fu, 2007). Based on prominent cultural factors discussed below identified in the participant population culture, Japan, three dimensions are used in the current study including two of Hofstede's (1980) original dimensions, *individualism-collectivism* and *power-distance*, and Hall's (1976) *communication context* dimension.

Individualism-Collectivism

Individualism-collectivism focuses on the relationship between individuals and groups. In Hofstede's (1980) model, *individualism* is the opposite of *collectivism*. *Individualistic* cultures encourage the making of decisions based on the needs of individuals, and in these cultures, everyone is expected to look after themselves. Furthermore, debate and expression of personal opinion are highly valued by *individualistic* cultures. Conversely, in *collectivistic* cultures, loyalty to a group and decision making revolving around what is best for the group are encouraged. Similarly, *collectivistic* cultures place an emphasis on maintaining social harmony in personal interactions and avoiding potentially confrontational or face-threatening interactions.

This chapter is interested in the *individualism-collectivism* dimension as Triandis (1995) suggests that it is the most relevant dimension in developing hypotheses concerning the relationship between culture and social behavior. The *individualism-collectivism* dimension can also be used to explain and predict why some cultures are more willing to adhere to societal and group norms than others (Gudykunst, Matsumoto, & Ting-Toomey, 1996; Lowry, Zhang, Zhou, & Fu, 2010). *Individualist* cultures, such as the United States, stress individual goals and needs, and *collectivist* cultures, such as China and Japan, emphasize group goals and social harmony (Gunawardena & Zittle, 1997; Kim & Bonk, 2002; Triandis, 1995). Finally, for the present study, the participant population consists of Japanese nationals, a highly collectivist culture (Hofstede, 1980; Nishimura, Nevgi, & Tella, 2008).

Power-Distance

Power-distance refers to the extent to which the less powerful members of institutions and organizations within a country expect and accept that power is distributed unequally (Hofstede, 1980; 1991). In other words, *power-distance* is the extent to which less powerful persons in a society accept inequality in power and consider it as normal (Gunawardena, Wilson, & Nolla, 2003). *Power-distance* is described as *high, low*, or *moderate*, with *high-power distance* being illustrated by cultures in which decisions are made by superiors without consultation with subordinates, and subordinates readily accepting this practice (Ford, Connelly, & Meister, 2003). Conversely, in *low-power distance* cultures, status differences among individuals are less of a factor and decisions are made in a more democratic manner.

Thus, in *low-power distance* cultures, those of lower social status are not fearful of disagreeing with superiors and are more participative in decision making. These levels of power difference can manifest in social status; employment positions, such as workers versus managers; and in many Asian cultures, Japan included, in elder-youth age-based relationships. The current participant population has been identified as having *high-power distance* (Hofstede, 1980; 1991).

Communication Context

Hall (1976) created a theoretical dimension of cultural variability noted as *high-* and *low-context communications* styles. This dimension has often been used in the study of culture in conjunction with Hofstede's dimensions and particularly with studies that examine culture in online learning environments (Gunawardena & Nolla, 2001; Kim & Bonk, 2002; Tu, 2001). Hall (1976) argues that the influence of context involves the degree to which protocol and tradition dictate how communication should proceed. In *high-communication context* cultures, communication style is influenced by the closeness of human relationships, well-structured social hierarchy, and strong behavioral norms (Kim, Pan, & Park, 1998). In a *high-communication context* culture the listener is expected to be able to read "between the lines" and understand the unsaid, thanks to his or her comprehension of context (Hall, 1976). In *low-communication context* cultures, such as the United States, communication occurs predominantly through explicit statements in text and speech. In regard to the current population of Japanese nationals, Hall and Hall (1990) have ranked them at the top of the high-context culture scale.

Use of Cultural Dimensions in Previous Studies on Culture and Distance Learning

As noted above, studies that have looked at online learning and culture have often made use of the dimensions used in the present study. In their study of online learners from the United States, Finland and South Korea, Kim and Bonk (2002) connect both *individualism-collectivism* and *communication context* dimensions with the distance learning concept of *collaborative learning*. They note that members of *collectivist* cultures value harmony, solidarity and being interconnected with others; they tend to be indirect, implicit, and reserved when communicating online and use predominantly *high-context communication*. Furthermore, individuals in *collectivist* and *high-context communication* cultures tend to give importance to relationships over tasks in online learning environments, the opposite of individualist, *low-context communication* cultures. Kim and Bonk (2002) found this true as Korean participants focused on group relationships while North American and Finnish students focused on tasks.

This is not to say, however, that the goals of learners in *collectivist* cultures are not achievement-based. While learners from *collectivist, high-power distance* cultures are more reluctant to speak up in class and instead try to preserve harmony and maintain social face, they are also often highly focused on achieving individual academic goals (Fang, 2007). In fact, studies on Asian culture and distance learning have shown that students find social connections enjoyable in online classrooms but often are hard pressed to make them. However, many students strive for personal achievement and keep their academic interaction centered on their instructors while viewing interactions with peers as primarily social (Bray, Aoki & Dlugosh, 2008; Fang 2007; Jung & Suzuki, 2006).

Gunawardena and Nolla (2001) examined grouping processes across North American and Mexican cultures connecting the *individualism-collectivism* dimension with *collaborative learning*. They found that learners from the United States had many more expressions of differing opinions compared to their *collectivist* Mexican peers, who reported finding much less conflict in the *collaborative learning* process. Anakwe and Christensen (1999) also note that relationship building is a primary goal of *collectivist* cultures and suggest that instructors should give students from *collectivist* cultures more time to develop social relationships prior to beginning *collaborative learning* tasks in online environments as they often suffer psychologically from being thrown into groups with peers they don't already know. In another study of graduate students from the United States and Taiwan, both *individualism-collectivism* and *communication context* dimensions were noted as a prominent factor influencing collaborative behaviors of learners (Chen, Hsu, & Caropreso, 2006). It was found that Taiwanese students tended to produce longer messages with more personal context reference compared to *individualistic* students from the United States, who made use of shorter messages focusing on content over personal relations. Finally, Thompson and Ku (2005) noted that *collectivist* behaviors such as maintaining group harmony were the primary factors in Chinese graduate students in the United States being less critical and giving less feedback in collaborative projects compared with US students.

A body of the work on culture and distance learning also points to *power distance* being a limiting factor on collaboration. Studies have found that in *low-power distance* cultures, such as the United States, students feel no problems in directly addressing or even questioning and contradicting their peers and instructors in online environments (Gunawardena & Nolla, 2001; Wang, 2007). On the other hand, *high-power distance* cultures such as those found in Asia suffer from the opposite. In a cross-cultural study examining *power distance* and distance learning, Wang (2007) found that learners from *high-power distance* cultures were often afraid to approach their instructors for help. This is directly attributed to learners' perceptions of being unequal to their instructors. Liang and McQueen (2000) similarly note Chinese students often refrain from saying anything that might challenge the authority of their professors. Lastly, multiple studies of culture and distance learning point to learners from *high-power distance* cultures as valuing instructor input and feedback much more than they do that of their peers (Bray, Aoki & Dlugosh, 2008; Liang and McQueen, 2000; Thompson & Ku, 2005).

Still, while many previous studies have highlighted culturally influenced links to behavior patterns in online settings, none have focused on potential problems linked to these behaviors in social constructivist online learning environments as the current study does.

Rationale behind Choice of Population

The primary reason behind choosing a Japanese participant population is that Japanese culture has heightened cultural factors of *collectivism*, *high-power distance*, and *high-communication context,* which are in direct contrast to cultural dimensions of *individualism*, *low-power distance* and *low-communication context* found in learners in the United States (Hall, 1976; Hofstede, 1991; Hofstede & McCrae, 2004). It is believed that these specific cultural dimensions will influence behaviors in *collaborative learning* with respect to potential conflicts with key social constructivist ideals such as student-centered learning and socially negotiated knowledge. Finally, despite a more recent national focus on distance learning in Japan, Japanese participants have rarely been used in culturally based distance learning studies and thus a greater body of research is needed in the area.

Distance Learning in Japan

While generally regarded as a technologically advanced country, Japan has been slow to adopt distance learning. A 2007 survey study by the Japanese National Institute of Media Education found that roughly 42% of private universities and 69% of national universities in Japan offered distance learning courses (Brown, Hartman, Aoki, & Yamada, 2009). Conversely, in the United States, 87% or more of all accredited universities offer distance learning programs (Allen and Seaman, 2013).

In examining Japanese learner perceptions, Jung and Suzuki (2006) found that students tend to discourage others from taking online courses and instead place emphasis on traditional face-to-face courses as many students preferred to see their professors face-to-face; a factor likely stemming from *high-power distance* and *high-communication context* dimensions. In another study on Japanese learners, Bray, Aoki and Dlugosh (2008) examined predictors indicative of learner satisfaction. Here they found that the only advantage Japanese learners saw in distance education was personal convenience while factors found to be difficult or discouraging were: (1) difficulties with time management, specifically in that without a classroom and regular class time, motivation to study was difficult; (2) difficulties with teacher interaction, namely not getting immediate feedback; and (3) problems with student interaction, primarily difficulties in making friends to discuss course matters with. Finally, in line with Fang's (2007) findings, Bray, Aoki and Dlugosh (2008) reported that 23% of Japanese students preferred to study alone and keep their interaction limited to the course instructor in order to focus on achievement. Using factor analysis, they found that students who had better computer skills and found it easier to communicate with the instructor were more satisfied with learning. Furthermore, students with a preference for social interaction were less satisfied with learning online compared with those who prefer to study alone. This final result would suggest that online learning is not necessarily conducive to interaction and collaboration between students, as opposed to teacher-centered models found in face-to-face-classes.

Methodology

Participants and Setting

Participants consisted of $N = 21$ sophomore and junior-level undergraduate-level Japanese students enrolled in classes at a university in the greater Tokyo area. These data used in the study consist of the combined total student generated postings from two classes on the topic of political science. These classes were a two-part sequence for mid-level undergraduates. In both cases the same full-rank professor taught the classes and most of the same students were in both classes with one student who was present in the first class not present in the second. While billed as an online class, students met in a face-to-face class with the professor twice a month during the semester for exams and questions.

The setting of the class mimicked that of other Japanese online courses, and was unique compared to Western settings as it did not take place within the context of a learning management system. Instead discussions from both classes took place on a single separate discussion forum designed specifically for the class. Discussions served as a required part of the class. They were worth 10% of the total grade of the class and served as the only weighted material in the class outside of exams. This is not unusual in Japanese courses where tests still consist of a majority of weighted grades (Nemoto, 1999). The professor would post lecture videos and reading assignments to the forums for students to watch and comment on if they needed further insights or clarification. Students were also allowed to post topics freely if they wished. While there was no minimum amount of posting required, students were expected to "maintain regular contact with the class" to receive credit for participation.

Instrumentation

The current study makes use of a *discourse analysis*-based coding scheme used by Kim and Bonk (2002) in their study of inter-cultural collaboration. The coding scheme was originally developed by Curtis and Lawson (2001) to analyze students' collaborative behaviors, or behaviors seen as being representative of *collaborative learning* in online environments, and to identify their online interactions. Since its original creation, the Curtis and Lawson (2001) coding scheme has been used in multiple CMC-based studies (Pawan, Paulus, Yalcin & Chang, 2003; Serce & Yildirim,2006; Serce et al., 2008; So, 2005; Wang, 2010). The coding scheme consists of 15 behaviors that fall under five behavioral categories, and focuses on behavioral and socio-linguistic factors, as opposed to grammatical constructions. It merits use across multiple languages without loss of reliability as noted by Kim and Bonk (2002) who used the scheme for English, Dutch, and Korean speakers. Finally, a strict undergraduate participant population chosen as the instrument used in this current study was tested and validated primarily on college undergraduates (Kim & Bonk, 2002; Yen & Tu, 2008; Yoo, Donthu, & Lenartowicz, 2010).

In collecting and analyzing linguistic data in the form of discussion board postings, it is expected that the study will be able to better represent key points found in Hofstede's (1980) dimensions of culture. For instance, group harmony behaviors such as *group skills*, which are noted as expressions that encourage group activity and cohesiveness, can be seen as in line with the *collectivistic* of placing high importance on maintaining social harmony. On the other hand, behaviors such as *challenging others* can be seen as an antithesis to *collectivist* principles. Use of the Curtis and Lawson (2001) coding scheme allows for a more complete analysis of the cultural dimension of the target population in a distance learning setting that can then be compared with the social constructivist distance learning pedagogical values outlined earlier in the chapter.

Data Analysis

Before analysis began, the linguistic data was coded. This coding was conducted in three steps by the researcher and two native Japanese speakers. In cases of *discourse analysis*, particularly when examining individual utterances, the number of participants involved does not matter as much as the amount of language data produced (Biber & Conrad, 2008). In Kim and Bonk's (2002) look into cross-cultural learning, they coded $N = 105$ postings from Korean students, $N = 135$ from Finnish students, and $N = 336$ from students from the United States. A total of $N = 302$ of posts were analyzed consisting of the entire data for both classes, with $N = 137$ in the first class and $N = 165$ in the second class. The next learner-learner interactions were discerned from learner-instructor interactions. It should be noted again that this study separates learner-generated linguistic interactions with peers from those with instructors as *high-power distance* is expected to produce markedly different interactions for the two types of interactions.

Finally, all linguistic data in the form of utterances, or sentences, were coded into the behavioral categories noted in the Curtis and Lawson (2001) coding scheme. In order to determine inter-rater reliability, an analysis using the Cohen's Kappa statistic was performed to determine consistency among raters. The inter-rater reliability for the raters was found to be Kappa = 0.88 (p <.0.01), 95% CI (.504, .848), meeting Landis and Koch's (1977), and Altman's (1991) standards for almost perfect agreement.

The linguistic data were analyzed as it has been in each of the previous studies it has been used in (Curtis & Lawson, 2001; Kim & Bonk 2002; Pawan, Paulus, Yalcin, & Chang 2003; Serce et al., 2008; Serce & Yildirim, 2006; Wang, 2010). Analysis of the linguistic data consists of occurrence counts of each type of behavior in each subcategory and category in the coding scheme, as well as what percentage of the total set of possible codes each category and sub-category makes up of the entire data set.

Results

Theoretically the concept of *collaborative learning* was tied to Hofstede's (1980; 1991) cultural dimensions of *power-distance, individualism-collectivism* and Hall's (1976) *communication context*. Overall, results found in analysis of the data are characteristic of a *high-power distance, collectivistic, high communication-context* culture.

Observing the overall results shown in Table 7.1, a total of $N = 1013$ utterances were coded with $N = 917$ (90.5 %) being learner-learner interactions and $N = 96$ (9.5%) being learner-instructor interactions. These data would seem to support previous reports by Nakane (2007) and Bray, Aoki, and Dlugosh (2008) as to Japanese classrooms being heavily teacher-centered spaces where learners rarely directly address their teachers. This theme of a teacher-centered classroom can also be seen in examining specific behavior categories and codes.

The *planning* behavior category accounts for nearly half of all postings in the learner-learner group. $N = 456$ (49.7%) learner-learner utterances were coded as *planning*, further broken down into individual code sub-categories as $N = 201$ (21.9%) *group skills*, $N = 95$ (10.4%) *organizing work*, and $N = 160$ (17.4%) *initiating activities*. These high levels of *group skills* and to a lesser extent *initiating activities* would support the theory of participant population as being highly *collectivistic* as the *group skills* code consists of expressions that encourage group activity, solidarity and cohesiveness, all in line with *collectivistic* thought. Looking at the learner-instructor results for the *planning* category a total of $N = 28$ (29.2%) of utterances occurred with individual code sub-categories consisting of $N = 21$ (21.9%) *group skills*, $N = 5$ (5.2%) *organizing work*, and $N = 2$ (2.1%) *initiating activities*. Again, consistent with the *collectivistic* trait of maintaining social harmony, a majority of utterances here consisted of *group skills*.

A total of $N = 145$ (15.8%) learner-learner utterances in the *contributing* category occurred. Individual code sub-categories consisted of *help giving* $N = 32$ (3.5%), *feedback giving* $N = 36$ (3.9%), *exchanging resources* $N = 33$ (3.6%), *sharing knowledge* $N = 27$ (2.9%), *challenging others* $N = 6$ (0.7%), and *explaining/elaborating* $N = 11$ (1.2%). Given the *collectivistic*, high-communication context culture of the participants, it is not surprising that the *challenging others* code is the least occurring behavior in the entire learner-learner data set. The cultural dimensions associated with the participants also helps to explain the low levels of *explaining/elaborating*, the second least occurring code in the learner-learner data,

TABLE 7.1 Overall results of the Curtis and Lawson (2001) coding scheme

Behavior categories	Codes	Code totals learner	Code (%) learner	Code totals teacher	Code (%) teacher	Code totals both	Code (%) total
Planning	Group skills	201	21.9%	21	21.9%	222	21.9%
	Organizing work	95	10.4%	5	5.2%	100	9.9%
	Initiating activities	160	17.4%	2	2.1%	162	16.0%
	Sub-total	456	49.7%	28	29.2%	484	47.8%
Contributing	Help giving	32	3.5%	9	9.4%	41	4.0%
	Feedback giving	36	3.9%	9	9.4%	45	4.4%
	Exchanging resources	33	3.6%	1	1.0%	34	3.4%
	Sharing knowledge	27	2.9%	0	0.0%	27	2.7%
	Challenging others	6	0.7%	0	0.0%	6	0.6%
	Explaining or elaborating	11	1.2%	4	4.2%	15	1.5%
	Sub-total	145	15.8%	23	24.0%	168	16.6%
Seeking input	Help seeking	28	3.1%	20	20.8%	48	4.7%
	Feedback seeking	18	2.0%	8	8.3%	26	2.6%
	Advocating efforts	15	1.6%	4	4.2%	19	1.9%
	Sub-total	61	6.7%	32	33.3%	93	9.2%
Reflection/ monitoring	Monitoring group effort	30	3.3%	1	1.0%	31	3.1%
	Reflecting on medium	21	2.3%	3	3.1%	24	2.4%
	Sub-total	51	5.6%	4	4.2%	55	5.4%
Social interaction	Social interaction	204	22.2%	9	9.4%	213	21.0%
	Sub-total	204	22.2%	9	9.4%	213	21.0%
Category Total			100.0%		100.0%		
Scheme Total		917	90.5%	96	9.5%	1013	100.0%

as students rarely challenged each other's statements. This pattern is echoed with greater emphasis in the learner-instructor data. Here, a total of a total of $N = 23$ (24.0%) learner-learner utterances in the *contributing* category were observed. Individual code sub-category results are as follows: *help* $N = 9$ (9.4%), *feedback* giving $N = 9$ (9.4%), *exchanging resources* $N = 1$ (1.0%), *sharing knowledge* $N = 0$ (0.0%), *challenging others* $N = 0$ (0.0%), and *explaining/elaborating* $N = 4$ (4.2%). In learner-instructor interactions, the additional cultural dimension of *power-distance* is combined with the *individualism-collectivism* dimension; thus, no occurrences of *challenging* the teacher were observed. Learners also follow the pattern noted by Bray, Aoki, and Dlugosh (2008) in which teachers solely dictate knowledge, thus possibly accounting for the lack of any *sharing knowledge* coded occurrences. It is interesting, however, to note the levels of *help giving* and *feedback giving* as $N = 36$ *feedback giving* codes occurred in learner-learner interactions, $N = 22$ of these were conversations about ideas for summer study group plans, as opposed to feedback on class content related ideas.

Data from the *seeking input* behavior category consisted of $N = 145$ (15.8%) learner-learner interactions. The three sub-category codes resulted in the following: *help seeking* $N = 28$ (3.1%), *feedback seeking* $N = 18$ (2.0%), and *advocating efforts* $N = 15$ (1.6%). These results also follow expected *collectivistic* patterns of student-teacher cultural roles, including high levels of *power-distance*, in Japan. As noted by Bray, Aoki, and Dlugosh (2008) for Japan and other East Asian cultures as a whole (Fang, 2007; Thompson & Ku, 2005), students see teachers as a sole source of knowledge in classroom environments, and place primary emphasis on teacher-based feedback, while paying little attention to peer feedback regarding academic matters. This would support the low number of utterances in both *help seeking* and *feedback seeking* codes. Additionally, as the *advocating efforts* code involves direct confrontation in identifying particular members whom the posters feel need to contribute more, and has the potential for social friction, it goes against the idea of social harmony found in *collectivistic* cultures. Along with the *challenging others* and *explaining/elaborating* sub-category codes, the entire code set of the *seeking input* category make up the least occurring interaction types in the data set. Building off of *power-distance* and traditional Japanese student-teacher roles, it is not surprising that *seeking input* is the highest ranked learner-instructor interaction behavior category, accounting for a third of total interactions $N = 32$ (33.3%). Individual sub-category codes occurred as follows: *help seeking* $N = 20$ (20.8%), *feedback seeking* $N = 8$ (8.3%), and *advocating efforts* $N = 4$ (4.2%). Given the culture dimensions of the participants, it is not surprising to see high levels of *help seeking* and to a lesser extent *feedback seeing* codes.

Results for the *reflection/monitoring* category were roughly equal in both types of interactions. Learner-learning data consisted of $N = 61$ (6.7%) total utterance with $N = 30$ (3.3%) *monitoring group efforts*, and $N = 21$ (2.3%) *reflecting on the medium* individual sub-category codes. Learner-instructor results in the *reflection/monitoring* behavior category found a total of $N = 4$ (4.2%) utterances with $N = 1$ (1.0%) *monitoring group efforts*, and $N = 3$ (3.1%) *reflecting on the medium* sub-category codes. The lack of *monitoring group efforts* is to be expected given the nature of learner-instructor interactions (e.g. the teacher is not a group member).

Finally, the *social interaction* category consists of personal discussions not relating to official class matters. Results here were difficult to anticipate as in a *collectivist* and high-communication context society the need for constant social harmony is important, however, given the Japanese learner perceptions of online courses noted by Jung and Suzuki (2006) students may also have felt more distant from the medium and thus felt the need to either refrain from personal discussions or overcompensate. A total of $N = 204$ (22.2%) learner-learner occurrences were coded for this behavior category. Again, the *social interaction* category only consists of a single code with the same name as the category. This makes *social interaction* the second most frequent category and the most frequent individual sub-category code of online interaction, in apparent contrast to Jung and Suzuki's (2006) findings. Learner-instructor utterances were comparatively about half of this, $N = 9$ (9.4%). This finding can be attributed to the higher rank the teacher holds on the *power-distance* continuum as students might feel less inclined to discuss personal matters with their superiors or be uncertain due to the ambiguous nature of asynchronous online CMC.

Discussion

What types and levels of collaborative learning are occurring in the Japanese distance learning classroom?

In examining the most frequently occurring behavioral categories in learner-learner interactions, *planning* and *social interaction* were the most common. Combined, the *planning* sub-category *group skills* and *social interaction* codes made up nearly 45% of all occurring codes. This supports the idea of the participant population as being a *collectivistic* and high-communication context culture placing emphasis on social harmony, interconnectedness, and personal relationships over tasks. When looking at the least frequently occurring codes in learner-learner, *challenging others*, *explaining/elaborating*, and *feedback seeking* were the least prevalent. This supports previous research on *collectivistic* and high-communication context cultures. Furthermore, in the few cases where challenges were made, they were often done so with a great attempt to avoid potential conflict and no challenges were ever met with a direct response. Data also suggest some levels of *power-distance* in learner-learner collaborative interactions, as in an example where an elder student openly teases underclassmen, creating potential social disharmony, yet is received with apparent respect. Overall, learners were very focused on creating and maintaining social bonds while avoiding potential conflicts.

To what extent is collaborative learning occurring in the Japanese distance learning classroom?

Overall, the patterns and levels of *collaborative learning* occurring in the Japanese distance learning classroom reflect the hypothesis that key cultural dimensions and aspects of national culture influence learner collaboration. As influenced by levels of *power-distance* and traditional Japanese student-teacher roles, the Japanese distance learning classroom is very teacher-centered, with the teacher being the keeper and distributor of knowledge. Students are also very social with each other and place a very high priority on solidarity and group harmony falling in line with expected collaborative behaviors of a *collectivistic* and high-communication context culture. The Japanese distance learning classroom presents a model very different from distance learning models found in the United States, wherein *individualistic, low-power distance* learners thrive on student-centered environments and active debate, as Japanese learners' collaborative interactions are heavily influenced by their culture and Japanese learners aim to actively avoid cornerstone behaviors associated with social constructivist ideals such as debate, contrast of ideas, and social negotiation of knowledge.

Limitations

Limitations of the present study are characteristic of the nature of research presented. Findings from the study focus on a homogeneous group, where all learners share common cultural factors, thus the generalizability of these results may be limited in cross-cultural or mixed culture environments. While many East Asian cultures share similar cultural dimensions with Japan and even some unique cultural factors, such as student-teachers roles, complex issues related to cultural, social, and academic use of technology are also factors in the generalizability of the study. This is not to say the findings in the present study may not be applicable to other East Asian cultures, as they may well serve as a foundation for future inquiry; rather, more cultural research in distance learning in East Asia is needed.

Practical Implications and Recommendations

Garrison and Akyol (2009) have suggested a need for technology and pedagogy to mutually influence each other in the creation of successful higher education curriculum. The present study has found that cultural factors also significantly influence how Japanese learners consider and experience a distance learning environment, and would argue that considerations of technology and pedagogy alone are not sufficient in the creation of a theoretical model of distance education. The results of the current study support the hypothesis that social constructivism, the driving pedagogy in distance learning, is not compatible with the cultural characteristics of Japanese learners. Cultural factors are tied deeply to how learners perceive technology and how they interact with their peers and instructors. Furthermore, findings in the current study have established that a one-size-fits-all social constructivist model for distance learning pedagogy will not work for Japanese learners and likely other cultures that exhibit similar cultural dimensions as well. Therefore in the creation of a new theoretical model, the present study would propose to add in consideration of cultural factors as a prominent element of the concept of distance learning.

While a theoretical model of culturally inclusive distance learning is needed, the salient cultural factors explored in the current study, while strongly linked to issues in distance learning, are by no means all-inclusive. Each culture has multiple elements that could impact distance learning in a unique manner such as illustrated by Patricia Young's work on culture-based models (2008). It is hoped, however, that the theoretical and empirical inquiry in the current study will not only bring light to the importance of cultural factors in distance learning, but will also provide a framework for future research in the field. A final point of consideration would be that individual cultures would benefit from exploring and designing theoretical, pedagogical, and practical models of distance learning to meet the unique needs of their learners.

References

Al-Oteawi, S. M. (2002). *The perceptions of administrators and teachers in utilizing information technology in instruction, administrative work, technology planning and staff development in Saudi Arabia*. (Doctoral dissertation). Ohio University, Athens, OH, USA.

Allen, I. E., & Seaman, J. (2013). Changing course: Ten years tracking online education in the United States. New York, NY: Pearson.

Altman D. G. (1991). Practical statistics for medical research. London, UK: Chapman and Hall.

Anakwe, U. P., & Christensen, E. W. (1999). Distance learning and cultural diversity: Potential users' perspective. *International Journal of Organizational Analysis, 7*(3), 224–243.

Andersson, A. (2008). Seven major challenges for e-learning in developing countries: Case study eBIT, Sri Lanka. *International Journal of Education and Development using ICT, 4*(3).

Biber, D., & Conrad, S. (2008). Register, genre and style. New York, NY: Cambridge University Press.

Bray, E., Aoki, K., & Dlugosh, L. (2008). Predictors of learning satisfaction in Japanese online distance learners. *International Review of Research in Open and Distance Learning, 9*(3), 53–87.

Brown, M., Hartman, J., Aoki, K., & Yamada, T. (2009, April). The emergence of e-learning in Japan. Presented at EDUCASE Learning Initiative, Orlando, Florida.

Chen, A., Mashhadi, A., Ang, D., & Harkrider, N. (1999). Cultural issues in the design of technology-enhanced learning environments, *British Journal of Educational Technology, 30*(3), 217–230.

Chen, S., Hsu, C., & Caropreso, E. J. (2006). Cross-cultural collaborative online learning: When the West meets the East. *International Journal of Technology in Teaching and Learning, 2*(1), 17–35.

Curtis, D. D., & Lawson, M. J. (2001). Exploring collaborative online learning. *Journal of Asynchronous Learning Networks, 5*(1), 21–34.

Fang, L. (2007). Perceiving the useful, enjoyable, and effective: A case study of the e-learning experience of tertiary students in Singapore. *Educational Media International, 44*(3), 237–253.

Ford, D.P., Connelly, C.E., & Meister, D.B. (2003). Information systems research and Hofstede's culture's consequences: An uneasy and incomplete partnership. *IEEE Transactions on Engineering Management, 50*(1), 8–25.

Garrison, D.R. (2000). Theoretical challenges for distance education in the 21st century: A shift from structural to transactional issues. *International Review of Research in Open and Distance Learning, 1*(1).

Garrison, D.R., & Archer, W. (2000). *A transactional perspective on teaching-learning: A framework for adult and higher education.* Oxford, UK: Pergamon.

Garrison, D.R., & Akyol, Z. (2009). Role of instructional technology in the transformation of higher education. *Journal of Computing in Higher Education, 21*(1), 19–30.

Gudykunst, W., Matsumoto, Y., & Ting-Toomey, S. (1996). The influence of cultural individualism-collevtivism, self construals, and individual values on communication styles across cultures. *Human Communication Research, 22*(4), 510–543.

Gunawardena, C.N., & McIsaac, M. (2003). Theory of distance education. In M. Moore & B. Anderson, (Eds.), *Handbook of research for educational communications and technology* (pp. 355–396). Mahwah, NJ: Lawrence Erlbaum Associates, Inc.

Gunawardena, C.N., & Nolla, A.C. (2001). A cross-cultural study of group process and development in online conferences, *Distance Education. 22*(1), 85–102.

Gunawardena, C.N., Wilson, P., & Nolla, A.C. (2003). Culture and online education. In M. Moore & B. Anderson (Eds.), *Handbook of distance learning* (pp. 753–775). Mahwah, NJ: Lawrence Erlbaum Associates, Inc.

Gunawardena, C.N., & Zittle, F.J. (1997). Social presence as a predictor of satisfaction within a computer-mediated conferencing environment. *The American Journal of Distance Education, 11*(3), 8–26.

Hall, E., & Hall, M. (1990). *Understanding cultural differences: Germans, French and Americans.* Yarmouth, MA: Intercultural Press.

Hall, E.T. (1976). *Beyond Culture.* Garden City, NY: Anchor.

Hofstede, G. (1980). *Culture's consequences: International differences in work-related values.* Beverly Hills, CA: Sage Publications.

Hofstede, G. (1991). *Cultures and organizations: Software of the mind.* London, UK: McGraw-Hill.

Hofstede, G. (1994). *Cultures and organizations.* London, UK: Harper-Collins Business.

Hofstede, G., & McCrae, R. (2004). Personality and culture revisited: Linking traits and dimensions of culture. *Cross-Cultural Research, 38*, 52–88.

Jung, I., & Suzuki, K. (2006). Blended learning in Japan and its application in liberal arts education. In C. Bonk and C. Graham (Eds.), *The handbook of blended learning* (pp. 267–280). San Francisco, CA: John Wiley & Pfeiffer.

Kim, K., & Bonk, C. (2002) Cross-cultural comparisons of online collaboration. *Journal of Computer-Mediated Communication, 8*(1). Accessed on March 22 2010 from: http://jcmc.indiana.edu/vol8/issue1/index.html

Kim, D., Pan, Y., & Park, H.S. (1998). High- versus low-context culture: A comparison of Chinese, Korean and American cultures. *Psychology & Marketing, 15*(6), 507–521.

Landis, J.R., & Koch, G.G. (1977). The measurement of observer agreement for categorical data. *Biometrics, 33*, 159–174.

Liang, A., & McQueen, R.J. (2000). Computer assisted adult interactive learning in a multi-cultural environment. *Adult Learning, 11*(1), 26–29.

Lowry, P.B., Zhang, D., Zhou, L., & Fu, X. (2010). Effects of culture, social presence, and group composition on trust in technology-supported decision-making groups. *Information Systems, 20,* 297–315.
Nakane, I. (2007). *Silence in intercultural communication: Perceptions and performance.* Amsterdam, The Netherlands: John Benjamins.
Nemoto, Y. (1999). *The Japanese education system.* Parkland, FL: Universal Publishers.
Nishimura, S., Nevgi, A., & Tella, S. (2008). *Communication style and cultural features in high/low context communication cultures: A case study of Finland, Japan and India.* University of Helsinki. Department of Applied Sciences of Education Research Report 299.
Pawan, F., Paulus, T.M., Yalcin, S., & Chang., C. (2003). Online learning: Patterns of engagement and interaction among in-service teachers. *Language Learning and Technology, 7*(3), 119–140.
Serce, F.C., Swigger, K., Alpslan, F., Brazile, R., Dafoulas, G., & Lopez, V. (2008, July). *Exploring the communication behavior among global software development learners.* Presented at Information technology based higher education and training.
Serce, F.C., & Yildirim. S. (2006). A web-based synchronous collaborative review tool: A case study of an on-line graduate course. *Educational Technology & Society, 9*(2), 166–177.
Shattuck, K. (2005). *Cultures meeting cultures in online distance education: Perceptions of international adult learners of the impact of culture when taking online distance education courses designed and delivered by an American University.* Pennsylvania State University, University Park (Doctoral dissertation).
So, H. (2005). The content analysis of social presence and *collaborative learning* behavior patterns in a computer mediated learning environment. In L. Chee-Kit, D. Jonassen, & M. Ikeda (Eds.), *Towards sustainable and scalable educational innovations informed by the learning sciences* (pp. 186–201). New York, NY: IOS Press.
So, H.J., & Brush, T. (2007). Student perceptions of *collaborative learning,* social presence and satisfaction in a blended learning environment: Relationships and critical factors. *Computers and Education, 51,* 318–336.
Thompson, L., & Ku, H. (2005). Chinese graduate students' experiences and attitudes toward online learning. *Educational Media International, 42*(1), 33–47.
Triandis, H.C. (1995). *Individualism and collectivism.* Boulder, CO: Westview Press.
Tu, C.H. (2001). How Chinese perceive social presence: An examination of interaction in online learning environment. *Educational Media International, 38*(1), 45–60.
Vygotsky, L.S. (1978). *Mind and society: The development of higher mental processes.* Cambridge, MA: Harvard University Press.
Wang, M. (2007). Designing online courses that effectively engage learners from diverse cultural backgrounds. *British Journal of Educational Technology, 38*(2), 294–311.
Wang, M. (2010). Online collaboration and offline interaction between students using asynchronous tools in blended learning. *Australasian Journal of Educational Technology, 26*(6), 830–846.
Wong, L., & Trinidad, S. (2004). Using web-based distance learning to reduce cultural distance. *Journal of Interactive Online Learning, 3*(1), 3–16.
Woo, Y., & Reeves, T. (2007). Meaningful interaction in web-based learning: A social constructivist interpretation. *Internet and Higher Education, 10,* 15–25.
Yen, C.J., & Tu, C.H. (2008). Online social presence: A study of score validity of the computer-mediated communication questionnaire. *Quarterly Review of Distance Education, 9*(3), 297–310.

Yoo, B., Donthu, N., & Lenartowicz, T. (2010). Measuring Hofstede's five dimensions of cultural values at the individual level: Development and validation of CVSCALE. *Journal of International Consumer Behavior*. Accessed on December 23 2010 from: http://people.hofstra.edu/Boonghee_Yoo/cvscale.pdf

Young, P. A. (2008). The culture based model: Constructing a model of culture. *Educational Technology & Society, 11*(2), 107–118.

Zhang, D., Lowry, P. B., Zhou, L., & Fu, X. (2007). The impact of individualism—collectivism, social presence, and group diversity on group decision making under majority influence. *Journal of Management Information Systems, 23*(4), 53–80.

8
CULTURE AND COMPUTATIONAL THINKING

A Pilot Study of Operationalizing Culturally Responsive Teaching (CRT) in Computer Science Education

Leshell Hatley, Cynthia E. Winston-Proctor, Gina M. Paige, and Kevin Clark

Computers and computing devices are predicted to be pervasive in the world young people will engage and work in as adults (Committee on Prospering in the Global Economy of the 21st Century, 2007; National Science Board, 2010; PCAST, 2010; CSTA, 2012; Modi, Schoenberg, & Salmond, 2012). One pressing educational priority within the United States is increasing the number of young people motivated to enter, continue, and flourish in computing and computer science fields. Thus, there is growing interest across the country to introduce technical, mathematical, scientific, and computing skills and concepts (e.g. Computational Thinking (CT) to all youth as early as possible—in elementary and middle school) throughout formal and informal education settings. In addition to these CT skills, members of the Computer Science Education (CSEd) Research Community suggest broadening the scope of instructional investigation, when teaching these age groups, to include empirical investigations into research regarding socio-cultural and situated learning, distributed and embodied cognition, disposition, attitudes towards computer science, and impact on learner identity (Grover & Pea, 2013). In response, the aim of this chapter is to report on an investigation using a design-based research approach to build a cultural responsive model for teaching and learning CT and computer programming skills with African-American middle school students in informal learning environments (i.e. a two-week summer camp). Design-based research is an emerging paradigm that includes methods that bridge theoretical research and educational practice (The Design Based Research Collective, 2003). Few scholars have adopted this approach to study the experiences of African American in science, technology, engineering, and mathematics (STEM; see Clark & Moore, 2007; Winston, Philip, & Lloyd, 2007).

What is CT?

Ten years ago, Jeannette Wing (2006) declared that CT "represents a universally applicable attitude and skill set everyone, not just computer scientists, would be eager to learn and use." But CT is not new. According to Google Book's nGram Viewer (Michel et al., 2011) the concept of CT first appeared in books in the early 1950s. Since the 1950s, as the use of computers and computing devices increased, the attempt to define and therefore operationalize the term "computational thinking" also dramatically increased. With the ubiquitous growth and usage of computers and computing technologies over the past several decades, there is a growing need to understand how to teach and apply these concepts and technologies to communicate, and to access, process, and represent information. The Computer Science Teachers Association (CSTA) distinguished the above CT skills in grades K-12 as the general ability to manipulate data, regardless of school topic. This manipulation includes the ability to *collect data, analyze data, represent data,* and *decompose* problems into smaller sub-problems, along with being able to understand and create abstractions (reducing information and detail to focus on concepts relevant to understanding and solving problems), algorithms and procedures, automation, parallelization, and simulations (CSTA, 2012). Moreover, it is universally recognized that the ability to use and/or create with these technologies to address a need or solve a problem requires CT skills and programming knowledge.

Increasing the Number of Students of Color in Computer Science

Moreover, there is special impetus in the attempt to engage students of color and other underrepresented populations in computer science careers. In fact, the private business sector within the United States allocated $240 million to the overall U.S. 2015 fiscal year STEM education budget, specifically targeting the educational and entertainment sectors of children from underrepresented groups (Wasserman, 2015). Research suggests that African-Americans and other underrepresented communities are not majoring in computer science at the same rates as their white counterparts, and that schools in economically challenged districts have less access to advanced computer science courses (as cited in Scott, Sheridan, & Clark, 2014). According to the 2014 Taulbee Report (Zweben & Bizot, 2015), the principal source of information on the enrollment, production, and employment of those in Computer Science and Computer Engineering, 1.1% of Ph.D.s in Computer Science (CS) and 1.5% of Ph.D.s in Computer Engineering were awarded to African-Americans/Blacks, while 0.9% of Ph.D.s in Computer Science and 1.5% of Ph.D.s in Computer Engineering were awarded to Hispanics, and 0.1% Ph.D.s in Computer Science and 0% Ph.Ds. in Computer Engineering were awarded to Native

Americans (Zweben & Bizot, 2015). As the country works to increase the number of underrepresented communities in STEM and CS careers and as more K-12 schools adopt CT and programming courses into their curriculum, it is crucial to understand the dynamics and impacts of successful teaching and learning strategies that specifically target and appeal to populations of color.

About this Study

The pilot study presented here sought to help bridge the gap between the need to increase the number of underrepresented communities and the desire for stronger instructional strategies in K-12 learning environments. More precisely, the aim of this study was to research a socio-cultural approach to the teaching and learning of CT and programming skills. More importantly, this study attempted to integrate notions of cultural relevance and individual and collective identity into the ways in which CT and computer programming skills are taught.

The Role of Culture in Pedagogy

For years, researchers have shared enormous amounts of data revealing that cultural patterns influence the way information is perceived, organized, processed, and used, resulting in what are called learning or cognitive styles (Adams, 1995; Barba, 1993; Boykin, 1977; Brown, Kloser, & Henderson, 2010; Gay, 2000; Gay, 2002; Hale, 1982; Ladson-Billings, 1995a; 1995b; Lee, 1993; Lee, 1997; Lee, 2003; Pinkard, 1999; Silva, Moses, Rivers, & Johnson, 1990). These researchers conclude that in order to maximize the learning potential of any learner, whether in or out of school, the learning environment and method of instruction should match or be consistent with the cultural experiences of that learner. Doing so is an instructional strategy called cultural scaffolding, culturally relevant and/or culturally responsive teaching (CRT). This concept is the basis of this study.

CRT

CRT has become a mantra for many educators and scholars concerned with the learning and academic achievement of culturally and linguistically diverse students (Adams, 1995; Barba, 1993; Boykin, 1983; Gay, 2002; Ladson-Billings, 1995a, 1995b; Lee, 1997; Leonard, Davis, & Sider, 2005). These researchers have found that students of different cultural backgrounds process information differently. For instance, reading researchers have consistently found that African-American and European-American children differ in storytelling styles, knowledge of print conventions, oral language, and question asking styles (Boykin, 1977; Gay, 2002; Hale, 1982; Lee, 1993; Lee, 1997; Lee, 2003; Pinkard, 1999). Applying culturally responsive strategies to reading, science, and math instruction proves beneficial for students from several cultures (Fullilove & Treisman, 1990; Reis & Kay, 2007;

Tharp, 1989; Treisman, 1985). Moreover, there are a number of centers, institutes, and teacher education facilities nationwide pushing for the CRT approach as a prominent school reform strategy (Werner, Campe, & Denner, 2005; Wiggins, Follo, & Eberly, 2007).

Culturally Responsive Pedagogy (CRP)

Gloria Ladson-Billings (1995a, 1995b) discovered and coined the phrase *Culturally Relevant Pedagogy* (CRP) after her ethnographic study of eight exemplary teachers of African-American classrooms, all female—five African-American and three European-American. From this study, her theory of *Culturally Relevant Pedagogy* identified the existence of three essential criteria for instruction that contribute to African-American student success: 1) develop students academically, 2) nurture and support cultural competence, and 3) develop a sociopolitical or critical consciousness.

Ladson-Billing's *Culturally Relevant Pedagogy* draws on the history of African-American life as well as contemporary understandings of unique ways of communicating, behaving, and knowing, and prepares students as critical thinkers to change society, not merely fit into it. It builds upon the cultural knowledge, prior experiences, frames of reference, and performance styles of ethnically diverse students (Ladson-Billings, 2001). According to many prominent African-American education researchers, culturally relevant pedagogy is argued to be central to the academic success of African-American students as well as other historically marginalized students.

Learning Styles and Culture of African-American Children

Research on learning styles has been conducted for several decades. The literature defines learning styles as biological and developmental characteristics and preferences that affect how students learn (Ellison, Boykin, Towns, & Stokes, 2000; Hale 1982; Serpell, Sonnenschein, Baker, & Ganapathy, 2002). These preferences can help with classroom instruction and assessments, along with the design of classroom settings and responses to a learner's individual need for quiet or sound, bright or soft light, warm or cold temperatures, seating arrangements, mobility, and/or grouping preferences (Dunn, Dunn, & Price, 1989; Dill & Boykin, 2000; Hale 1982).

Boykin (1977) suggests nine Afro-cultural ethos (cultural characteristics) that contribute to distinctive learning styles of African-American students:

1. **Spirituality**—intuition, supreme force
2. **Harmony**—versatility and wholeness
3. **Movement**—rhythm of everyday life
4. **Verve**—intense stimulation, action, colorfulness

5. **Affect**—premium on feelings, expression
6. **Communalism**—social orientation, group duty, identity, sharing
7. **Expressive individualism**—distinct, genuine, personal
8. **Orality**—oral and aural modes of communication
9. **Social time perspective**—time is marked by human interaction

Boykin's seminal uncovering provided a foundation for decades of empirical research used to highlight effective methods of instruction for African-American students, especially those that can take advantage of their strengths: their cultures, learning styles, and modes of motivation and engagement. Integrating these Afrocultural characteristics into instructional design and delivery heightens learning, motivation, and engagement in African-American students. Boykin (1994a, 1994b) provide summaries of this work.

Boykin (1977) simply frames this foundation in *culture*. So, then, what is culture? According to Hofstede (1991), an influential Dutch writer on the interactions between national cultures and organizational cultures, "culture is the collective programming of the mind that distinguishes the members of one human group from those of another" (para. 1). Culture in this sense is a system of collectively held values. Thus, cultural relevancy in teaching and learning can connote the relevance of everyday experiences of a group of people with commonly held values. In the study presented here, African-American middle school youth in an informal learning environment (e.g. summer camp) make up the group of people with commonly held values.

Theoretical Framework: Preparing for CRT and CRP

In order to successfully operationalize CRT and CRP, which have similar objectives, Gay (2002) describes five tenets regarding knowledge, attitudes, and skills that can be used by educators as they prepare to teach students who are African, Asian, Latino, and Native American: 1) develop a knowledge base about cultural diversity, 2) include ethnic and cultural diversity content in the curriculum, 3) demonstrate caring and build learning communities, 4) communicate using ethnically diverse styles, and 5) respond to ethnic diversity in the delivery of instruction. These tenets are crucial to *cultural scaffolding,* which again means using students' cultures and experiences to expand their intellectual horizons and academic achievement (Gay, 2002; Lee, 2003).

Design Principles for Culturally Responsive Learning Environments

Lee (2003) expands these tenets of *cultural scaffolding* and uses them as rationale in the creation of a design framework for modeling culture when designing culturally responsive learning environments. These *cultural modeling design principles* have particular emphasis on computer-based learning environments, but can be used when designing classroom-based and other learning environments. These design principles are presented in Table 8.1.

Under the heading 'Generic design' to the left side of Table 8.1 are instructional design tasks for designing learning environments, be they digital or physical. They involve determining and analyzing the content, instructional strategies, and learner activities for teaching any subject domain. To the right side of the table are tasks oriented from a culturally responsive design rationale (Gay, 2002). Specifically, these tasks require the designer to 1) review and consider the prior knowledge and ways of knowing of the intended learner, 2) embed engaging and motivational learning activities, and 3) provide content that leads to social and civic empowerment—all from a culturally responsive perspective. This means details about prior knowledge and characteristic ways of knowing are gleaned from the learners' culture; engagement is designed from the learners' cultural

TABLE 8.1 Lees's (2003) cultural modeling design principles

	Generic design	*Culturally responsive design rationale*		
	Task analysis	*Prior knowledge and cultural models as ways of knowing*	*Engagement and motivation*	*Social and civic empowerment*
Cultural modeling design steps	• Analyze generative constructs in the domain • Analyze problem solving based on expert novice differences	• Analyze cultural practices of target group and look for comparable models, analogies, naïve concepts, or misconceptions related to the academic problem to be solved • Use existing cultural models, scripts, and schemas as models, analogs, or counter-examples to be interrogated by students	• Structure learning activities in ways that invite students to be meta-cognitive, making their tacit thinking public • Structure instructional talk using community-based discourse norms, while incorporating discipline specific modes of reasoning	• Identify content for tasks that invite interrogation of community and/or personal needs

Source: Permission to reproduce this figure has been granted by Lee (2003).

practices (tacit or otherwise); and content selected for instructional delivery should be prepared in such a way as to provide civic and social development, engagement, and empowerment so that learners can connect themselves with the world around them. Taken together, these design principles satisfy the three essential criteria for instruction that contributes to African-American student success specified in Ladson-Billing's (1995a, 1995b) CRP and were used in the pilot study presented here.

CRC: Operationalizing CRT in CSEd

When it comes to the Computer Science instruction of African-American students, Scott et al. (2010) suggests three pillars of CRT as professional development for in-service teachers regarding the creation of informal STEM (technology) programs. These pillars implore the teachers to take responsibility for: 1) *reflective action*—teaching participants how to identify a topic within their own lived experiences, 2) *asset building*—building on their students' knowledge, and 3) *connectedness*—fostering a sense of community so students feel a responsibility to something larger than themselves. These three pillars were framed within the context of technology education to form the following Culturally Relevant Computing (CRC) goals:

1. Motivate and improve STEM learning experiences;
2. Provide a deeper understanding of heritage and vernacular culture, empowerment for social critique, and appreciation for cultural diversity;
3. Bring 1 and 2 together: to diminish the separation between the worlds of culture and STEM; and
4. Technology education must not only respond to these identity issues, but also satisfy pedagogical demands of the curriculum.

In 2014, these goals were re-conceptualized to form improved CRC theory and goals (Scott, Sheridan, & Clark, 2014), as listed below:

1. All students are capable of digital innovation.
2. The learning context supports transformational use of technology.
3. Learning about one's self along various intersecting socio-cultural lines allows for technical innovation.
4. Technology should be a vehicle by which students reflect and demonstrate understanding of their intersectional identities.
5. Barometers for technological success should consider who creates, for whom, and to what ends rather than who endures socially and culturally irrelevant curriculum.

Placed in the context of Lee's (2003) Cultural Modeling Design Principles, these five goals address students' prior knowledge and ways of knowing (goals one, two, and three), focuses content and its delivery in ways that are engaging and (goals one, two, three, four, and five), and provides social and civic empowerment (goals two, three, four, and five).

CS2: Computational Thinking, Science, Culture, and Story CAMP

The research described above informed the theoretical framework for the conceptualization, design, and implementation of this pilot study. CS2: Computational Thinking, Science, Culture, and Story was a pilot project within a larger design-based research project goals to investigate how elements of the Black Cultural Ethos (BCE), characteristics of CRT, CRP, and CRC can inform the creation of instructional strategies, instructional tactics, and learning activities of CT skills, science, and identity. This study is based in the three goals of CRC, rooted in the nine elements of BCE, and employs Gay's five tenets of CRT. This pilot research study was designed to discover various instructional strategies and learning activities that could be efficient in helping to teach CT and programming skills. Using the form of a two-week computer programming camp for African-American middle school students, the researchers designed a culturally and personally relevant CT curriculum, instructional strategies, learner activities, and beginner computer programming tasks aligned with CT, science, culture, and story. The camp focused on deploying the following elements of the CS2 model: (1) teaching and learning CT and programming skills using the Scratch programming environment (CT); (2) expanding students' knowledge about how to use DNA as a cultural tool to determine one's African Ancestry; (3) introducing complex psychological science phenomenon (e.g. personality, cultural identity, narrative psychology) to promote participants' personal and adolescent development (*Science & Culture*); and storytelling as a means of self-expression and self-representation (*Story*).

CS2: Overview of Setting, Participants, and Methods

CS2 was implemented during the summer months at a northeastern public charter school as one of the school's summer sessions. CS2 pilot study participants comprised of four middle school students: three African-American students and one student of Nigerian-American whose parents were raised in Nigeria and Grenada. There were three girls and one boy, three matriculating 8th graders and one matriculating 9th grader. A team of instructors, researchers, and camp facilitators included a university professor, an entrepreneur, three undergraduate students, one Ph.D. student, and the lead CT instructor and researcher, who was a Ph.D. candidate at the time. Students, instructors, and facilitators met in one large room with laptops, a projector, and access to the Internet for two weeks during the summer month of July. Camp was in session for two weeks from

Monday-Friday during the hours of 9am–1pm, with a 30-minute lunch break each day. Data collection occurred throughout the entire two weeks of camp, as African-American middle students learned, collaborated on, and completed several beginner programming tasks during summer camp. Various video and audio recording methods were used to capture every moment and was used to help describe the "actual process" of teaching and learning CT and programming (and other) skills. Pre- and post-test measures were implemented along with other qualitative data collection approaches throughout the study.

CS2 Instructional Elements: What is Scratch?

The Lifelong Kindergarten Group at the MIT Media Lab created Scratch, a visual programming environment for youth, in 2007. Now at version 2.0, Scratch is an online visual programming language, user community, and learning environment used to teach computer programming concepts to students of all ages. Instead of typing text and using a command line interface to create and run computer programs, learners drag and drop visual programmable bricks, which look like puzzle pieces on the computer screen, and snap them together like legos to create a program block (multiple program puzzle pieces stacked together) of instructions to be executed. Figure 8.1 illustrates the distinct difference between text and visual programming (text is on the left, visual programming block on the right).

Using visual programming interfaces has been proven to be better absorbed by young students learning to program as they do not have to worry about the syntax (i.e. specific programming formats and rules in text-based programming languages) of a particular language or the challenge of debugging their code (Hu, Winikoff, & Cranefield, 2013). In Scratch, if two puzzle pieces do not logically flow, their puzzle pieces will not fit together, giving instant feedback regarding a learner's programming logic. The only syntax required is that the puzzle pieces fit together.

```
define dance (speed)
set [dist v] to ((speed) * (distan
repeat until ((timer) > [10])
    move (dist) steps
    wait (1) secs
    move (() - (dist)) steps
    play note (42 v) for (0.5) be
end
```

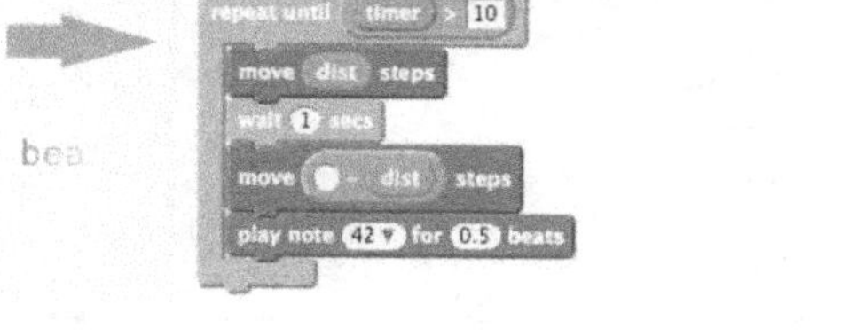

FIGURE 8.1 Program test and Scratch puzzle pieces (blocks) created to perform the exact same action

CS2 Instructional Elements: What is African Ancestry?

Using the power of DNA and the most comprehensive database of indigenous African genetic sequences in existence, African Ancestry traces the genetic ancestries of maternal and paternal lineages back 500–2,000 years ago. African-Americans are the only group in the United States that cannot use traditional methods to research family histories. Genetic technology allows them to break the genealogical brick wall of American history. African Ancestry is the only company that can trace genetic ancestry to a specific present-day African country of origin, and to specific African ethnic groups.

CS2 Curriculum

Table 8.2 illustrates the day-to-day CS2 curriculum and how these elements were used in learning objectives and activities.

TABLE 8.2 CS2 curriculum based on CT and programming learning objectives

Content area	Broad topics	Camp day
Camp CS2	*Morning*: Introductions (People, Camp CS2, Research Project)	Day 1
Computational Thinking/ Scratch	*Afternoon*: Pre-Assessment *Afternoon*: What is Programming, Introduction to Scratch (Layout, Blocks, Sprites, etc.)	Day 1
African Ancestry	*Morning*: Introduction	Day 1
Psychological Science	*Afternoon*: Introduction	Day 1
Computational Thinking/ Scratch	*Morning*: Scratch Community & Remixing, Timing, Look Blocks, Costumes	Day 2
Psychological Science	*Afternoon*: Story, Story Structure, Autobiographical Memory, Narrative Psychology	Day 2
Computational Thinking/ Scratch	*Morning*: Reverse Engineering, Algorithm, Pseudo code *Afternoon*: Pen Tool, Move Blocks, Sound Blocks; Conditionals (If/Then/Else), Sensing Blocks	Day 3
Psychological Science	*Morning*: Personality Traits Assessment	Day 4
African Ancestry	*Afternoon*: DNA, Genes, West-African Geography, Paternal, Maternal, Biotechnology, Culture	Day 4

Content area	Broad topics	Camp day
Psychological Science	*Morning*: Personality Traits, Identity	Day 5
Computational Thinking/ Scratch	*Afternoon*: Vocabulary (Pattern, Simultaneous/ Parallel Processing) Students' view of what is needed to be successful in Scratch	Day 5
Computational Thinking	*Morning*: Emotional Intelligence Self-Assessment	Day 6
Computational Thinking/ Scratch	*Afternoon*: Computer Parts, How a Computer Works and Manipulates Data (Input, Process, Storage, Output, Move), What is Data?, Student Reactions to Scratch	Day 6
Computational Thinking/ Scratch	*Morning*: Vocabulary Review, Variables, Lists (Arrays), *Afternoon*: Random Number Generator, Pair Programming	Day 7
Computational Thinking/ Scratch	*Morning*: Decomposition, Data Representation, Abstraction, Bits & Bytes, *Afternoon*: REVIEW: Conditionals, Lists, and How a Computer Works	Day 8
Computational Thinking/ Scratch	Students Work All Day on the End of Camp Project (African Ancestry)	Day 9
Computational Thinking/ Scratch	More Project Time (if needed) and *Demo Day*. Parents invited to attend	Day 10

CS2: CRC in Action

As a result of 15+ years of experience teaching African-American PreK-12th grade students, the lead instructor and researcher firmly believes the first goal of CRC: *All students are capable of digital innovation*. As such, every instructor and facilitator maintained high expectations throughout the two weeks of camp: to deliver CRC education, and more specifically the second goal of CRC, ensuring the learning context supports transformational use of technology, as CS2's primary learning objective centered around CT and programming skills using Scratch. CRC's third goal, learning about one's self along various intersecting socio-cultural lines allows for technical innovation, was implemented using African Ancestry's® DNA process. This process along with a psychological test to discover personality traits and emotional intelligence were used for discovering one's origin and identity. Class discussions, programming assignments, and a final camp project were used to satisfy CRC's fourth and fifth goals.

CS2: CRT in Action

Rooted in the nine elements of BCE, CS2 focused most on *communalism* (collaboration, sharing, group identity) as a valued "way of knowing" often expressed by African-American youth. This was implemented using pair problem-solving and pair programming (Denner, Werner, Campe, & Ortiz, 2014; Williams and Kessler, 2000). Culturally and personally relevant class discussions and learner activities were used to engage and motivate students and programming assignments were designed to focus attention on personal needs and interests. For example, students focused on reverse engineering concepts during an attempt to solve a problem related to proving that a musician wrongfully sampled another musician's original song. This was during a time when these types of cases were reported in current news cycles. Content used to identify reflection and interrogation of personal need involved programming projects that shared information about their families and career interests. Doing so, CS2 satisfied Lee's (2003) Cultural Modeling Design Principles for creating learning environments. Other elements of the BCE were also emphasized within CS2's instructional strategies and learner activities.

CS2: Instructional Strategies and Learning Activities

CRC elements and Cultural Modeling Design principles were combined with content in science and psychological science (narrative and personality) from culturally relevant and adolescent development perspectives. When designing the instructional strategies and learning activities of CS2, Gay's (2002) five tenets of CRT were employed: 1) developing a knowledge base about cultural diversity, 2) including ethnic and cultural diversity content in the curriculum, 3) demonstrating caring and building learning communities, 4) communicating with ethnically diverse styles, and 5) responding to ethnic diversity in the delivery of instruction.

Instructional strategies and learner activities attempted during Camp CS2 and how they map onto Boykin's (1977) BCE are illustrated in Table 8.3. Please note that the Spirituality, Harmony, and Affect were not used.

Results and Conclusion: CRT/CRP and CRC

Descriptive analysis of the multiple sources of data revealed some very interesting patterns. Empowerment and self-pride were evident results of CS2. One of our beginning icebreaker activities involved the discussion of slavery. Not only did students speak low and mumble during this conversation but their body language illustrated shame and powerlessness. For instance, heads were bowed down and bodies slouched during these conversations. Initially students were asked from where were they and their families. Their responses mentioned the surrounding

TABLE 8.3 Mapping of instructional strategies and learner activities to elements of the BCE

Element of BCE	Instructional strategies	Learner activity
Movement	Culturally and personally relevant discussions (about topics from everyday life) and how they related to CT and programming tasks	Enact topic or pseudo-code
Verve	Embodied cognition (modeled by instructors), e.g. throwing a large ball to whoever should answer the next question	Enactment, embodied cognition
Communalism	Participants stood at whiteboard together while instructor sat in seat and asked questions. All participants had to answer before anyone could sit down ("Flipped Placement")	Pair programming
Expressive	Referring to each participant using their career goals (e.g. chemist, animator)	Scratch project to describe career goals or personal story
Orality	Group (oral) assessment and demo day	Group (oral) assessment, presentations, and demonstrations
Social time	None	Joke and story programming assignments

area along with some of the southern states. When pressed to describe where their ancestors were from, even before arriving to these locations, many students were clueless. However, after learning about African Ancestry and the process used to test DNA to determine what area of West Africa is linked to the biological make-up of a person, the students showed obvious pride and empowerment during speculations of where their families might originate as well as the characteristics that may have made up their originating tribe. These experiences, along with learning about their personality and other traits, and being referred to as a person practicing their career interests (e.g. animator, engineer), planted seeds of empowerment and pride in each student.

Results and Conclusion: CT and CP

Only one of the four students had heard of and used Scratch prior to CS2. Nonetheless, throughout camp, it was obvious that students were challenged with problem-solving when attempting the CT and programming activities. They were challenged with knowing the steps needed to solve problems and were also unfamiliar with how to break a problem into smaller problems (i.e. decomposition). As a result, the instructional team quickly realized the need to introduce and model each problem-solving step. The next instructional goal was to describe how these problem-solving steps transfer to CT and programming within Scratch. The instructional and research team realized effective teaching strategies and learner activities involved explanations, modeling, checklists, and dissecting Scratch programs that already existed. Thus, teaching and learning became possible with deconstructing a program that already existed, explaining the various concepts related to that program, and using what was learned to create a new program. As a result of this pilot study, we share recommended instructional strategies (Table 8.4), and learner activities (Table 8.5) that teachers can use when delivering similar courses to African-American students. In Table 8.4, the left column lists the instructional strategy and the right column shares whether or not that instructional strategy is *culturally relevant* (CR) or enhances the three elements of CT skills: *programming skills* (PS), *inquiry skills* (IS), and/or *communication skills* (CS). These attributes are represented with their respective abbreviations.

Table 8.5 illustrates several learner activities are mapped onto the same attributes of CR and CT skills, using the same highlighted abbreviations which were used to describe the instructional strategies in Table 8.4. These learner

TABLE 8.4 Instructional strategies and how they map across cultural relevance and CT skills

Instructional strategy	Attribute covered
Give learning style, learning context preference, personality trait, emotional intelligence, and interests questionnaires before the start of any instructional undertaking. Responses can inform instructional content.	CR
Share the steps needed to brainstorm, design (i.e. pseudo-code), program, and test computer programs in a checklist format.	PS, IS, CS
Introduce and continue to use inquiry words like *evaluate*, *explore*, *analyze*, *explain*, *model*, and *elaborate*, and add them to a problem-solving and programming checklist.	IS
Model and explain all programming tasks; provide scaffolding. Doing so is very similar to explaining *"worked examples"* in a math course.	PS
Provide a set of programming tasks along with the inquiry steps needed and potential different approaches used to complete them. Make these available with checklist for student practice.	PS, IS
Sequence instructional material and culturally/personally relevant elements appropriately. Once introduced, they should remain in play.	CR
Describe and model how presentations and explanations of the steps completed in problem solving and programming.	CS

TABLE 8.5 Learner activities and how they map across cultural relevance and CT skills

Learner activities	Attribute covered
Use images and descriptions of the Scratch puzzle pieces used when learners are writing their algorithms and pseudo-code.	PS, CS
Use embodied cognition, drawing, and discussion to brainstorm and communicate solution ideas.	CR, PS, CS
Program "worked examples" as practice, labeling and discussing CT and programming elements used. This will aid in strengthening decomposition, inquiry, reverse engineering, and programming skills.	PS, IS, CS
Individual and group "think-alouds" and note taking should be used as learner activities for each concept or skill taught.	CR, PS, IS, CS
Reflect (out loud or written)	CR, PS, CS

activities to CR and CT skills attribute mappings are featured in Table 8.5, where the learner activity is on the left and the attributes of CR and CT skills they refer to are listed on the right.

Results and Conclusion: Overall

Overall, not only did students learn how to use and navigate the Scratch environment effectively, they were also equipped with checklists that enabled them to design solutions to problems and select the best approach to translate their solutions into Scratch programs. They used these and additional CT skills to create unique and efficient programs. End-of-camp presentations allowed them to express their ideas and present their final projects. As a result, their self-efficacy, sense of belonging to the CT and computer science community, and interest in pursuing computer science-related career fields increased.

This pilot study provides preliminary evidence that the design principles used to develop the CS2 model offer culturally and developmentally appropriate teaching and learning opportunities anchored in cutting-edge computer science problem-based learning and a commitment to students' personal development (e.g. emotional intelligence, cultural identity development, and career motivation). Future cycles of model development will include refining the instructional strategies and exploring how to deploy the model in other informal learning environments in which students of color reside (e.g. community centers, churches). Also, this project illuminates the theoretical and practical benefits of the novel integration of the disciplines of psychology, genetics, and history to promote excellence and success in computer science education.

References

Adams, J., 1995. *Risk*. London: UCL Press.
Barba, R.H. (1993). A study of culturally syntonic variables in the bilingual/bicultural science classroom. *Journal of Research in Science Teaching, 30*(9), 1053–1071.
Boykin, A.W. (1977). Experimental psychology from a Black perspective: Issues and examples. *Journal of Black Psychology, 3*(2), 29–49.
Boykin, A. W. (1983). The academic performance of Afro-American children. In J. Spence (Ed.), Achievement and achievement motives (pp. 321–371). San Francisco: Freeman.
Boykin, A.W. (1994a). Afro-cultural expressions and its implications for schooling. In E. Hollins, J. King, & W. Hayman (Eds.), *Teaching diverse populations: formulating a knowledge base*. Albany, NY: State University of New York Press.
Boykin, A.W. (1994b). Harvesting culture and talent: African American children and school reform. In R. Rossi (Ed.), *Schools and students at risk: Context and framework for positive change* (pp. 116–138). New York, NY: Teachers College Press.
Brown, B.A., Kloser, M., & Henderson, J.B. (2010). *Building bridges towards cognition: cultural continuity and the language-identity dilemma*. Stanford, CA: Stanford University Press.
Clark, K., & Moore, J. (Eds.) (2007). Looking beyond the digital divide: Participation and opportunities with technology in education [Special Issue]. *Journal of Negro Education, 76*(1).
Committee on Prospering in the Global Economy of the 21st Century (2007). *Rising above the gathering storm: Energizing and employing America for a brighter economic future*. Washington, DC: The National Academies Press.
Computer Science Teacher Association (CSTA) (2012). *Computer Science K-8: Building a Strong Foundation*. Retrieved September 22, 2012 from http://csta.acm.org/Curriculum/sub/CurrFiles/CS_K-8_Building_a_Foundation.pdf
Denner, J., Werner, L., Campe, S., & Ortiz, E. (2014). Pair programming: Under What conditions is it advantageous for middle school students? *Journal of Research on Technology in Education, 46*(3), 277–296.
Dill, E.M., & Boykin, A.W. (2000). The comparative influence of individual, peer tutoring, creating complex and communal learning contexts on the text recall of African American children. *Journal of Black Psychology, 26*(1), 65–78.
Dunn, R.S., Dunn, K.J., & Price, G.E. (1989). *Learning style inventory (LSI)*. Price Systems, Incorporated (PO Box 1818, Lawrence 66044).
Ellison, C.M., Boykin, A.W., Towns, D.P., & Stokes, A. (2000). *Classroom cultural ecology: The dynamics of classroom life in schools serving low-income African American children*. Report no. 44, CRESPAR.
Fullilove, R.E., & Treisman, P.U. (1990). Mathematics achievement among African American undergraduates at the University of California, Berkeley: An evaluation of the Mathematics Workshop Program. *Journal of Negro Education, 59*(3), 463–478.
Gay, G. (2000). *Culturally responsive teaching: Theory, research, & practice*. New York: NY. Teachers College Press.
Gay, G. (2002). Preparing for culturally responsive teaching. *Journal of Teacher Education, 53*(2), 106–16.
Grover, S., & Pea, R. (2013). Computational thinking in K–12: A review of the state of the field. *Educational Researcher, 42*(1), 38–43. Handbook, 2010–11 Edition, Computer Scientists.

Hale, J. E. (1982). *Black children: Their roots, culture, and learning styles.* Baltimore, MD: JHU Press.

Hofstede, G. (1991). *Organizations and cultures: Software of the mind.* New York, NY: McGraw-Hill.

Hu, M., Winikoff, M., & Cranefield, S. (2013). A process for novice programming using goals and plans. *Proceedings of the Fifteenth Australasian Computing Education Conference* (pp. 3–12). Darlinghurst, Australia: Australian Computer Society, Inc.

Ladson-Billings, G. (1995a). But that's just good teaching! The case for culturally relevant pedagogy. *Theory into practice, 34*(3), 159–165.

Ladson-Billings, G. (1995b). Toward a theory of culturally relevant pedagogy. *American Educational Research Journal, 32*(3), 465–491.

Ladson-Billings, G. (2001). *Crossing over to Canaan: The journey of new teachers in diverse classrooms.* The Jossey-Bass Education Series. Jossey-Bass, Inc., 350 Sansome Street, San Francisco, CA 94104.

Lee, C. D. (1993). *Signifying as a scaffold for literary interpretation: The pedagogical implications of an African American discourse genre* (Research Report Series). Urbana, IL: National Council of Teachers of English.

Lee, C. D. (1997). Bridging home and school literacies: A model of culturally responsive teaching. In J. Flood, S. B. Heath, & D. Lapp (Eds.), *A handbook for literacy educators: Research on teaching the communicative and visual arts* (pp. 330–341). New York: Macmillan.

Lee, C. D. (2003). Toward a framework for culturally responsive design in multimedia computer environments: Cultural modeling as a case. *Mind, Culture, and Activity, 10*(1), 42–61.

Leonard, J., Davis, J. E., & Sidler, J. L. (2005). Cultural relevance and computer-assisted instruction. *Journal of research on Technology in Education, 37*(3), 263–284.

Michel, J.-B., Shen, Y. K., Aiden, A. P., Veres, A., Gray, M. K., Pickett, J. P., Aiden, E. L. (2011). Quantitative analysis of culture using millions of digitized books. *Science, 331*(6014), 176–182. Retrieved September 24, 2015 from http://doi.org/10.1126/science.1199644

Modi, K., Schoenberg, J., & Salmond, K. (2012*). Generation STEM: What girls say about science, technology, engineering, and math.* New York, NY: Girl Scouts of the USA. Retrieved September 24, 2012 from http://www.girlscouts.org/research/pdf/generation_stem_full_report.pdf

National Science Board (2010). *Preparing the next generation of STEM innovators: Identifying and developing our nation's human capital.* Retrieved September 23, 2012 from http://www.nsf.gov/nsb/publications/2010/nsb1033.pdf

Pinkard, N. D. (1999). Lyric Reader: An architecture for creating intrinsically motivating and culturally responsive reading environments. *Interactive Learning Environments, 7*(1), 1–30.

President's Council of Advisors on Science and Technology (PCAST). (2010). *Prepare and inspire: K-12 education in science, technology, engineering, and math (STEM) for America's future.* Retrieved September 22, 2012 from http://www.whitehouse.gov/administration/eop/ostp/pcast

Reis, N. M., & Kay, S. (2007). Incorporating culturally relevant pedagogy into the teaching of science: The role of the principal. *Electronic Journal of Literacy Through Science, 6*(1), 54–57.

Scott K. A., Sheridan K. M., and Clark K. (2014). *Learning, media and technology, 40*(4), 412–436.

Scott, K. A., Clark, K., Hayes, E., Mruczek, C., & Sheridan, K. (2010). Culturally Relevant Computing programs: Two examples to inform teacher professional development. In D. Gibson & B. Dodge (Eds.), *Proceedings of Society for Information Technology & Teacher Education International Conference 2010* (pp. 1269–1277). Chesapeake, VA: Association for the Advancement of Computing in Education (AACE).

Serpell, R., Sonnenschein, S., Baker, L., & Ganapathy, H. (2002). Intimate culture of families in the early socialization of literacy. *Journal of Family Psychology, 16*(4), 391.

Silva, C. M., Moses, R. P., Rivers, J., & Johnson, P. (1990). The algebra project: Making middle school mathematics count. *Journal of Negro Education, 59*(3), 375–391.

Tharp, R. G. (1989). Psychocultural variables and constants: Effects on teaching and learning in schools. *American Psychology, 44*(2), 349.

The Design Based Research Collective. (2003). Design based research: An emerging paradigm for educational inquiry. *Educational Researcher, 32*, 5–9.

Treisman, P. (1985). A study of the mathematics achievement of Black students at the University of California, Berkeley. Unpublished doctoral dissertation, University of California, Berkeley, Professional Development Program.

Wasserman, S. (2015, March 27). *White House gets $240 Million from Private Sector for STEM Education.* Retrieved September 23, 2015 from http://www.engineering.com/Education/EducationArticles/ArticleID/9853/White-House-gets-240-Million-from-Private-Sector-for-STEM-Education.aspx

Werner, L. L., Campe, S., & Denner, J. (2005, October). Middle school girls + games programming = information technology fluency. In *Proceedings of the 6th Conference on Information Technology Education* (pp. 301–305). ACM.

Wiggins, R. A., Follo, E. J., & Eberly, M. B. (2007). The impact of a field immersion program on pre-service teachers' attitudes toward teaching in culturally diverse classrooms. *Teaching and Teacher Education, 23*(5), 653–663.

Wing, J. M. (2006). Computational thinking. *Communications of the ACM, 49*(3), 33–35. Retrieved April 5, 2014 from http://doi.org/10.1145/1118178.1118215

Williams, L. A., & Kessler, R. R. (2000). The Effects of 'Pair-Pressure' and 'Pair-Learning' on Software Engineering Education, *Proceedings of Thirteenth Conference on Software Engineering Education and Training*, pp. 59–65.

Winston, C. E., Philip, C. L., & Lloyd, D. L. (2007). Integrating design based research and the identity & success life story research method: toward a new research paradigm for looking beyond the digital divide and race self complexity within the lives of Black students. *Journal of Negro Education, 76*(1), 31–43.

Zweben, S., & Bizot, B. (2015). 201 Taulbee Survey. *Computing Research News, 27*(5). Retrieved November 27, 2015 from http://cra.org/wp-content/uploads/2015/06/2014-Taulbee-Survey.pdf

9

FOUNDATIONAL THEORIES OF SOCIAL MEDIA TOOLS AND CULTURAL COMPETENCY

A Systematic Literature Review

Sandra G. Nunn, Lequisha Brown-Joseph, and Michelle Susberry Hill

Introduction

In today's world, the use of social media tools can influence education, society, and the global community by providing users with enhanced skills to create and share information. According to Rodriguez (2013), social media uses different tools and platforms to allow more open interactions not only to share information but also to collaborate with other users. While social media enhances increased communication among users at many levels throughout the global community, an important issue is whether the growing use of social media promotes cultural competency and improved cross-cultural communication. Scholars must consider if social media tools allow users the ability to acknowledge cultural heritages, implement multicultural perspectives, and shows users how to respect different cultural paradigms (Gay, 2000).

In prior research, Arroyo-González and Hunt-Gómez (2009) noted that cultural competencies and technological use would grow through the use of computer technology in the 21st century. The increased use of social media tools allows users to share information more openly to collaborate with other users (Graham, 2014). For example, social media helps to engage users such as students during the educational process (Sandlin & Peña, 2014), enhances intercultural experiences (Chan & Nyback, 2015), and fosters increased innovation (Mount & Garcia-Martinez, 2014). In turn, cultural competency represents a respect and sensitivity to the diversity of individuals and groups from different cultural and religious settings (Stennis, Purnell, Perkins, & Fischle, 2015).

Because cultural competency must transcend this diversity to facilitate greater ability to overcome cultural boundaries and achieve enhanced communication, achieving cultural competency can involve a complicated process (Delphin-Rittmon, Andres-Hyman, Flanagan, & Davidson, 2013). Through prior studies, the educational process has affirmed the importance of implementing culturally competent practices to overcome cultural barriers (Ford, Stuart, & Vakil, 2014; Lewthwaite, Owen, Doiron, Renaud, & McMillan, 2014). For example, Rodrigo and Nguyen (2013) determined how virtual communication can help support the development of cultural competency. This cultural competency includes the use of cultural intelligence because of the ability of an individual to relate and work effectively across cultures (Baugher, 2012).

While the emergence of the Internet has allowed for global communication among users, a communication gap still exists because users of social media tools cannot address various cultural norms and ideologies. "What can be difficult . . . is understanding how to communicate effectively with individuals who speak another language, or who rely on different means to reach a common goal" (Cross-Culture Communication, 2016, para. 1). According to Goodrich and de Mooij (2013), "different cultures show varying emphasis on different types of online information and develop local variations of social media that cater to particular cultural usage" (p. 114). Because of cultural differences and language differences, users may encounter difficulties in achieving effective communication; therefore, users may lack the ability to transcend and overcome barriers to seamless communication throughout the world. For this reason, scholars recognize that development of cultural competency can help to address global issues (Baugher, 2012). By fostering cultural competency, global users can achieve greater cultural understanding among people in different geographic regions and promote improved awareness of unique perspectives. Therefore, it can also benefit users in various environments including education and business. For example, the use of cultural competency can help users understand how people in different cultures learn or how people in other cultures conduct business. Given these considerations, it is important to address how social media tools can better integrate cultural competency into the social media experience. By doing so, users can enhance communication and information exchange in the global community.

Background

Social Media

The way we exchange information has evolved over the years to how we communicate today. Some of the earliest forms of communication involved sending messages by messengers or by horseback. But technology innovations soon allowed the telegraph and then the telephone to replace these old communication systems (Cheshire, 2009). With the emergence of computer technology, the use of social media provided a means to send electronic information through networking websites. According to Power (2014), social media uses various web-based instruments to enable a platform for users to mutually and virtually interact to exchange information.

The emergence of online games in the 1970s provided the initial foundation for the earliest forms of social media. People used a virtual world for online chatting while engaging in role-playing games such as Multiuser Dungeon (MUD). Additional communications emerged with the creation of Bulletin Board Systems (BBS) in 1978 and Usenet in 1988. In 1986, Listserv launched and was considered the first electronic mailing. However, the first social media networking sites began in the 1990s. As social media began to evolve, users observed the creation of websites such as MoveOn, Epinion, MySpace, LinkedIn, Facebook, YouTube, and Twitter. By 2010, Facebook had more than 500 million active users and ranked as the most visited site in the world. Later, Twitter took the stage with its use of microblogs. The different options and short snippets helped Twitter to become popularized among regular users as well as celebrities who used Twitter to provide updates about themselves (Edosomwan, Prakasan, Kouame, Watson, & Seymour, 2011). Now, Twitter boasts millions of users globally because of its ease of use on today's smartphones and computers.

As shown above, social media has significantly changed the way in which diverse people, communities, and different organizations communicate in society today (Ngai et al., 2014). According to Kaplan and Haenlein (2010), "social media is a group of internet based applications, that build on the ideological and technological foundations of Web 2.0 and allow the creation of the creation and exchange of user-generated content" (p. 61). Therefore, the use of social media allows individuals to create, share ideas, and exchange information in a digital community (Ngai, Tao, & Moon, 2014). By definition, Web 2.0 is a tech term that "refers to the second generation of the World Wide Web" ("Web 2.0," 2016, para. 1) that consists of blogs, social networking sites, web-based applications, and user content sites. Stated differently, Web 2.0 signifies the foundation of 21st-century communication on the Internet. The use of this protocol migrated from a brainstorming conference in 2004 of like-minded individuals who decided the future of the Internet was important and worked together to provide clarity. As such, Web 2.0 can be visualized as a set of values that bring together an authentic constellation of websites that validate some or all of the values in a variety of ways that stem from the heart of the platform (O'Reilly, 2005). Web 2.0 allows users to collaborate, participate in groups, engage in two-way communication, become actively involved, and engage with user-generated content. "Web 2.0 also utilizes social networking tools to further increase the level of viewer participation" (Matusky, 2015, para. 2).

Cultural Competency

Cultural competency emerged out of the movement of multicultural education. While current definitions of cultural competency differ, some scholars describe cultural competency as different behaviors that join and allow individuals to collaborate in cross-cultural environments (Cross, Bazron, Dennis, & Isaacs, 1989). Cultural competency stems from the word culture that shows different definitions. Thus, culture represents an individual's unique behavior to include how a person thinks and communicates. Culture also represents an individual's attitudes, beliefs, concepts of the universe, experiences, hierarchies, material objects and possessions, meanings, notions of time, religion, roles, spatial relations, and values about a larger group (Li & Karakowsky, 2001).

Similarly, Blum (1997) noted that "multiculturalism is a response not only to diversity itself, but to striking social, economic and educational inequalities in efforts to provide a learning environment for diverse learners" (p. 1). Multiculturalism represents the synthesis of different cultures through the borrowing of pieces and the resulting transformation of the combined parts into a new idea (Multiculturalism, 2011). Similarly, cross-culturalism relates to cultural differences and comparisons.

Cultural competency exists within many aspects of American culture. Outside of the education realm, cultural competency impacts a variety of professional industries such as health care, advertising, churches, social work, and counseling. Because cultural competency can apply to many industries, a challenge exists to promote and support the ongoing challenge of multicultural organizational development. Currently, scholars suggest seven important strategies to support organizational and systemic cultural competency. Four of these strategies assert that the organization can provide executive-level accountability and support, encourage participation and partnerships among the community and other stakeholders, conduct assessments of organizational cultural competency, and develop action plans to promote cultural competency. The remaining three strategies propose that organizations can ensure linguistic competency, establish and retain a culturally competent workforce, and develop a system strategy for managing grievances (Delphin-Rittmon et al., 2013). However, new considerations of cultural competency continue to emerge as technology and social media continue to evolve throughout the global community. Certainly, one of these considerations is how the use of cultural competency can benefit the educational process.

According to Gallegos, Tindall, and Gallegos (2008), cultural competency is commonly embedded in the foundation of many organizations' and programs' mission statements. As a result of the Civil Rights Movement, scholars reported the emergence of new social directions in the 1980s. In turn, federal mandates produced a chain reaction of local government actions, city initiatives, business changes, and organizational upgrades that made the inclusion of cultural competency objectives in some programs a requirement for funding. In other cases, the inclusion of cultural competency represented a movement to make specific connections to society culturally relevant. The paradigm shifts of becoming more culturally competent not only advanced how one connects with all aspects of society but also revealed what drives how people communicate in different environments such as education and business as well as between individuals.

It is important for individuals to understand that the values connected with the concept of cultural competency are the driving force of future Internet and online communications worldwide. To integrate cultural competency with social media, a program or organization must include five essential elements. The first element should focus on valuing diversity within the program or organization. Second, the program or organization must have the ability to self-assess the culture within the entity. Third, the program or organization must demonstrate awareness of the dynamics relative to cultural interaction. Fourth, the program or organization must facilitate the institutionalization of cultural knowledge. Finally, the program or organization must ensure that the development of services properly reflects appropriate cultural diversity and understanding. These elements should be reflected throughout the entire program not only within the delivery system but also in the attitudes, policies, services, and structures (Gallegos et al., 2008). Social media and cultural competency have the ability to go hand in hand when it comes to communication. The ideologies of how social media and cultural competency is interpreted together by society have the capacity to reveal how the world will continue to communicate and share information.

Relevance and Importance of this Literature Review

This literature review demonstrates relevance and importance in several ways. First, given the importance of communication in different situational contexts, scholars must understand how the integration of social media and cultural competency applies in today's world. For example, they must consider how integrated theoretical constructs can affect educators, students, business users, and other individuals. Another important consideration of social media usage is the ability to communicate ideas and information across multicultural boundaries not only to learn but also to expand the individual's worldview in the global community. In other words, users can communicate seamlessly with other users throughout the world. Further, unlike in the past, the use of social media allows for a real-time experience of sharing information to engage in a learning process across geographical boundaries rather than sitting in a singular classroom environment. The advantage of this method is that a student in the United States can engage with a student in another part of the world to share information in a cross-cultural environment. By doing so, students not only benefit from learning course concepts but also learn how to adapt to different cultural considerations to enhance communication and understanding.

Though the researchers identified the insights noted above, a review of the literature regarding social media and other research regarding cultural competency reveals a gap relating to the integration of cultural competency considerations with social media usage. The use of social media requires a new understanding of how users must process culture and communicate with others in the world (Jenkins, Clinton, Purushotma, Robison, & Weigel, 2009). For this reason, this literature review provides a comprehensive overview of the relevant current literature to provide insights into the theoretical basis of social media tools and cultural competency. Through the study of the literature, the researchers reveal how practitioners can use current theory to integrate cultural competency with social media tools to improve communication within different aspects of the global community including education, business, and individual use. Further, this literature review provides potential directions for future research about this topic.

Method

Using the method outlined by Cooper (1988) as the framework, this literature review used the following procedure to synthesize the literature: (1) formulate the problem, (2) collect data, (3) evaluate the appropriateness of the data, (4) analyze and interpret the relevant data, and (5) organize and present the results.

Formulating the problem. The problem established by the research team was that social media tools do not appear to integrate cultural competency considerations adequately enough to encourage enhanced levels of communication and understanding within the global community. To address the problem, the researchers identified two research questions to serve as the focus of the literature review.

1) What foundational theories support the use of social media tools in achieving cultural competency?
2) How might cultural competency theories affect how individuals use social media tools in productive and meaningful ways?

Data collection. The goal of data collection was to find all empirical studies including quantitative, qualitative, mixed methods, and literature reviews including theories regarding the integration of cultural competency and social media since inception. The keywords used included *social media history*, *social* *media theories, cultural competency history, cultural competency theories, social media and cultural competency,* and *social media and cultural competency theories.* The databases used included Google Scholar, Educational Resources Information Center (ERIC), ProQuest, and EBSCO HOST.

Data evaluation and analysis. To locate information most applicable to this literature review, the research team examined only peer-reviewed articles based on specific topics relative to social media and cultural competency. Germinal articles focusing on theory for social media, cultural competency, and the integration of these topic areas were researched as well as peer-reviewed articles written subsequent to the germinal articles. Only those articles considered the most relevant for purposes of this literature review were used. Based on the described procedure, 44 articles were found. Of the 44 articles found on cultural competency and social media theories, 17 focused on social media theories and related content, 8 focused on cultural competency and related content, and 19 focused on theories relative to the integration of social media and cultural competency. These articles were included in the scope of this literature review. Articles that did not discuss the specific theories and related information deemed necessary for this literature review were excluded.

Results

Social Media Theories

Various theories can help explain how social media can affect how users communicate to exchange and share information in educational and social contexts. Some theories pre-date the emergence and use of social media; however, these early theories can also serve as the foundation to understand how communication and learning takes place in educational and social environments. The more contemporary theories go further to explain social media communications relative to technological and social perspectives. Some of the seminal theories consist of Social Learning Theory (Bandura, 1963; Bandura, 1977), Vygotsky's Theory (Vygotsky, 1978a), Theory of Planned Behavior (Ajzen, 1985), and Social Constructivism Theory (Sivan, 1986). More contemporary theories consist of Social Presence Theory (Gunawardena, 1995) and the Unified Theory of Acceptance and Use of Technology Model (AlAwadhi & Morris, 2008). A description of these theories explores the important components of each theoretical construct and how the theory can apply to social media usage.

Social learning theory. As an early theoretical construct developed prior to Internet-based communications, Social Learning Theory can help explain many different types of environments to include the current usage of social media. In Social Learning Theory, Bandura (1963) posited that learning consists of cognitive processes that emerge within social environments either from user observations or through direct learning processes. Social Learning Theory (Bandura, 1977) involves the interaction between the user and the information. It is with these temporary sensory stimuli that users can create mental images. This symbolism is usually carried out with graphics, chats, and videos. Scholars noted that Social Learning Theory exists when there is a belief that one can achieve an outcome using all resources in the process (Deaton, 2015). This theory is widely used today to describe how users learn from social media by observing and learning from others on different social media sites (Edwin, 2014).

Vygotsky's theory. Vygotsky's Theory (Vygotsky, 1978a) leans toward society and culture promoting cognitive growth. This increase occurs through the interactions between others that can potentially improve learning. Cognitive growth does not happen in isolation (Taylor, King, & Nelson, 2012). It happens through collaborating with others. Within this collaboration, learning takes place because of the interactions with others through the back and forth exchanges that occur with the use of social media (Megele, 2014). Vygotsky's Theory explains that the interactions should be between a learner and a teacher, or a more knowledgeable person. These interactions help the student gain knowledge. Specifically, emphasis should be placed on the new insights gained rather than what the learner already knows (Lefebvre, Bolduc, & Pirkenne, 2015). Because new knowledge is readily available in social media, this theory proves useful to explain how social media can help benefit the educational process.

Theory of planned behavior. The Theory of Planned Behavior (Ajzen, 1985) suggests that an individual attitude level lends itself to how various influences can affect people's actions and behaviors. When using social media, people provide positive and negative ideas (Ghosh, Varshney, & Venugopal, 2014). Because this concept relates to associations, people may listen more attentively to negative information rather than positive information. With many universities online, it is important that media sharing concentrates on academic studies instead of personal experiences. For example, many people look at user reviews to make decisions. This aspect impacts the behavior of users who are basing their actions on the opinions of unknown others. The credibility of these users is also unknown (Ghosh et al., 2014). Therefore, social media use in a controlled learning environment can mitigate this challenge.

Social constructivism theory. Social Constructivism Theory (Sivan, 1986) involves the collaborative construction of knowledge. This theory suggests that instead of memorizing information, learners gain from the information presented to them through collaborative interactions. Therefore, learning takes place through interactions in a social setting (Gaytan, 2013). Because social media involves the interaction of different users to communicate and share information, this theory aligns well with the concept of how users can learn using social media applications.

Social presence theory. Social Presence Theory (Gunawardena, 1995) suggests that users have a sense of awareness through the interactions in their online groups. With this theory, using social media tools should allow for a sense of community building within the groups. This community building is similar to a community in a neighborhood or classroom (Smith & Tirumala, 2012). Frequent communications within these communities lead to relationships; therefore, the interactions determine the quality of the relationships (Short, Williams, & Christie, 1976). Ultimately, social media tools provide the platform for the existence of Social Presence Theory.

UTAUT. The Unified Theory of Acceptance and Use of Technology (UTAUT) Model (AlAwadhi & Morris, 2008) addresses the intended use of social media through five determining factors that influence a user's intention and use behaviors. The five elements consist of performance expectancy, effort expectancy, social influence, facilitating conditions, and behavioral intention moderated by age, experience, gender, and user voluntariness. Of the five factors, social influence addresses user perceptions of others in social interactions using technology systems. Hanson, West, Neiger, Thackeray, Barnes & McIntyre (2011) noted that social networking sites and media sharing sites reveal visitors who have a common association in the group or organization. Pressure from peers and purposeful use with an expected outcome were often factors in social media use. Other factors include ease of use and the sustainability of the infrastructure of the system that supports the social media use (Hanson et al., 2011).

Cultural Competency Theories

Different theories can help explain the social implications of shared culture and cultural competency. The following four theories provide a sampling of theoretical constructs that help promote cultural competency in various contexts. This section explores certain germinal theories such as Expectation States Theory (Berger et al., 1972), Social Impact Theory (Latané, 1981), Dynamic Social Impact Theory (Latané, 1996), and Social Systems Theory (Luhmann, 1995). These theories can help explain how social interaction can help promote cultural competency by enhancing cultural understanding between individuals.

Expectation states theory. Expectation States Theory (Berger, Cohen, & Zeldich, 1972) shows how interactions between diverse groups of people can influence the emergence of interpersonal hierarchies. While this theory can apply to different groups based on age or gender, it can also apply to ethnic groups with different cultural backgrounds. For this reason, this theoretical concept can apply to cultural competency because cultural considerations can influence beliefs and stereotypes.

Social impact theory. Social Impact Theory (Latané, 1981) explains the social implications of how other individuals can influence another person. In this theory, the probability that a person will react to social influences increases according to the importance of the group, the closeness of the group, and the number of people in the group with respect to the individual experiencing any influences. This theory relates to cultural competency because it serves as the foundation of Dynamic Social Impact Theory which, as shown in the next section, relates very strongly to cultural considerations.

Dynamic social impact theory. The Dynamic Social Impact Theory (Latané, 1996) explains how cultural elements such as beliefs, practices, and values can emerge by sharing these cultural ideologies through the interaction of individuals. According to Harton and Bullock (2007), the Dynamic Social Impact Theory proposes that local social influence creates culture. Four occurrences define the theory as: (a) regional differences in cultural components, (b) emergent associations between components, (c) consolidation, and (d) ongoing diversity. Therefore, cultures are developed and can change daily from the bottom up via communication with neighbors, friends, and coworkers.

Social systems theory. Social Systems Theory (Luhmann, 1995) does not focus on behaviors of individuals or groups but rather describes how communication occurs within social systems. According to Gallegos et al. (2008), a system may become more culturally competent by valuing diversity, possessing the ability to self-assess culture, demonstrating awareness of the dynamics of cultural interaction, institutionalizing cultural knowledge, and understanding cultural diversity. In turn, Durkheim (1858/1984; 1897/1951) believed that society exerted a dominant force on individuals by way of social integration theory. Durkheim also believed group norms, beliefs, and values make up a cooperative consciousness, or a collective way of understanding and responding to the world.

Theories that Integrate Cultural Competency with Social Media Tools

A review of the literature reveals how several theories can help to explain the integration of cultural competency with social media tools. Many theoretical constructs appear to support the use of social media while others focus on cultural competency. However, several theoretical frameworks also support the integration of cultural competency with social media tools. These germinal theories include the SIDE Model (Lea & Spears, 1991), Social Identity Theory (Tajfel & Turner, 1979; Tajfel & Turner, 1986), Cultures-of-Use Theory (Thorne, 2003), Hofstede's Cultural Dimensions Theory (Hofstede, 1983), and Diffusion of Innovation Theory (Rogers, 1962). Social Capital Theory (Bourdieu, 1986) and Cultural Capital Theory (Bourdieu, 1979) also serve to address the integration of cultural competency with social media. Moreover, additional theories include Collaborative Learning (Vygotsky, 1934/1962; Vygotsky, 1978b), Model of "Community of Inquiry" (Garrison, Anderson, & Archer, 2000; Garrison & Anderson, 2003), and

Cross-Cultural Collaboration (Vygotsky, 1978b). A description of these theories appears below.

SIDE model. This theory emerged from studies in communication and social psychology to explain how anonymous and identifiable components can influence group behavior. As a technology theory, the SIDE Model helps to explain how computer-based communications can affect society. In another context, the SIDE Model posits that high virtual environments can contribute to increase cultural knowledge acquisition as well as application (Lea & Spears, 1991; Krumm, Terwiel, & Hertel, 2013). Because this theory describes how people communicate in a virtual community as well as how users share cultural knowledge, it aligns with the integration of social media and cultural competency.

Social identity theory. Social Identity Theory focuses on the assimilation of others into a social group where differences are overlooked in favor of the group (Tajfel & Turner, 1979; Tajfel & Turner, 1986; Krumm et al., 2013). This theory asserts that three different processes of social categorization, social identification, and social comparison help people to identify with one group or another (Tajfel & Turner, 1979). Therefore, Social Identity Theory possesses implications for how people perceive different cultural groups such as in the case of members of virtual teams (Krumm et al., 2013). For this reason, this theory may prove relevant because users can integrate cultural competency considerations with virtual-based communications.

Cultural capital theory. Cultural Capital Theory embodies cultural value by explaining the connection between social privilege and academic success (Bourdieu, 1979; Prieur & Savage, 2011). One aspect of this theory addresses how a newer focus regarding cultural engagement includes new technology, different forms of culture, and a system of values (Prieur & Savage, 2011). For example, some researchers propose the possibility of information technology as a form of cultural capital (Emmison & Frow, 1998). "Information technology ... embodies social capital as it opens doors to new relationships, both physical and virtual" (Kvasny & Truex, 2000, p. 288). Given these considerations, this theory shows applicability to the integration of social media with cultural competency.

Social capital theory. Social Capital Theory posits how forces can bring groups together in a positive way for all parties involved (Bourdieu, 1986; Gauntlett, 2011). According to this theory, greater networking and association can increase the level of social capital in any given situation. Further, this theory posits that social capital can also include virtual as well as actual resources (Bourdieu & Wacquant, 1992). Through the use of social networks, people can engage in collective efforts to achieve value. When viewing this theory, users can apply these concepts to include virtual communications that can also enhance cultural interactions among groups of people.

Cultures-of-use theory. Mitchell (2012) noted how the Cultures-of-Use Theory first proposed by Thorne (2003) explained how the use of social media helped users to engage in language and cultural learning. Using social networking, users could improve language skills and cultural competency as well as enhance social contact through online interactions (Mitchell, 2012). Thorne (2003) further noted:

> People engaged with and mediated by material culture in all its forms mark the profitable point of departure for research in the area of communicative practice and intercultural understanding. . . . Cultural artifacts such as global communication technologies are produced by and productive of socio-historically located subjects. Such artifacts take their functional form and significance from the human activities they mediate and the meanings that communities create through them.
>
> (p. 58)

Based on the foregoing, this theory can apply in different contexts such as education or business to show how the use of social media can help to enhance cultural competency among users.

Hofstede's cultural dimensions theory. Hofstede's Cultural Dimensions Theory (Hofstede, 1983; Sawyer, 2011) explores cross-cultural communication from six cultural dimensions to include power distance, individualism/collectivism, masculinity/femininity, uncertainty avoidance, long-term/short-term orientation, and indulgence/self-restraint. Using these cultural dimensions allows users to make comparisons between different countries and cultures. Understanding these differences allows people to understand other cultures, establish expectations, and learn how to interact toward people of different cultures. While this theory often helps to address international business applications, it also relates to cross-cultural communication. Therefore, this theory can apply to the integration of social media and cultural competency.

Diffusion of innovation theory. The Diffusion of Innovation Theory (Rogers, 1962; Sawyer, 2011) explores how technological advancements as well as innovative ideas through social media use can spread throughout a networking group in the global community thus allowing people to share ideas and multicultural awareness. Srite and Karahanna (2006) noted that cultural differences can affect how people perceive and adopt the diffusion of innovative information technology. "Peoples' decision to adopt a technology includes the external impressions, such as cultural values and norms that people are subject to" (Lekhanya, 2013, p. 1565). Therefore, learning through social interactions helps to promote the diffusion of technology (Romer, 1986). In this theoretical construct, people can adopt new ideas through various means to include word-of-mouth, personal interactions, shared cultural values, and interactions through interpersonal communications networks. Under the premise of this theory, the integration of social media communications and cultural competency align. Therefore, this theory can prove beneficial in educational and business contexts.

Collaborative learning. The use of Collaborative Learning (Vygotsky, 1934/1962; Vygotsky, 1978b; Yang, Kinshuk, Yu, Chen, & Huang, 2014) provides the theoretical basis for cross-cultural learning in a virtual environment. Yang et al. (2014) posited how collaborative learning using Web 2.0 technology and four strategies can enhance cultural competency. The strategies involved establishing cultural awareness, determining the task model needed for the online learning process, using appropriate language resources, and considering the influences of different cultures on learning interactions. According to a National Education Association (2008) policy brief, becoming more culturally competent in education is important for several reasons. First, students can enhance individual levels of diversity. Second, culture plays a critical role in the learning process. In addition, cultural competency can lead to effective teaching of all students in all types of environments. Also, culturally competent educators are able to develop deeper rapport with families and communities. Finally, culturally competent teaching aids student achievement. For these reasons, use of the Collaborative Learning model can serve as an effective theoretical foundation in the learning process to enhance the achievement of cultural competency using technology and social media tools. Use of this model can help transcend barriers and enhance cross-cultural understanding.

Model of community of inquiry. Another model for cross-cultural learning includes the Model of "Community of Inquiry" (Garrison et al., 2000; Garrison & Anderson, 2003; Yang et al., 2014). This model focuses on how computer-mediated communications can support the learning process. Through the use of three components consisting of cognitive presence, social presence, and teaching presence, educators and researchers can establish how communications using computerized interactions between individuals can promote education (Ling, 2007). Use of the three components helps to establish the educational environment, support discourse, and regulate learning to enhance the educational experience for educators and learners (Garrison et al., 2000). The Model of Community of Inquiry sets the climate between social presence and teaching presence, supports discourse between social presence and cognitive presence, and allows the selection of learning content between cognitive presence and teaching presence (Garrison et al., 2000). For this reason, this model enables students to achieve deep and meaningful learning. Further, use of this model shows how creating a community of inquiry can help foster the sharing of information and cultural ideologies in different cross-cultural environments. For example, students in a classroom in one country can use technology-based tools such as social media to communicate with students in a classroom in another country to engage in interactive learning processes. Students can share ideas, learn about each other's cultures, and collaborate together to achieve learning outcomes in a cross-cultural environment.

Evaluation methods for cross-cultural collaboration. Another important aspect of cross-cultural collaboration utilizing social media for learning purposes concerns the Evaluation Methods for Cross-Cultural Collaboration (Vygotsky, 1978b; Yang et al., 2014). Successful cross-cultural collaboration through social media can only exist if educators and users can monitor the effective exchange of information and learning in a technology-based environment (Nguyen-Ngoc & Law, 2007). This concept focuses on the ability of educational stakeholders such as educators, researchers, and students to show accountability regarding cultural competency by evaluating the effectiveness of social media exchanges of culture, ideas, and learning.

Discussion

Examination of the results from this study provided the information needed to address the two questions posed at the beginning of this literature review. A discussion regarding the results follows.

Research Question 1

What foundational theories support the use of social media tools in achieving cultural competency?

To address the first research question, a review of the section entitled *Theories that Integrate Cultural Competency with Social Media Tools* revealed the foundational theories that could help to support the use of social media tools in achieving cultural competency. Within this section, researchers identified ten theories that appeared to provide the basis for integrating social media and cultural competency. In reviewing these theoretical concepts, certain common components emerged to show how these ten theories address the first research question. The most prominent element demonstrated by the theories consisted of a focus on cultural competency. Other elements noted within each theoretical concept revealed a focus on information exchange either through learning, social interaction, or virtual communication.

For example, an examination of Table 9.1 shows the ten theories that relate to cultural, cross-cultural, and multicultural concepts. Cultural Capital Theory (Bourdieu, 1979), Cultures-of-Use Theory (Thorne, 2003), the SIDE Model (Lea & Spears, 1991), Social Capital Theory (Bourdieu, 1986), and Social Identity Theory (Tajfel & Turner, 1979; Tajfel & Turner, 1986) relate to cultural aspects. Collaborative Learning (Vygotsky, 1934/1962; Vygotsky, 1978b), Cross-Cultural Collaboration (Vygotsky, 1978b), Hofstede's Cultural Dimensions Theory (Hofstede, 1983), and the Model of Community of Inquiry (Garrison et al., 2000; Garrison & Anderson, 2003) focus on cross-cultural concepts. Finally, Diffusion of Innovation Theory (Rogers, 1962) addresses multicultural awareness.

A further review of Table 9.1 shows how the ten theories relate to information exchange with respect to learning, social interaction, or virtual communication.

TABLE 9.1 Theories that integrate cultural competency with social media tools

Theory	Description	Original source(s)	Additional source(s)
Collaboration Learning	Describes basis of cross-cultural learning in virtual environment	Vygotsky (1934/1962); Vygotsky (1978b)	Yang et al. (2014)
Cross-Cultural Collaborations	Describes cross-cultural learning	Vygotsky (1978b)	Yang et al. (2014)
Cultural Capital Theory	Embodies cultural value by explaining the connection between social privilege and academic success	Bourdieu (1979)	Bourdieu & Wacquant (1992); Prieur & Savage (2011)
Cultures-of-Use Theory	Explains how social media helps users engage in language and cultural learning	Thorne (2003)	Mitchell (2012)
Diffusion of Innovation Theory	Explores how technological advancements and innovative ideas through social media use allow people to share ideas and multicultural awareness	Rogers (1962)	Sawyer (2011)
Hofstede's Cultural Dimensions Theory	Explores cross-cultural communication from six dimensions including: power distance, individualism/collectivism, masculinity/femininity, uncertainty avoidance, long-term/short-term orientation, and indulgence/self-restraint	Hofstede (1983)	Sawyer (2011)
Model of "Community of Inquiry"	Describes cross-cultural learning	Garrison et al. (2000); Garrison & Anderson (2003)	Yang et al. (2014)
SIDE Model	High virtual environments help increase cultural knowledge acquisition and application	Lea & Spears (1991)	Krumm et al. (2013)
Social Capital Theory	Describes how forces can bring groups together in a positive way	Bourdieu (1986)	Gauntlett (2011)
Social Identity Theory	Focuses on assimilation of others into a social group where differences are overlooked	Tajfel & Turner (1979); Tajfel & Turner (1986)	Krumm et al. (2013)

Review of the description reveals that Collaborative Learning relates to cross-cultural learning through the use of a virtual-based system of communication (Vygotsky, 1934/1962; Vygotsky, 1978b). Similarly, the use of Cross-Cultural Collaboration (Vygotsky, 1978b) and the Model of Community of Inquiry (Garrison et al., 2000; Garrison & Anderson, 2003) reflects use of cross-cultural learning in an educational environment. Similarly, the Cultural Capital Theory (Bourdieu, 1979), Social Capital Theory (Bourdieu, 1986), and Social Identity Theory (Tajfel & Turner, 1979; Tajfel & Turner, 1986) show how cultural exchanges occur through social interactions between individuals or social groups of people. In addition, the SIDE Model (Lea & Spears, 1991), Cultures-of-Use Theory (Thorne, 2003), and Diffusion of Innovation Theory (Rogers, 1962) reveal that virtual communications and social media allow users to share cultural knowledge and engage in multicultural awareness. Finally, Hofstede's Cultural Dimensions Theory (Hofstede, 1983) show the different dimensions by which cross-cultural communication occurs which could, depending on the situation, potentially include information exchange through learning, social interaction, or virtual communication. By examining the descriptions of each theoretical construct, users will find that the use of technology and social media can also align with the cultural components of each theory depending on the situational context.

Research Question 2

How might cultural competency theories affect how individuals use social media tools in productive and meaningful ways?

To address the second question, researchers examined the cultural competency theories identified to understand how these theoretical constructs can influence how people use social media tools in productive and meaningful ways. Many people familiar with social media can communicate with other individuals within a collective educational, business, social, cultural, or language group. However, individuals may face difficulties when they attempt to communicate with people in different cultures or countries because of language and cultural differences. What may mean one thing to one cultural group may hold an entirely different meaning to another cultural group. Therefore, users from different cultures need to learn how to engage with people from other cultural backgrounds as well as how and when to use different communication styles when engaged in cross-cultural interactions. However, users must recognize that "the inclusion of . . . culture into the practice and education process is both a simple matter and a complex undertaking" (Gallegos et al., 2008, p. 57). Educators and learners may have to use additional approaches such as additional coursework that helps to enhance individual understanding of different cultures in the global community. Once this cultural foundation is established, users can better understand how these theories can help bridge gaps in multicultural environments to find common meaning and achieve greater levels of mutual understanding. The theories explored in this chapter provide different approaches regarding how to use social media technology and cultural competency to overcome cultural barriers to learning and understanding. By understanding how cultural interactions take place, users can adapt communications within multicultural environments to become more sensitive to different cultural customs and communications styles. Further, users can become more adaptable and flexible to enhance the ability to communicate effectively.

Recommendations

While this literature review identified as many theories as possible that met the criteria, readers must recognize that this area of research will continue to evolve given the dynamic nature of social media growth and the rise of globalization. Because of innovation, social media and different communication techniques continually change in how people use these strategies to share information and ideas in cross-cultural learning as well as business-oriented environments. Further, scholars must recognize that communication in different multicultural contexts through social media still constitutes a new paradigm for many people. Therefore, further research needs to be done to determine which of the theories identified in this study will prove more viable in different situations.

If users from diverse settings don't find specific social media tools relevant to them or the users' social media knowledge and skillsets, then the user may not feel comfortable in using these tools. Therefore, the user may opt not to use certain social media tools available to them. For example, Yoo and Huang (2011) did research on different cultural groups and found that students from various countries shared information differently on social media. While American students are more likely to share personal information, others prefer to share information on political interests. In addition, these same students learn differently and they incorporate the social media tools in the classroom based on their personal experiences from their country. Knowledge about cultural differences increases the awareness of what is comfortable to share within the groups especially in classroom settings (Yoo & Huang, 2011). For this reason, aligning the concepts of cultural competency to the use of social media tools will encourage more diverse users to integrate social media tools into their everyday lives. It will also enhance the operations of programs, organizations, businesses, and educational institutions both nationally and globally. By ensuring the alignment of social media and cultural competency in these theoretical constructs, educators and other users can help to enhance greater levels of information and cross-cultural exchanges among people throughout the world. For example, ascribing the concepts of cultural competency to digital citizenship curriculums can help users to become more culturally relevant and enhance the learning environment.

Hung and Yuen (2010) state that being part of a community establishes a feeling of increased motivation to do better academically. Students are more likely to complete their studies or graduate with this added sense of belonging. If students perform better because they feel a greater sense of belonging and online tools can connect different cultures globally, then further research may provide information about which social media tools enhance learning and bring cultures together. Also, researchers could conduct a live study to determine the perspectives of individuals that use social media tools regularly and identify users' feelings regarding the integration of cultural competency in their everyday usage. By doing so, researchers could gain greater insights into ways to enhance the social media experience with the integration of cultural competency.

Contributions and Implications of the Study

This study helps the reader to understand the theoretical basis for social media, cultural competency, and the integration of these concepts. Given the growth of social media in the global community, scholars can understand how the integration of cultural competency with social media usage complements cross-cultural communication, learning, and understanding among users in different geographical and cultural contexts.

For example, the theories identified in this literature review show how the use of social media tools combined with cultural competency can benefit the educational process. According to Edwards (2003), users become culturally competent when they make a conscious effort to understand those who are culturally different. It is also helpful when representatives of the group are in the group or directly work with the group. These theoretical concepts help to set the tone for traditional, hybrid, and online learning models to take form within a set of concepts or a framework of culturally relevant teaching. Moody (2010) elaborates on the advantages of using social media tools in the classroom. She states that the utilization of a variety of instruments such as Twitter, YouTube, and Facebook provide instruction to reach students who possess different learning styles. When social media integrates cultural competency, users become more open-minded and receptive to new ideas. Students may be more likely to participate and collaborate online than in actual face-to-face encounters (Felder & Brent, 2005). According to Moody (2010), interests in class increases when the instructor presents information using tools that students already use for entertainment. Additionally, the possibility of collaborating and discussing biases with a culturally diverse group is more likely to prove more successful when done using online tools rather than traditional instruction. Given these implications, this literature review helps to provide the foundational theories that educators and other users will find most relevant and useful as the use of social media and other available technology expands in cross-cultural settings. Further, as the literature continues to evolve, scholars may identify additional theoretical constructs that may prove relevant to this topic area.

Acknowledgement

Acknowledgement is given to Drs. Marianne Justus and Mansureh Kebritchi at the Center for Educational and Instructional Technology Research, School of Advanced Studies, University of Phoenix, for their support in developing and publishing this study.

References

Ajzen, I. (1985). From intentions to actions: A theory of planned behavior. In J. Kuhl & J. Beckmann (Eds.), *Action control: From cognition to behavior* (pp. 11–39). Berlin, Germany: Springer Berlin Heidelberg.

AlAwadhi, S., & Morris, A. (2008). The use of the utaut model in the adoption of e-government services in Kuwait. *Proceedings of the 41st Hawaii International Conference on System Sciences, USA*, 1–11. doi: 10.1109/HICSS.2008.452

Arroyo-González, R., & Hunt-Gómez, C. I. (2009). Research on written communication. *The International Journal of Learning, 16*(3), 167–184.

Bandura, A. (1963). *Social learning and personality development.* New York, NY: Holt, Rinehart, and Winston.

Bandura, A. (1977). *Social learning theory.* Englewood Cliffs, NJ: Prentice-Hall.

Baugher, S. L. (2012, Spring). Cultural competency: Globally and locally. *Journal of Family & Consumer Sciences, 104*(2), 10–12.

Berger, J., Cohen, B. P., & Zeldich, M. (1972). Status characteristics and social interaction. *American Sociological Review, 37*(3), 241–255. doi:10.2307/2093465

Blum, L. (1997). Multicultural education as values education. Working Paper: Harvard Project on Schooling and Children. Retrieved from http://law.scu.edu/wp-content/uploads/socialjustice/BlumMEVE.pdf

Bourdieu, P. (1979). *La distinction: Critique sociale du jugement.* Paris, France: Editions de Minuit.

Bourdieu, P. (1986). The forms of capital. In J. C. Richardson (Ed.), *Handbook of theory and research for the sociology of education* (pp. 241–258). New York, NY: Greenwood Press.

Bourdieu, P., & Wacquant, L. J. D. (1992). *An invitation to reflexive sociology.* Chicago, IL: University of Chicago Press.

Chan, E. A., & Nyback, M. H. (2015, June). A virtual caravan—A metaphor for home-internationalization through social media: A qualitative content analysis. *Nurse Education Today, 35*(6), 828–832. doi:10.1016/j.nedt.2015.01.024

Cheshire, W. P. (2009, June). Accelerated thought in the fast lane. *Ethics and Medicine, 25*(2), 75–78.

Cooper, H. (1988). The structure of knowledge synthesis: A taxonomy of literature reviews. *Knowledge in Society, 1*, 104–126.

Cross, T. L., Bazron, B. J., Dennis, K. W., & Isaacs, M. R. (1989, March). *Towards a culturally competent system of care: A monograph on effective services for minority children who are severely emotionally disturbed* [Monograph]. Retrieved from http://eric.ed.gov/?id=ED330171

Cross-Culture Communication (2016). *MindTools.* Retrieved from https://www.mindtools.com/CommSkll/Cross-Cultural-communication.htm

Deaton, S. (2015, April-June). Social learning theory in the age of social media: Implications for educational practitioners. *Journal of Educational Technology, 12*(1), 1–6.

Delphin-Rittmon, M. E., Andres-Hyman, R., Flanagan, E. H., & Davidson, L. (2013, March). Seven essential strategies for promoting and sustaining systemic cultural competence. *Psychiatric Quarterly, 84*(1), 53–64. doi:10.1007/s11126-012-9226-2

Durkheim, E. (1858/1984). *The division of labor in society.* New York, NY: The Free Press.

Durkheim, E. (1897/1951). *Suicide.* New York, NY: The Free Press.

Edosomwan, S., Prakasan, S. K., Kouame, D., Watson, J., & Seymour, T. (2011). The history of social media and its impact on business. *The Journal of Applied Management and Entrepreneurship, 16*(3), 79–91.

Edwards, K. (2003). Increasing cultural competence and decreasing disparities in health. *Journal of Cultural Diversity, 10*(4), 111–113.

Edwin, H. (2014, December 30). Why you should encourage social learning. *eLearning Industry.* Retrieved from http://elearningindustry.com/4-important-reasons-encourage-social-learning

Emmison, M., & Frow, J., (1998). Information technology as cultural capital. *Australian Universities Review, 1*(1998), 41–45.

Felder, R. M., & Brent, R. (2005). Death by PowerPoint. *Chemical Engineering Education, 39*(1), 28–29.

Ford, B. A., Stuart, D. H., & Vakil, S. (2014, Fall). Culturally responsive teaching in the 21st century inclusive classroom. *Journal of the International Association of Special Education, 15*(2), 56–62.

Gallegos, J. S., Tindall, C., & Gallegos, S. A. (2008). The need for advancement in the conceptualization of cultural competence. *Advances in Social Work, 9*(1), 51–62.

Garrison, D. R., & Anderson, T. (2003). *E-Learning in the 21st century: A framework for research and practice* (1st ed.). London, UK: Routledge/Falmer.

Garrison, D. R., Anderson, T., & Archer, W. (2000). Critical inquiry in a text-based environment: Computer conferencing in higher education. *The Internet and Higher Education, 2*(2–3), 87–105.

Gauntlett, D. (2011). *Making is connecting: The social meaning of creativity.* Cambridge, UK: Polity Press.

Gay, G. (2000). *Culturally responsive teaching: Theory, research, & practice.* New York, NY: Teachers College Press.

Gaytan, J. (2013). Integrating social media into the learning environment of the classroom: Following social constructivism principles. *Journal of Applied Research for Business Instruction*, *11*(1), 1–6.

Ghosh, A., Varshney, S., & Venugopal, P. (2014, August). Social media WOM: Definition, consequences and inter-relationships. *Management and Labour Studies*, *39*(3), 293–308. doi:10.1177/0258042X15577899

Goodrich, K., & de Mooij, M. (2013). How 'social' are social media? A cross-cultural comparison of online and offline purchase decision influences. *Journal of Marketing Communications*, *20*(1–2), 103–116. doi: 10.1080/13527266.2013.797773

Graham, M. (2014). Social media as a tool for increased student participation and engagement outside the classroom in higher education. *Journal of Perspectives in Applied Academic Practice*, *2*(3), 16–24.

Gunawardena, C. N. (1995). Social presence theory and implications for interaction and collaborative learning in computer conferences. *International Journal of Educational Telecommunications*, *1*(2), 147–166.

Hanson, C., West, J., Neiger, B., Thackeray, R., Barnes, M., & McIntyre, E. (2011). Use and acceptance of social media among health educators. *American Journal of Health Education*, *42*(4), 197–204.

Harton, H. C., & Bullock, M. (2007). Dynamic social impact: A theory of the origins and evolution of culture. *Social and Personality Psychology Compass*, *1*(1), 521–540. doi: 10.1111/j.1751-9004.2007.00022.x

Hofstede, G. (1983, Autumn). The cultural relativity of organizational practices and theories. *Journal of International Business Studies*, *14*(2), 75–89.

Hung, H. T., & Yuen, S. C. Y. (2010). Educational use of social networking technology in higher education. *Teaching in Higher Education*, *15*(6), 703–714.

Jenkins, H., Clinton, K., Purushotma, R., Robison, J. A., & Weigel, M. (2009). *Confronting the challenges of participatory culture: Media education for the 21st century*. Retrieved from https://www.macfound.org/media/article_pdfs/JENKINS_WHITE_PAPER.PDF

Kaplan, A. M., & Haenlein, M. (2010). Users of the world unite: The challenges and opportunities of social media. *Business Horizons*, *53(1)*, 59–68.

Krumm, S., Terwiel, K., & Hertel, G. (2013). Challenges in norm formation and adherence: The knowledge, skills, and ability requirements of virtual and traditional cross-cultural teams. *Journal of Personnel Psychology*, *12*(1), 33–44. doi:http://dx.doi.org/10.1027/1866-5888/a000077

Kvasny, L., & Truex III, D. (2000). *Information technology and the cultural reproduction of social order: A research paradigm*, 277–293. Retrieved from https://faculty.ist.psu.edu/lyarger/kvasny2000.pdf

Latané, B. (1981). The psychology of social impact. *American Psychologist*, *36*, 343–356.

Latané, B. (1996). Dynamic social impact: The creation of culture by communication. *Journal of Communication*, *46*(4), 13–25. Retrieved from http://www2.psych.ubc.ca/~schaller/528Readings/Latane1996.pdf

Lea, M., & Spears, R. (1991). Computer-mediated communication, de-individuation and group decision-making. *International Journal of Man Machine Studies*, *34*, 283–301.

Lefebvre, P., Bolduc, J., & Pirkenne, C. (2015). Pilot study on kindergarten teachers' perception of linguistic and musical challenges in nursery rhymes. *Journal for Learning through the Arts: A Research Journal on Arts Integration in Schools and Communities, 11*(1), 1–17.

Lekhanya, L.M. (2013). Cultural influence on the diffusion and adoption of social media technologies by entrepreneurs in rural South Africa. *International Business & Economics Research Journal, 12*(12), 1563–1574.

Lewthwaite, B., Owen, T., Doiron, A., Renaud, R., & McMillan, B. (2014, April). Culturally responsive teaching in Yukon first nation settings: What does it look like and what is its influence? *Canadian Journal of Educational Administration and Policy*, (155), 1–34.

Li, J., & Karakowsky. L. (2001). Do we see eye-to-eye? Implications of cultural differences for cross-cultural management research and practice. *The Journal of Psychology: Interdisciplinary and Applied, 135*(5), 501–517. doi: 10.1080/00223980109603715

Ling, L.H. (2007). Community of inquiry in an online undergraduate information technology course. *Journal of Information Technology Education, 6*, 153–168.

Luhmann, N. (1995). *Social systems*. Stanford, CA: Stanford University Press. Retrieved from http://uberty.org/wp-content/uploads/2015/08/Niklas_Luhmann_Social_Systems.pdf

Matusky, R. (2015, April 3). Web 2.0 vs. web 3.0—What really is the difference? [Web log post]. Retrieved from http://randymatusky.com/2015/04/03/web-2-0-vs-web-3-0-what-really-is-the-difference/

Megele, C. (2014). Theorizing Twitter chat. *Journal of Perspectives in Applied Academic Practice, 2*(2), 46–51.

Mitchell, K. (2012). A social tool: Why and how ESOL students use facebook. *CALICO Journal, 29*(3), 471–493.

Moody, M. (2010). Teaching Twitter and beyond: Tips for incorporating social media in traditional courses. *Journal of Magazine & New Media Research, 11*(2), 1–9.

Mount, M., & Garcia-Martinez, M. (2014). Social media: A tool for open innovation. *California Management Review, 56*(4), 124–143. doi:10.1525/cmr.2014.56.4.124

Multiculturalism: What does it mean. (2011, February 7). *BBC News Magazine*. Retrieved from http://www.bbc.com/news/magazine-12381027

National Education Association. (2008). *An NEA policy brief: Promoting educators' cultural competence to better serve culturally diverse students*. Retrieved from http://www.nea.org/assets/docs/PB13_CulturalCompetence08.pdf

Ngai, E.W.T., Tao, S.S.C., & Moon, K.K.L. (2014). Social media research: Theories, constructs, and conceptual frameworks. *International Journal of Information Management, 35*, 33–44.

Nguyen-Ngoc, A.V., & Law, E.L.C. (2007). Evaluation of cross-cultural computer-supported collaborative learning: Preliminary findings for icamp challenges. In C. Montgomerie & J. Seale (Eds.), *Proceedings of EdMedia: World Conference on Educational Media and Technology 2007* (pp. 1887–1896). Association for the Advancement of Computing in Education (AACE). Vancouver, Canada. Retrieved from https://www.learntechlib.org/p/25628

O'Reilly, T. (2005, September 30). Design patterns and business models for the next generation of software [Web log post]. Retrieved from http://www.oreilly.com/pub/a/web2/archive/what-is-web-20.html

Power, A. (2014). What is social media? *British Journal of Midwifery, 22*(12), 896–897.
Prieur, A., & Savage, M. (2011). Updating cultural capital theory: A discussion based on studies in Denmark and in Britain. *Poetics, 39*(6), 566–580. doi: 10.1016/j.poetic.2011.09.002
Rodrigo, R. & Nguyen, T. (2013). Supporting more inclusive learning with social networking: A case study of blended socialised design education. *Journal of Learning Design, 6*(3), 29–44.
Rodriguez, S. (2013). Making sense of social change: Observing collective action in networked cultures. *Sociology Compass, 7*(12), 1053–1064. doi:10.1111/soc4.12088
Rogers, E.M. (1962). *Diffusion of innovations* (1st ed.). New York, NY: Free Press.
Romer, P. (1986). Increasing returns and long-run growth. *Journal of Political Economy, 94*(5), 1002–1037.
Sandlin, J.K., & Peña, E.V. (2014). Building authenticity in social media tools to recruit postsecondary students. *Innovative Higher Education, 39*(4), 333–346. doi:10.1007/s10755-014-9280-9
Sawyer, R. (2011). *The impact of new social media on intercultural adaptation* (Senior Honors Projects, Paper 242). Retrieved from http://digitalcommons.uri.edu/srhonorsprog/242
Short, J., Williams, E., & Christie, B. (1976). *The social psychology of telecommunications.* New York, NY: John Wiley & Sons.
Sivan, E. (1986). Motivation in social constructivist theory. *Educational Psychologist, 21*(3), 209–233.
Smith, J.E., & Tirumala, L.N. (2012, Spring/Summer). Twitter's effects on student learning and social presence perceptions. *Teaching Journalism & Mass Communication, 2*(1), 21–31.
Srite, M., & Karahanna, E. (2006). The role of espoused national cultural values in technology acceptance. *MIS Quarterly, 30*(3), 679–704.
Stennis, K.B., Purnell, K., Perkins, E., & Fischle, H. (2015, Fall). Lessons learned: Conducting culturally competent research and providing interventions with black churches. *Social Work & Christianity, 42*(3), 332–349.
Tajfel, H., & Turner, J.C. (1979). An integrative theory of intergroup conflict. In S. Worchel & W.G. Austin (Eds.), *The social psychology of intergroup relations* (pp. 33–47). Pacific Grove, CA: Brooks/Cole Publishing Company.
Tajfel, H., & Turner, J.C. (1986). The social identity theory of intergroup behaviour. In S. Worchel & W.G. Austin (Eds.), *Psychology of intergroup relations* (pp. 7–24). Chicago, IL: Nelson-Hall.
Taylor, R., King, F., & Nelson, G. (2012). Student learning through social media. *Journal of Sociological Research, 3*(2), 29–35. doi: http://dx.doi.org/10.5296/jsr.v3i2.2136
Thorne, S.L. (2003, May). Artifacts and cultures-of-use in intercultural communication. *Language Learning & Technology, 7*(2), 38–67. Retrieved from http://llt.msu.edu/vol7num2/pdf/thorne.pdf
Vygotsky, L.S. (1934/1962). *Thought and language.* Cambridge, MA: MIT Press.
Vygotsky, L.S. (1978a). Interaction between learning and development. *Readings on the Development of Children, 23*(3), 34–41.
Vygotsky, L.S. (1978b). *Mind in society: The development of higher psychological processes.* Cambridge, MA: Harvard University Press.

Web 2.0. (2016). *TechTerms*. Retrieved from http://techterms.com/definition/web20

Yang, J., Kinshuk, Yu, H., Chen, S., & Huang, R. (2014). Strategies for smooth and effective cross-cultural online collaborative learning. *Journal of Educational Technology & Society, 17*(3), 208–221.

Yoo, S.J., & Huang, W.D. (2011). Comparison of web 2.0 technology acceptance level based on cultural differences. *Educational Technology & Society, 14*(4), 241–252.

10

iDESIGN

Designing and Implementing a Culturally Relevant Game-Based Curriculum

Roberto Joseph and James Diamond

iDesign is a three-year, National Science Foundation-funded project to create a video game design curriculum for after-school computer clubhouses. The project seeks to provide increased opportunities for underserved students to develop the computer science competencies they will need in order to successfully navigate an increasing technological world. At present, only a quarter of the elementary, middle, and high schools in the United States offer computer science classes, and only 4300 of 37,000 high schools offer Advanced Placement computer science classes. The iDesign project, situated in Culturally Relevant Pedagogy and game-based learning, aims to disseminate a framework for after-school programming and curricula that can be adopted by schools to strengthen students' Science, Technology, Engineering, and Mathematics (STEM) skills. The ability to innovate and create with technology is important for students' future success and their capacity to make a difference in a global world. This chapter describes the iDesign project, the model on which it is based, and the early results from the implementation.

iDesign Overview

iDesign's priority is to give young people who are often underrepresented in STEM opportunities to learn and apply concepts and design practices that are common in computer programming in the context of serious game design and development. Ten secondary schools in the New York metropolitan area are partnering on the project, most in multi-ethnic, low-income communities. The schools involved have been selected based on recommendations by the New York Department of Education because they serve low-income students, including a large percentage of underrepresented minority students, and because they have experienced rapid academic improvement under the state system in recent years. These schools indicated that they were motivated to create rich new learning environments that would improve their students' strategic thinking, intellectual understanding, and appreciation for STEM learning.

The project engages 150 6th-9th grade students each year (about 450 students over three years) and 14 of their teachers in after-school clubs that represent a paradigm shift from traditional K-12 educational settings. Students engage in information technology experiences that move them beyond technological literacy (computer use) to technological fluency (creating with computers). In iDesign, students learn to express their understanding about topics in which they are interested through game design and coding. The project leadership hypothesizes that successful experiences with game design and programming in the context of culturally relevant instructional practices will increase students' interests in exploring STEM-focused academic or career pathways in the future.

Higher education faculty in educational technology, computer science, and teacher education at Hofstra University lead the project working with Global Kids, Inc., a non-profit educational organization for global learning and urban youth development based in New York City. The New York State After-School Network (NYSAN) is responsible for connecting the iDesign project to networks of after-school and community-based organizations across New York State and nationally, and Education Development Center's Center for Children and Technology (EDC|CCT) serves as the research and evaluation partner on the project.

The *iDesign* project integrates **Culturally Relevant Pedagogy** and **Game-Based Learning** as a strategy that will support the preparation of underrepresented students for the kind of technical fluency that will help them master content that they might not otherwise acquire in traditional classrooms (Ladson-Billings, 1995; Gay, 2002; Prensky, 2003; Lee, 2007; Mayo, 2007). Culturally Relevant Pedagogy is defined by Gay "as using the knowledge, prior experiences, frames of reference, and performance styles of ethnically diverse students to make learning more relevant and effective" (2002, p. 29). Game-Based Learning uses an appealing range of interactive media to engage the interest of students and help them reach a more nuanced understanding. Examples of culturally relevant games are *Tempest in Crescent City*, in which local heroes rise to the challenge of Hurricane Katrina; *ElectroCity*, where players learn about energy, sustainability, and environmental management; and *America 2049*, a Facebook game.

The iDesign Model

The pedagogical foundation of the iDesign curriculum is a set of three, interrelated instructional routines: (1) Introduction to the principles of game design; (2) Investigating topics of personal relevance and learning to translate them into computer games; and (3) Executing the game design using computer programming and computational thinking. In this project, the core technologies for engaging in these routines are *Gamestar Mechanic*, a digital game and online community that familiarizes youth with principles of game design and systems thinking; *Scratch*, a free programming language and online community created specifically to introduce 8-16-year olds to computer programming; and *TaleBlazer*, a platform for making and playing location-based mobile Augmented Reality (AR) games.

The one-year curriculum for students in the game design after-school program is composed of three modules, and each module requires 8–10 weeks of meeting time for a total of 24–30 weeks. The curriculum is available online, so that teachers can review the program modules whenever they need to, and students can learn in a format and pace that appeals to their individual learning style. The curriculum modules are aligned with the Common Core New York State Standards, which emphasize literacy and mathematics as they relate to college and work readiness in a globally competitive society. For example, the students learn crucial communication skills by performing effective Web-based research and blogging regularly about their work. The design practices are the project's implicit "technological fluency" objectives. Figure 10.1 illustrates how the curriculum sequences activities within the components with respect to the target skills and practices. Below we summarize each of the core components.

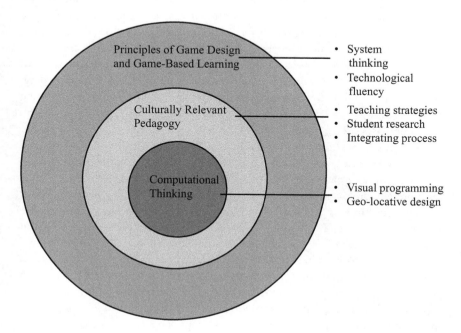

FIGURE 10.1 iDesign Model: three curriculum components of the culturally-relevant game design program

Principles of game design. The *iDesign* curriculum uses design activities to engage youth who might be interested in digital games but who are otherwise put off by STEM content; to help them build systems thinking skills; and to connect design experiences in the clubs with an awareness of the potential to repeat those kinds of experiences in future careers and academic paths. James Gee points out that well-designed games encourage players to think about relationships rather than isolated events. Each action of a player impacts on future actions and the actions of other players (Gee, 2008). In *Playing and Making Games for Learning*, Yasmin Kafai makes the point that young game designers develop technological fluency—not only knowing how to use technological tools, but developing new ways of thinking based on use of these tools. She states that "game-making activities offer an entry point . . . into the digital culture, not just as consumers but also producers" (Kafai, 2006, p. 39). Resnick, Rusk, and Cook also emphasize that youth need to proceed from using technological tools to "knowing how to construct things of significance with those tools" (1998).

In the iDesign model the first steps to learning how to design games includes two broad sets of materials: non-digital materials for brainstorming game design ideas and digital game development tools, such as *Gamestar Mechanic*. Non-digital paper-based and physical activities are introduced throughout the early lessons for participants to complete with partners or in teams to familiarize students with game design principles. For example, in one activity, club members change one feature of *Tic-Tac-Toe* or *Rock, Paper, Scissors* to experience how the alteration changes the entire game. Students are learning that changing one aspect of a game affects all other aspects of the game, which helps students think about games as systems. At this point students are using brainstorming, storyboarding, and flowcharting skills to familiarize them with methods for drafting and iterating their games.

iDesign uses existing digital tools to introduce students to game development and computational computer development. These tools were selected because they are web-based, so students can continue to engage in developing their games at home or elsewhere, as long as they have access to the Internet. These tools are also free, and were developed and tested for effectiveness by experts at such institutions as the Massachusetts Institute of Technology (MIT) and the Institute of Play. As a beginning tool Gamestar Mechanic teaches students about what makes a game a game. Players assume the role of "mechanics" whose job is to fix broken games in the game world; that is, they play the role of game designers. Figure 10.2 pictures the game's editor screen. For any broken game—and, eventually, new games that players have created—a player adjusts at least one of the five game design elements: Goals (a player's objectives); Rules (permissible actions); Space (the setting); Components (the game objects); and Mechanics (play actions). Players switch between Edit and Play mode as they

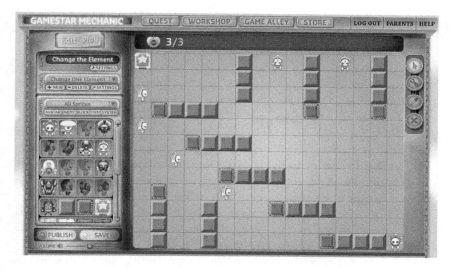

FIGURE 10.2 Gamestar Mechanic editor interface

make adjustments to elements and test their effects on the game. Students can save their original games to the Gamestar Mechanic website for others to play and comment on.

Culturally relevant themes and activities. The second component of the curriculum is to help students develop their game ideas in a way that is relevant to their life experiences. The project takes its definition of Culturally Relevant Pedagogy from Ladson-Billings (1995), who defined it as,

> A pedagogy of opposition . . . not unlike critical pedagogy but specifically committed to collective . . . empowerment. Culturally relevant pedagogy rests on three criteria or propositions: (a) Students must experience academic success; (b) students must develop and/or maintain cultural competence; and (c) students must develop a critical consciousness through which they challenge the status quo of the current social order.
>
> (p. 160)

Cultural competency "requires that students maintain some cultural integrity . . . the teacher use[s] it as a bridge to school learning" (pp. 160–161). The goal of critical consciousness requires that "students must develop a broader sociopolitical consciousness that allows them to critique the cultural norms, values, mores, and institutions that produce and maintain social inequities" (p. 162). According to Cross et al. (1989) essential elements are valuing diversity, having the capacity for cultural self-assessment, and being conscious of the dynamics inherent when cultures interact. Cultural competency assumes that the game designer is knowledgeable about the culture of the game and will seek to gain a deep understanding of the broader socio-cultural issues related to the setting of the game. Students are examining their own cultures with new eyes and building these insights into the world of the game.

To help participating youth begin to progress toward these goals, the iDesign curriculum encourages teachers to include videos that focus on social justice issues, such as racial segregation, poverty, and climate change. The curriculum activities shift toward a "research" phase in which students spend time on the Internet during the after-school meetings identifying and researching the topics they will represent in their games. The students can also begin to conduct fieldwork in their communities, interviewing local residents, and developing skills for searching/finding/evaluating information in books, journals, and on the Internet. In their after-school clubs, iDesign's students research topics that have greatly impacted their communities and design and develop games that immerse, engage, and allow users to think about their own local interests.

Computational thinking. The final component of the iDesign curriculum involves the use of game design to develop computational thinking concepts. Brennan and Resnick (2012) define seven such concepts that are highly useful in a wide range of programming projects: sequences, loops, parallelism, events, conditionals, operators, and data. The iDesign curriculum is sequenced for youth to advance from basic design principles to more complex programming in the *Scratch* environment.

Scratch is a visual programming language created by the MIT Media Lab's Lifelong Kindergarten group specifically to enable youth to practice computational thinking through design-based projects. Figure 10.3 illustrates the Scratch interface. Scratch employs building blocks (or, alternatively, puzzle pieces) as a visual metaphor for how developers construct programs. Youth insert blocks (pictured from the second column in Figure 10.3) and change parameters to create "scripts" (pictured in the third column) that control "sprites" (sprites are graphics, in this example, the space invaders graphics pictured in the first column). In principle, and with practice, youth are able to begin creating the complex scripts (or programs) that constitute a digital game. Because it is an online community, youth can save their creations on the Scratch site, share them with others, and give and respond to feedback.

Another game development tool used in the iDesign curriculum to develop students' computational thinking skills is *TaleBlazer, a geo-locative design interface* that uses a visual blocks-based coding system (pictured in Figure 10.4), that is similar to Scratch. TaleBlazer is an AR software platform that enables users to make and play location-based mobile games. Students create games using computer browsers, but they can only be played on mobile devices, such as a tablet or mobile phone. Because game play is based on a player's location, the device must be Global Positioning System (GPS)-enabled.

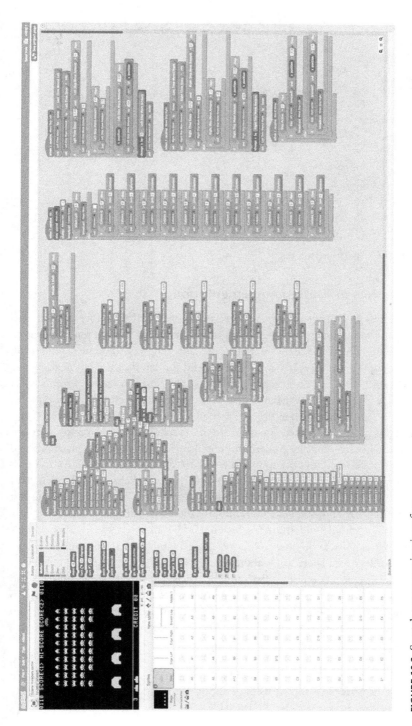

FIGURE 10.3 Scratch programming interface

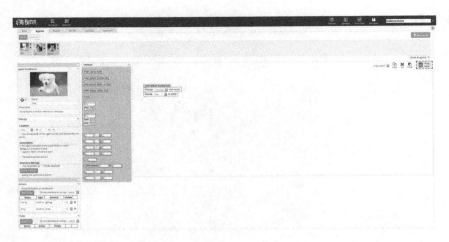

FIGURE 10.4 TaleBlazer interface

Early Results of iDesign Implementation

The iDesign club-leader positions were publicized within school districts and 14 teachers were chosen by their school administrators to run the ten after-school clubs (some schools have more than one club advisor). Teachers who took part in the program received an annual stipend funded by the National Science Foundation (NSF). All the teachers in the iDesign program had access to at least one school computer lab. Participating students worked individually on computers and in pairs and groups when doing paper and computer-based activities.

In terms of demographics, the majority of the schools served large populations of youth who are typically underrepresented in STEM academic programs and careers. For example, in year two of the project approximately 85 boys and girls (~50 boys and ~35 girls) attended the clubs regularly between October 2014 and June 2015. Of those, about 60% (n=50) were in the 6th grade, and the rest were in the 7th and 8th grades. Table 10.1 contains summary data about the participating schools and students. Seven middle and two elementary schools in New York City and Nassau County, Long Island participated. Although we did not collect data specifically about students' access to technology outside of school, most teachers reported that student access was mixed: some students had computers at home, others did not. All ten sites met once a week for 90 minutes after the school day was over. The clubs were regularly observed by the iDesign team members and staff from EDC, the external evaluator on the National Science Foundation project.

All of the teachers noted that their students enjoyed the hands-on activities, such as "remixing" Tic-Tac-Toe and Rock, Paper, Scissors. Teachers noted that the students often had mixed feelings about the examples of existing culturally relevant games introduced by Global Kids. The students felt that they were not

TABLE 10.1 School summary data (all names are pseudonyms)

School	Type	Grades	Demographic data	% students eligible for free or reduced-price lunch	# students in regular attendance at club
Anthony Middle School (1 teacher)	Public, Suburban	6–8	62% Hispanic; 36% Black; 2% Asian	86%	4 (7th–8th grades)
Jefferson Middle School (1 teacher)	Public, Urban	K–8	76% Black; 21% Hispanic; 2% White; 1% Asian or Asian/Pacific Islander	85%	7 (8th grade)
Obama Middle School (1 teacher)	Public, Suburban	6–8	56% Hispanic; 42% Black; 1% White	81%	10 (6th grade)
Franklin Middle School (1 teacher)	Public, Suburban	6–8	55% Black; 43% Hispanic; 1% Asian or Asian/Pacific Islander	66%	6 (7th–8th grades)
Adams Middle School (2 teachers)	Public, Suburban	7–8	54% Hispanic; 38% Black; 7% White; 1% Asian or Asian/Pacific Islander	61%	3 (7th–8th grades)
Buchanan Elementary School (1 teacher)	Public, Suburban	5–6	56% Hispanic; 34% Black; 8% White; 1% Asian/Pacific Islander	51%	10 (6th grade)
Lincoln Middle School (1 teacher)	Public, Suburban	K–6	49% Black; 24% Asian or Asian/Pacific Islander; 17% Hispanic; 8% White	26%	6 (6th grade)
Madison Elementary School (1 teacher)	Public, Suburban	K–6	60% White; 18% Hispanic; 11% Asian or Asian/Pacific Islander; 10% Black	9%	16 (6th grade)
Hamilton Middle School (2 teachers)	Public, Suburban	6–8	52% Asian or Asian/Pacific Islander; 41% White; 6% Hispanic	5%	20 (6th–8th grades)

always as much fun as students expected games to be. Three of the middle school teachers mentioned that they would periodically ask their students "what they thought the games were about" as a way to engage them in thinking about serious game topics, though none of them mentioned discussing game mechanics with students as they played. Several teachers supplemented the curriculum activities by introducing their own materials. For example, one teacher found an online version of Tic-Tac-Toe for her students to use during the remixing activity; another brought in construction paper and markers for one of the paper-based game design activities.

Gamestar Mechanic. Among the 6th–8th graders, Gamestar Mechanic was the most popular activity. One middle school teacher commented, "They loved Gamestar more than anything else. They were more interested in those games than the other games." Another teacher said that several of her students played through many of the levels at home, in between the clubhouse meetings. During clubhouse observations, we noted several students who became very engaged about their progress through the game levels. They became more excited about undertaking new quests when they realized that completing in-game quests gave them opportunities to acquire new sprites (i.e., objects for their own game designs).

Most teachers allowed their students to play Gamestar at their own pace during the club meetings. Students regularly played each other's games and made comments about their likes and dislikes. Several of the teachers whom we observed would ask students about how they were using specific game design elements as they walked around the lab. Only one teacher had a formal game critique session, however, during which students commented on design elements and made suggestions for change.

Scratch. Two iDesign high school teachers commented that their students preferred Scratch to Gamestar, mostly because Gamestar Mechanic was "too easy and you couldn't do that much." All of the teachers explained that they followed the instructional routines very closely when they introduced Scratch to their students because they were less comfortable with its features. We observed one high school teacher with previous programming experience working closely with a student who wanted to create a game on climate change. The student chose a question-and-answer format for the game. As she constructed her scripts in Scratch, the teacher answered questions about where to find specific blocks and gave her feedback during testing and debugging.

Student-Designed Games

In creating their own interactive games, learners must focus on building and testing their games within the environment. The game under development reflects the team's understanding of the nature of an issue, its constraints, and options to its resolution, defining the input variables, and understanding the

TABLE 10.2 Students' culturally and/or socially relevant game design ideas

	My game for change topic	My core game idea	I am inspired by . . .	My game is fun because . . .
Student 1	I identify with the community of girls being bullied in my middle school.	I am a middle school girl and I fight against bullying.	Bullying occurs many times and leaves students feeling stressed and worthless	It's a fast moving game, moving through halls and collecting points.
Student 2	I identify with the community of the Dominican Republic and Haiti facing violence.	I am a news reporter against violence in the Dominican Republic by stopping fights.	I would not like my family in the Dominican Republic to be fighting in a war.	It's a questionnaire that tests your thinking in stopping fights.
Student 3	I identify with the community of California and migrant workers in the fields.	I am a superhero who fights for civil rights in California.	I don't really understand why bosses of migrant workers treat them so unfairly.	You can parkour and take flight which lots of kids dream of doing.
Student 4	I identify with the community of my town, Valley Stream, facing mild crime.	I am a police officer; I fight against crime in a town by arresting criminals.		It's pretty cool to be a cop and arrest all the bad guys. The time limit also adds a bit of drama to the game.
Student 5	I identify with the community of New York facing police discrimination.	I am an activist. I fight against police discrimination in NY by protesting.	Currently police are being more hostile to minorities and not being reprimanded for unauthorized violence.	There are different possibilities to try out.
Student 6	I identify with the community of Puerto Rico facing wanting to become the 51st state.	I am a security guard I fight for Puerto Rico to become a state in Washington by protecting people giving speeches.	I've heard about it all over the news, my parents are always talking about it, and my aunt and uncle live in Puerto Rico and are always complaining about it.	You get to stop all the bad guys from fighting the protesters, and you get to collect the citizens to make them become a part of the protest.

viewpoints involved, and how competing resolutions may inform decision-making. Students work with story-telling, developing characters, evaluating plots, and working with digital images and music. They develop their abilities to receive and incorporate critiques while sharing their own designs.

Over the three-year iDesign project, the middle and high school students involved in the clubs worked on designing games on a number of topics that were important to them. As a major step in the development process, the students planned their games and created prototypes by responding to a series of prompts that helped them frame their game ideas around socially relevant topics. Table 10.2 summarizes their responses to some of these prompts.

Additional responses concerned the students' descriptions of the five elements of their games. For example, Student 1 identified her **goal** as "to make your way to the end of the cafeteria," **rules** as "not allowed to walk through walls or run into people," **components** as "popular girls, a nerd avatar, self-esteem points, a nerd friend," **mechanics** as "running and collecting," and **space** as "a cafeteria with different rooms." In another example, Student 6 identified her **goal** as "to get people to join the protest," **rules** as "can't hit anybody, use weapons, or kill people," **components** as "a crowd," **mechanics** as "people moving around and disappearing," and **space** as "in front of the congress building."

In responding to another prompt, which asked the students to identify the major difficulties they had with coding their game, Student 6 said, "the hardest thing to code in my game was making the sprites loop back and forth and up and down the screen." Student 1 said, "the hardest thing for me to code was the popular girls (enemies), because they had a lot of costume changes." Student 5 said, it was hard "to try to get each of the sprites to receive messages from other sprites."

Conclusion

The iDesign project was developed to achieve equity in STEM education for underrepresented youth. Members of non-dominant populations (such as girls, students of color, or those from high-poverty communities) in STEM pursuits often feel alienated when studying these topics in formal educational settings (Moje et al., 2004; Calabrese Barton & Tan, 2010). The project leadership hypothesizes that successful experiences with game design and programming in the context of culturally relevant instructional practices will increase students' interests in exploring STEM-focused academic or career pathways in the future.

As conceived, iDesign's student activities and learning objectives are influenced by *constructionist learning principles,* which posit that learning is strongest when young people have regular opportunities to apply the concepts and practices they have been taught to the design and development of personally meaningful products (Papert, 1991). Similarly, the curriculum is informed by the hands-on, materials-based ethos of the "Maker Movement," where learners build, test, and iterate on their designs. Each design and development cycle is an opportunity to deepen—with the support of educators and peers—the understanding of concepts as they play out through design. Martinez and Stager (2013) argued that, "making is a way of bringing engineering to young learners. Such concrete experiences provide a meaningful context for understanding abstract science and math concepts" (p. 3). In combination with culturally relevant instructional routines led by educators, these formats provide opportunities for youth who might otherwise feel intimidated by or distanced from STEM to develop personal connections to content and practices.

The next steps for the iDesign project are to learn what works best in order to improve the curriculum and provide useful examples, tools, and support for programs that want to implement an innovative game-based curriculum. In the project's third and final year, we are conducting summative tests of the impact of participation in iDesign on students' STEM interests, as well as their use of a subset of computational thinking concepts and practices. The games that the students have developed will provide a rich example of the use of the culturally relevant game-based model.

References

Brennan, K., & Resnick, M. (2012). New frameworks for studying and assessing the development of computational thinking. Proceedings of the 2012 annual meeting of the American Educational Research Association, Vancouver, Canada.

Calabrese Barton, A., & Tan, E. (2010). We be burnin': Agency, identity and learning in a Green energy program. Journal of the Learning Sciences, 19(2), 187–229.

Cross, T., Barzon, B., Dennis, K., & Isaacs, M. (1989). Towards a culturally competent system of care: A monograph on effective services for minority children who are severely emotionally disturbed. National Institute of Mental Health, Child and Adolescent Service Program (CASSP) Technical Assistance Center, Georgetown University Child Development Center.

Gamestar Mechanic (n.d.). Retrieved March 27, 2016, from http://gamestarmechanic.com/

Gay, G. (2002). Preparing for culturally responsive teaching. Journal of Teacher Education, 53(2). 106–16.

Gee, J. (2008). What video games have to teach us about learning and literacy. New York: Palgrave Macmillan.

Kafai, Y.B. (2006). Playing and making games for learning: Instructionist and constructionist perspectives for game studies. Games and Culture, 1(1): 34–40.

Ladson-Billings, G. (1995). But that's just good teaching! The case for culturally relevant pedagogy. Theory into Practice, 34(3), 159–165.

Lee. C.D. (2007). Culture, literacy and learning taking bloom in the midst of the whirlwind. New York: Teachers College Press.

Martinez, S.L., & Stager, G. (2013). Invent to learn: Making, tinkering and engineering in the classroom. Torrance, CA: Constructing Modern Knowledge Press.

Mayo, M.J. (2007). Games for science and engineering education. Communications of the ACM, 50(7), 30–35.

Moje, E., Ciechanowski, K., Kramer, K., Ellis, L., Carrillo, R., & Collazo, T. (2004). Working toward third space in content area literacy: An examination of everyday funds of knowledge and discourse. Reading Research Quarterly, 39(1), 38–70.

Papert, S. (1991). Situating constructionism. In S. Papert & I. Harel (Eds.), Constructionism (pp. 1–11). Norwood, NJ: Ablex.

Prensky, M. (2003). Digital game-based learning. ACM Computers in Entertainment, 1(1), 1–4.

Resnick, M., Rusk, N., and Cook, S. (1998). The computer clubhouse: Technological fluency in the inner city. In Schon, D., Sanyal, B., & Mitchell, W. (Eds.), High technology and low income communities (pp. 266–286). Cambridge: MIT Press.

Scratch—Imagine, Program, Share. (n.d.). Retrieved March 27, 2016, from https://scratch.mit.edu/

TaleBlazer. (n.d.). Retrieved March 27, 2016, from http://taleblazer.org/

11
BOYS AND VIDEO GAME PLAY

Re-engaging Boys in the Classroom

Shulong Yan, Yelim Mun, Jason A. Engerman, and Alison Carr-Chellman

A crisis is prevalent for boys in K-12 traditional education. In the traditional school system, boys are facing cognitive as well as non-cognitive challenges, which some researchers suggest are due to a skewed focus on improving educational equity for girls (Connell, 1996). Over the past several decades, educational research has paid more attention on girls' academic achievements particularly among middle school girls' Science, Technology, Engineering, and Mathematics (STEM) learning. While this has been an extremely important focus, unintended consequences have created less attention on challenges that boys face in classrooms. As a result, the current educational reality includes boys who are significantly underperforming their girl counterparts (Martin, Ruble, & Szkrybalo, 2002; Sommers, 2013). This paper takes up the deeper understanding of the "boy crisis" and examines video games as one possible avenue for increasing learner engagement particularly among disenfranchised boys.

The challenges boys face compared to girls occur in various forms. For example, boys between the ages of 3 and 17 are diagnosed with Attention Deficit Hyperactivity Disorder (ADHD) three times more often when compared to girls (Bloom, Cohen, & Freeman, 2012). They are also far more likely to be retained and suspended from school because of their misbehaviors (Kindlon & Thompson, 2009). Spelke (2005) summarizes that females and males have subtle cognitive differences in terms of verbal and mathematical problem solving, and memory processing skills during their development. At the same time, he also concludes that all genders have equal academic capacity. In other words, both boys and girls have equivalent academic potentials yet one group is lagging behind the other. Given the small cognitive differences between boys and girls, it is not enough to understand why boys are academically far behind girls.

In the domains of psychology, scholars admit that relying solely on biological explanations for the current boy crisis is problematic. From a sociocultural perspective, the study of the boy crisis in education should also include the cultural and historical factors that influence their learning (Sawchuk & Stetsenko, 2008). Therefore, another group of scholars investigated the culture within schools and classrooms for possible explanations (Buchmann, DiPrete, & McDaniel, 2008). It is imperative to call attention to the need to explain this crisis and develop possible solutions from a cultural perspective (Weaver-Hightower, 2003).

The argument being advanced in this chapter is that although girls' educational rights still deserve explicit attention, an equal amount of emphasis should be given to the crisis that boys are currently facing. This is because improving girls' performance while neglecting boys' needs impairs gender equality in schools (Cassell & Jenkins, 2000). Furthermore, we acknowledge that the notion of boy culture is broad and diverse. In some cases, the term "boy culture" can be considered overreaching, even essentializing, which is not our intent. However, we are referring to the general population of boys who fit into a general tendency, although certainly not all boys fit the same profile. Of course, then we are talking about tendencies within groups that can vary significantly. In this chapter, we discuss the nature of boys in regard to play. Following this, we explain how video games may help mitigate the achievement gap. Lastly, the chapter concludes with suggestions and implications for school districts, educators, and educational researchers towards educational reform.

Boys' Culture and the Traditional Education System: The Incompatibility

Boys' culture is a collection of beliefs, values, and behaviors that are accepted by boys within a particular society (Gilbert & Gilbert, 1998). From a sociocultural perspective, boys construct their views of being boys through social practices such as interaction with male role models, peer interaction, and school education (Connell, 1996). Schools are major formal spaces where boys spend half of their developmental lives before they reach manhood. However, these systems often fail to provide space and opportunity for identity formation. The conflict between boys' culture and the current educational system may be seen to be inevitable. In addition, with the absence of male role models, boys might face difficulties engaging within traditional school settings (Connell, 1996). In this section, we attempt to unpack three elements to describe this situation: the importance of male role models, *rough-and-tumble* play as a form of peer interaction for boys, and the incompatible school culture.

The Importance of Male Role Models

Boys' culture varies due to historical and geographical trends. How boys view themselves as male "is a matter of constructing oneself in and being constructed by the available ways of being male in a particular society" (Gilbert & Gilbert, 1998,

p. 46). Within a cultural setting, boys learn the social norms that allow community acceptance. As they learn to be part of a culture and group, they internalize the dominant social norms as *the* way of being. Finally, those norms become a part of their identities. Societal ritual that is facilitated by adult males becomes an important part in their transition to manhood (Kimmel & Davis, 2011). In other civilized societies, males often go through a societal ritual to guide them into adulthood. These rites are typically facilitated by adult males within that given culture.

Boys in the United States are taught that crying and showing sensitivity to emotional pain are signs of weakness. Kindlon and Thompson (2009) mention, in their book *Raising Cain,* that a boy desires and requires healthy emotional connections. According to several authors, the impact of societal notions of masculinity has led to the development of a boy population in sore need of empathy, emotional intelligence, and positive male role models (Kimmel & Davis, 2011; Kindlon & Thompson, 2009). Unfortunately, in the formal U.S. school environment, the intentional guided development of boys from childhood into adulthood is less frequent. In the last 15 years the number of male classroom teachers at the elementary level has been cut in half, leaving boys to make the transition to manhood with fewer positive male role models. In comparison to formal education, the guidance of male role models towards boys' identity in an informal environment is more prevalent in communities such as boy scouts and sports teams.

Limited role models for boys can affect the way in which boys learn to cope with stressors, interact with peers, and develop self-esteem. Despite these negative pressures, there are natural ways in which boys interact and behave that alleviates stressors, builds empathy and can help build positive relationships among peers.

Rough-and-Tumble Play as a Form of Peer Interaction

Generally, play helps children develop social skills and allows boys to release excessive energy and emotional stress (Pellegrini, 1988). Boys have an inclination for *rough-and-tumble* play (DiPietro, 1981). Scholars such as Hamburg and Van Lawick-Goodall define boys' *rough-and-tumble* play behaviors as "pushing, pulling, hitting, chasing, and wrestling" without physical harm (as cited in DiPietro, 1981, p. 50). We view "aggressive play" and *rough-and-tumble* play in a similar way. However, there is a clear distinction between how we use "aggressive" and the way "aggression" is defined in most literature. Traditionally, aggression refers to behaviors that intended to cause physical or mental pain to someone else. Aggressive play in this chapter, however, means play that is rough but within the rules and under self-control.

Boys are frequently regarded as physically more active than girls from their infancy to adolescence (Eliot, 2010). One possible explanation for this is given through primatology. Male primates, who are considered our closest relatives, are most likely to pursue a medium-sized prey as compared to females who hunt smaller animals (Sax, 2007). In order to survive through adulthood, their participation in this intense activity required the young male primates to practice rough hunting skills (Sax, 2007). Similarly, boys learn to explore rules and establish boundaries via *rough-and-tumble* play (Olson, Kutner, & Warner, 2008). Studies have shown that boys who have been deprived of this form of aggressive play encounter problems when socializing with male peers. In fact, these males show more violent behaviors in adulthood (Pellis & Pellis, 2007). They experience difficulties in getting along with playmates. Particularly, they have difficulty adjusting their emotions and behaviors and deciding when to terminate their aggressive play (Flanders et al., 2010). By experimenting with what is appropriate and socially acceptable behavior through aggressive play, boys learn the social rules and norms. Pellegrini's (1988) research has shown that the children who are rejected by peers have a higher tendency to act aggressively as compared to popular children.

The Incompatible School System

Traditional schools are dominated primarily by a feminine ethos that is often alienating to boys (Epstein, 1998). Boys are under pressure at school to perform, at the same moment that they face a system with limited male role models to look for guidance on how to cope with negative emotions such as frustration and stress. Subconsciously, boys resist a female teacher's nurturing maternal nature (Gilbert & Gilbert, 1998). This resistance somewhat represents a boy's perception of toughness and coolness especially when he refuses to be seen as a "mama's boy" (Cassell & Jenkins, 2000). At the same time, most female teachers fail to detect boys' emotional needs that may further suppress boys; and the suppression generates powerlessness and alienated feelings (Kindlon & Thompson, 2009). According to Epstein (1998), boys are in an acrimonious position in that "school is a terrible place for boys. In school they are trapped by 'the matriarchy' and are dominated by women who cannot accept boys as they are. The women teachers mainly wish to control and to suppress boys" (Epstein, 1998, p. 7). To deal with this suppression, boys turn off their attention to schools and focus mainly on different activities such as physical education, recess, and video games, where they participate in collaborative activities, master strategies and control environments, and begin to feel powerful again (Newkirk, 2002). In the virtual world of gaming, it is legitimate for boys to escape from unpleasant reality and satisfy their violent fantasy play desires (Gee, 2003; Yee, 2006). The space created by video games makes boys feel safe to explore who they are, what the acceptable social norms are, and how to cope with negative emotions (Erikson, 1968; Gee, 2003).

Boys' natural aggressive play has been widely prohibited and misunderstood. There are two possible explanations—the Zero Tolerance policies and the opposition to *rough-and-tumble* play by the majority of female teachers, parents, school administrators and policy makers. Zero Tolerance policies began in K-12 schools in the United States by Congress as part of the Gun-Free Schools Act of 1994 (Kang-Brown, Trone, Fratello, & Daftary-Kapur, 2013). The policy was enacted to suppress disruptive behaviors and the possession of unacceptable things like guns, knives, and other life threatening weapons. The notion of Zero Tolerance is laudable, and it is essential that schools are safe places for students to learn. However, in some cases, Zero Tolerance has become a widely accepted and embedded philosophy within schools, which has resulted in numerous unfair prosecutions of students (Skiba & Peterson, 1999). Thus, it is not the presence of Zero Tolerance policies that cause issues for active learners; rather, it is the way that these policies are enforced and enacted that creates the forced disengagement of certain kinds of learners, most often boys. We do agree that schools should provide positive and safe academic environments for students; however, research in last the two decades has found that there is no positive correlation of zero tolerance and safe school settings for students (American Psychological Association Zero Tolerance Task Force, 2008). On the contrary, boys' natural aggressive play has been stigmatized as a severe disruptive behavior and prohibited at school under this policy.

Along with Zero Tolerance policies, sometimes the feminized nature of teachers and classrooms can also feel incompatible with boys' physical aggression and active energy levels (Logue & Harvey, 2009). Feminized teachers in traditional schools are more likely to have a difficult time understanding boys' exuberant behaviors and kinesthetic learning requirements (Engerman, Mun, Yan, & Carr-Chellman, 2015; Epstein, 1998). Teachers tend not to acknowledge boys' aggressive play as a necessary part of their developmental maturation. Instead, schools tend to make concerted efforts to eliminate these behaviors in boys—calling them distraction, unfocused, problematic, and an impediment to a positive learning environment for everyone in the classroom. The social explanation that "boys will be boys" is sometimes used to describe boys' disruptive behaviors (Kelley, Loeber, Keenan, & DeLamatre, 1997; Singh, 2003). Rather than uncovering the real problem that distance these boys, sometimes schools judge boys as not following rules, violent, or aggressive. However, according to Kindlon and Thompson (2009), boys learn to use disruptive, violent, and aggressive behaviors to suppress negative emotion to show their toughness from social practice. Instead of treating them as troubled boys, we should educate our boys in healthy ways to be aware of and be able to regulate their emotions.

The increasing emphasis on standardized tests and teacher performance assessments influenced by the No Child Left Behind policy creates pressure for schools and teachers to control any behaviors that may distract from high performance on high stakes tests. This pedagogical evolution hinders boys' exploration of identity through play, which is the main activity for their identity formation, particularly in the early years. In schools, the contents of curriculum forces students to be seated still rather than be physically active (Logue & Harvey, 2006). This change decreases boys' opportunity to have physical movements in space (Cassell & Jenkins, 2000; Eliot, 2010). Teachers and school administrators are overly sensitive about aggressive behaviors so they restrain boys' true nature of exploration.

Rough-and-tumble play allows boys to explore social norms (Pellegrini, 1988). Play is fundamental because the autonomous space it offers enables boys to explore and construct their identity through social activities. However, teachers are pressured to guide their students to achieve high test scores, which often leads to authoritarian teaching methods. Even though this negative model of coercive learning influences both genders, boys have a harder time adjusting themselves to accommodate the change—in general they are less compliant.

The definition of literacy in school settings is narrow and it limits the multimodal literacy practice (Gilbert & Gilbert, 1998; Newkirk, 2002). The traditional school literacy typically does not resonate with boys' interests in part because what is expected at schools does not match their perception of masculinity. Boys then have little interest in literacy practices at school because of the difficulty of transforming the contents into their social conversations with other boys (Blair & Sanford, 2004). Most boys are interested in sports magazines, heroic comic books, and gaming magazines, which are considered as inappropriate in schools (Blair & Sanford, 2004). Some of those materials are even regarded as violent (Newkirk, 2002). However, violent fantasy play is normal for boys, similar to their nature of *rough-and-tumble* play (Jordan, 1995; Klinger, Hamilton, & Cantrell, 2001). Their violent fantasy play is too often seen by teachers as antisocial, void of empathy, and deficient in terms of cooperative attitudes (Newkirk, 2002). Researchers sometimes have difficulty in distinguishing between fantasy play and real violent behaviors, which can be one of the primary causes of tension and fear exploited by the media (Newkirk, 2002). In fact, fantasy play provides the opportunity for developing children's social skills and social cognition (Rubin, 1980).

Video Games as a Tool to Mitigate the Tension

Some researchers have blamed violent video games for escalating aggressive and vicious behavior in schools such as massive shootings (Anderson & Bushman, 2001; Anderson & Dill, 2000). They claim that boys are looking for images to model their identities while playing video games (Dill & Thill, 2007; Gilbert & Gilbert, 1998). However, people with accusations against video games are oversimplifying the phenomenon of boys' violent behaviors (Newkirk, 2002).

We admit that most video game designers are men and the early character creation in video games follow violent fantasy models. The customized characters, especially for boys, resonate as figures they admire and that satisfy their heroic fantasies. Following this logic, scholars conclude that boys who are inspired by those aggressive heroic characters would imitate what they see from video games in a real life (Gilbert & Gilbert, 1998). However, we argue that this logic is based on a behavioral perspective of boys' identity formation, which sees the process as simple, unthinking imitation based on what they have seen. This statement neglects the importance of human agency. Every human consistently makes sense of the outside world through internalizing the information in order to operate in his or her own way (Vygotsky, 1980; Weick, Sutcliffe, & Obstfeld, 2005). It is not what roles boys play that becomes the major concern; on the contrary, it is the practice boys engage in that shape their identity.

This leads to our second argument that this opinion would conceal the true diverse practices in video games that have positive potential to shape boys' culture. Later, we discuss details about what practices boys are mostly immersed in. Here, we think too often that the general public, as prompted by the media, tend to see video games as tools that create static, closed, and defined spaces. Video games actually tend to be more flexible, complicated, and adjustable than many other social media.

Rather, we suggest that gaming should be considered a positive outlet for emotion and aggression in controlled school environments. As such, video game play could be a solution rather than a problem. We believe it is a symptom of frustration and disenfranchisement rather than the *cause* of that alienation. It represents a world where the players/learners are in control and completely engaged. It is imperative that we do not praise video games while ignoring their potential for addictive behaviors; however, we must understand their importance as a potentially positive tool as well. A balanced perspective is most appropriate given the wide diversity of games out there as well as the significantly varied ways that games are used by players. Video games not only provide situated learning opportunities, they also create a collaborative, yet competitive peer interaction environment (Squire, 2003). In this environment, boys explore their identities, understand acceptable social norms of peer interaction, and develop strategies to cope with stress and frustration positively (Engerman, Mun, Yan, & Carr-Chellman, 2015; Gee, 2003). To investigate how peers interact in gaming environment and what learning happened in this environment, we conducted a three-phased phenomenological study with a group of athletic teenage boys from Northeastern Pennsylvania suburb.

Video Games Provide Situated Learning Spaces and Opportunities

Video games, as powerful learning tools, create environments that situate learning through deeper exploration (Shaffer, Halverson, Squire, & Gee, 2005). They can assist traditional teachers' roles as knowledge dispensers by embedding information within specific engaging activities. Games allow learners to engage deeply through exploration within designed learning experiences (Gee, 2003; Prensky, 2005; Squire, 2003; Squire, 2008; Steinkuehler & King, 2009). Educational researchers have laid both theoretical foundations as well as empirical groundwork for the educational value of video games (Barab, Pettyjohn, Gresalfi, Volk, & Solomou, 2012; Gee, 2003; Squire, 2008).

Learning in video games goes beyond abstract principles, languages, or symbols, and opens learning spaces to interpret meaning through concrete representation and experiential interaction (Gee, 2003; Shaffer et al., 2005). Instead of becoming disengaged through rote-learning assignments, boys are experiencing abstract concepts through visual representation, strategy creation, grit, and sharpening problem-solving skills through video games play (Engerman, 2016). The immediate feedback nature of video games reinforces learning potentials. As John Dewey and Albion Woodbury Small (1897) argue, schools should transform from fact-oriented to skill-oriented learning environments. Video games situate learning into contexts that enable users to make skill-oriented connections (Gee, 2003; Shaffer et al., 2005; Squire, 2011). For example, rather than replacing literacy, video game players situated their literacy learning into practice (Steinkuehler, 2005). Players have to immerse themselves in gaming environments while making sense of texts embedded in games in order to take actions (Squire, 2008). In the 21st century, the definition of literacy has extended from traditional printed language to visual symbols such as images and videos (Gee, 2003). The rich, in-game texts and off-game forum interactions require players to use literacy skills such as *discursive argumentation, researching, assembling,* and *synthesizing* resources for problem solving (Steinkuehler & King, 2009). Those literacy practices are largely emphasized in Common Core State Standards as well as traditional classroom learning, but the embeddedness within the gaming space tends to discount its validity to parents, teachers, and school leaders.

Our ongoing research also supports the claim that commercial games have the potential to map onto English Language Arts Literacy Standards (Engerman, MacAllan, & Carr-Chellman, 2014; Engerman, Mun, Yan, & Carr-Chellman, 2015). Games are, at times, inseparable from critical reading, as participants must make meaning out of the written information. In our studies, video games asked boys to read closely to determine what the text explicitly says and to make logical inferences from it (CCRA.R.1). They also had to determine central ideas or themes of a text and analyze their development by summarizing the key supporting details and ideas Career and College Readiness Anchors for Reading (CCRA.R.2) (Engerman & Carr-Chellman, 2014; NGA & CCSSO, 2015). Our findings also reveal that boys learn specific skills within history/social studies. Through playing games such as "Assassin's Creed" and "Call of Duty," our participants showed that even at the 11–12 grade levels they could determine the central ideas or information of a primary or secondary source. They were also able to provide an accurate summary that makes clear the relationship among the key details and ideas Reading in History for grades 11 and 12 (RH.11–12.2) (Engerman & Carr-Chellman, 2014; NGA & CCSSO, 2015). Our research shows that there are valuable skills learned in the commercial gaming space, particularly those that overlap with traditional school standards.

Video games also create emotional literacy opportunities for boys. Towards improving troubled boys' performance at schools, Kindlon and Thompson (2009) suggested that boys should be educated with emotional literacy. This would require boys to reflect on and express their feelings without hesitation, and be capable of responding to others' feelings (Kindlon & Thompson, 2009). From our qualitative data, we found that boys who game not only demonstrate their ability to "identify and name their emotions" (Kindlon & Thompson, 2009, p. 5), but also develop strategies to deal with their frustration and anger via playing video games. Parts of the interviews we conducted suggested that our participants experienced relaxation by playing video games when they felt stressed with school matters. Video games became an asylum for escaping the emotional turbulence that arose from school work and other social interaction. Interestingly, the boys in our study were not emotion-free when they played video games. On the contrary, even though they enjoyed being challenged, they claimed that video game experiences could be discouraging, even highly frustrating sometimes. From our interview data, boys suggested that they developed strategies to cope with the frustration built up from video games as well as finding them relaxing at other times. When feeling frustrated, they stopped playing, walked away, and returned with a calm mind.

Video Games Create Collaborative yet Competitive Environment

Video games simulate *rough-and-tumble* play virtually. Video games have played a large role in boy culture for decades (Lawry et al., 1995; Steinberg, Kehler, & Cornish, 2010). Video games have replaced "outdoor" space and become a new representative trend of boys' culture (Cassel & Jenkins, 2000). First, as the form of popular culture, they have engulfed the majority of boys' leisure time (Cummings & Vandewater, 2007). Although female gamers are increasing, male players are still the dominant population (Lenhart et al., 2008). According to a study from the Pew Internet & American Life Project (Lenhart et al., 2008), 97% of teenagers play video games on different devices and 99% of teenage boys are gamers. Second, video games assemble boys' culture (Cassell & Jenkins, 2000). *Rough-and-tumble* play is changing from more physical outdoor play to more indoor virtual play. Boys interact aggressively and competitively against the computer interface or with other players virtually. For them, physical engagement is necessary for meaning making and is a natural part of their development.

Also, video games provide collaborative peer interaction opportunities. From our data, even though boys play video games competitively and aggressively, they build up peer relationships via collaboration as well. The social function of game play was a major driving force for engagement. The boys in our study were primarily focused on not only building but also maintaining and improving their peer bonds through competitive interaction in their virtual worlds.

Different from traditional views that video games distance boys from social activities, video game play can complement traditional outdoor play and become a new interactive social event for them (Gee, 2003). The peer interaction boys involve in has been extended largely through a shift from single offline player games to multiplayer online games. Video games are designed in such a way that teamwork becomes necessary to achieve their goal of winning.

One of our participants understood that the teamwork skills gained in games were transferrable skills that they could draw from. The boys in our study recognized that communicating clearly, efficiently, and quickly were skills that were imperative for real world success within the team dynamic and gameplay was the engine helped refine these skills.

Instead of playing games alone, boys in our study engaged in collaborative teamwork with friends or other players online. Through active engagement with friends and even strangers, boys learn and reconstruct online communities' social norms into their rules of acceptable behaviors. Boys seek out spaces that allow them to explore and experience their identities. The autonomous environment video games create provides a *psychosocial moratorium* that allows boys to explore who they are and what role they play in society (Erikson, 1968; Gee, 2003). Boys from our study credit video game space for giving them an opportunity to experience failure without being judged. They use this space to build up their self-confidence because failure is valued as a part of success. The lesson they learn from video games is a trial-and-error approach for learning and practicing.

Implications

This chapter sheds light on the confrontation of boys' crisis in schools. Our overarching goal is to bring out awareness of the possible systemic change in school cultures including changing curricula and pedagogies, opening to *rough-and-tumble* play or other boys' natural behaviors, and acknowledging video games as learning tools in classrooms. Our call for reform asks that we could: (1) consider changes in school cultures to better accommodate boys and active children; (2) encourage parent, teachers, and administrators to go beyond an acceptance of their students' cultures to a place of *respect* for their cultures; (3) recognize the learning potential of video games, especially as a re-engagement tool to bring underperforming boys into significant engagement in their own learning.

First, we should consider changes in school cultures to better accommodate boys and active children. Teachers, parents, and school leaders are rarely gamers, which almost immediately creates a distance between these adults and the students. One solid empirical finding that is repeated over and over in school effectiveness research is the need for understanding and caring teachers (Gleason & Dynarski, 2002; James & Jurich, 1999). It requires teachers to develop a deep understanding towards their students and their culture, which will help engage disengaged learners (Kindlon & Thompson, 2009).

Second, we propose that it is our responsibility to create a culture-sensitive environment with self-learning engaging opportunities for all genders. There is much diversity within boy culture, especially as it pertains to masculinity. As Dewey mentioned, limiting children's own learning space is denying their learning capacity (Dewey & Small, 1897). At the organizational level, we suggest that schools should help create more open spaces. These spaces need self-guided learning opportunities that are sensitive to feminine and masculine cultures. Given the benefits of play that creates safe spaces for self-development and self-exploration, boys are allowed to have more autonomous space and freedom to learn in their natural way.

Last but not least, we should recognize the learning potential of video games, especially by regarding them as re-engagement tools for underachieving, disengaged students. This needs attention not only from policy makers and educators, but also from game designers. Video games serve as effective learning tools especially in the field of literacy, problem solving, and emotional literacy. We propose that video game designers should recognize the gendered patterns that exist in current games and take the patterns into account when designing video games. We believe that all genders would take advantage of engaging in the learning opportunities video games provide.

The aforementioned literature strengthens our argument that video games are an effective tool to assist learning. We propose that video games should be welcome into classrooms with an honest respect for boys' culture and deep understanding of the potential benefits and drawbacks of commercial video gaming in classrooms. Considering that the average gamers are in their 30s, we believe that the interest in applying games into classrooms among young teachers is growing. At the same time, prominent academic scholars are conducting extensive research on the potential power of video game learning and its application to formal education (Shaffer et al., 2005).

Conclusion

The boys' crisis in formal education is multilayered and complex. The interdependence of all the factors we have discussed in this chapter are intertwined in a way that the discussion we have here is just the tip of the iceberg. In this chapter, we tentatively describe boys' culture through the lens of how they see themselves, male perception, and their *rough-and-tumble* play activities. Current school systems include three aspects that we explored briefly—school rules, pedagogy, and curriculum design. These constructs tend to reject boys' culture in traditional learning experiences. Within the feminized classroom, boys can find themselves less comfortable in traditional school environments. We have suggested that video games reflect boys' culture and can bring learning opportunities into sharp focus. Therefore, we advocate for careful, balanced consideration of the implementation of commercial video gaming in classrooms. By bringing video games into classrooms, teachers can reconnect with active learners and express caring respect for their culture. Stakeholders including researchers, instructional designers, and educators in particular, can be more culturally sensitive towards the boys' culture and embrace their culture of active play and competition. In fact, these cultural facets can be leveraged for increased engagement and learning among a population that has been performing poorly in traditional classrooms. We believe video games are valuable learning tools and cultural artifacts, which have the potential to provide more culturally responsive learning experiences and more space for the development of boys.

References

American Psychological Association Zero Tolerance Task Force (2008). Are zero tolerance policies effective in the schools?: An evidentiary review and recommendations. *The American Psychologist, 63*(9), 852.

Anderson, C.A., & Bushman, B.J. (2001). Effects of violent video games on aggressive behavior, aggressive cognition, aggressive affect, physiological arousal, and prosocial behavior: A meta-analytic review of the scientific literature. *Psychological Science, 12*(5), 353–359.

Anderson, C.A., & Dill, K.E. (2000). Video games and aggressive thoughts, feelings, and behavior in the laboratory and in life. *Journal of Personality and Social Psychology, 78*(4), 772.

Barab, S., Pettyjohn, P., Gresalfi, M., Volk, C., & Solomou, M. (2012). Game-based curriculum and transformational play: Designing to meaningfully positioning person, content, and context. *Computers & Education, 58*(1), 518–533.

Blair, H.A., & Sanford, K. (2004). Morphing literacy: Boys reshaping their school-based literacy practices. *Language Arts, 81*(6), 452–460.

Bloom, B., Cohen, R.A., & Freeman, G. (2012). Summary health statistics for us children: National Health Interview Survey, 2011. *Vital and health statistics. Series 10, Data from the National Health Survey* (254), 1–88.

Buchmann, C., DiPrete, T.A., & McDaniel, A. (2008). Gender inequalities in education. *Annual Review in Sociology, 34*, 319–337.

Cassell, J., & Jenkins, H. (Eds.). (2000). *From Barbie to mortal kombat: Gender and computer games*. Cambridge, MA: MIT Press.

Connell, R. (1996). Teaching the boys: New research on masculinity, and gender strategies for schools. *The Teachers College Record, 98*(2), 206–235.

Cummings, H.M., & Vandewater, E.A. (2007). Relation of adolescent video game play to time spent in other activities. *Archives of Pediatrics & Adolescent Medicine, 161*(7), 684–689.

Dewey, J., & Small, A.W. (1897). *My Pedagogic Creed* (No. 25). New York, NY: EL Kellogg & Company.

DiPietro, J.A. (1981). Rough and tumble play: A function of gender. *Developmental Psychology, 17*(1), 50.

Dill, K.E., & Thill, K.P. (2007). Video game characters and the socialization of gender roles: Young people's perceptions mirror sexist media depictions. *Sex Roles, 57*(11–12), 851–864.

Eliot, L. (2010). The truth about boys and girls. *Scientific American Mind, 21*(2), 22–29.

Engerman, J. A. (2016). *Call of Duty for Adolescent Boys: An ethnographic phenomenology of the experiences within a gaming culture.* (Unpublished doctoral dissertation). Pennsylvania State University, University Park, PA.

Engerman, J. A., & Carr-Chellman, A. (2014). Boys and video games: What learning occurs from video game play and how might it map to the common core standards? In Spector, M. (Ed). In *Proceedings of the Association for Educational Communication and Technology on Research, Theory and Development* (pp. 280–287). Jacksonville, FL: Association of Educational Communications and Technology.

Engerman, J. A., MacAllan, M., & Carr-Chellman, A. (2014). Boys and their toys: Video game learning & the common core. In Ochsner, A., Dietmeier, J., Williams, C., Steinkuehler, C. (Eds). In *Proceedings of Games, Learning and Society Conference 10.0* (GLS 10.0) (pp. 504–510). Madison, WI: Games, Learning and Society.

Engerman, J. A., Mun, Y., Yan, S., & Carr-Chellman, A. (2015). Video games to engage boys and meet common core. In *Proceedings of International Society for Technology in Education.* Philadelphia, PA: International Society for Technology in Education.

Epstein, D. (1998). *Failing Boys?: Issues in gender and achievement.* Maidenhead: McGraw-Hill Education (UK).

Epstein, D., Elwood, J., Hey, V., & Maw, J. (1998). Schoolboy frictions: feminism and 'failing' boys. In *Failing Boys? Issues in gender and achievement* (3–18). Maidenhead: McGraw-Hill Education (UK).

Erikson, E. H. (1968). *Identity.* New York, NY: W.W. Norton & Company.

Flanders, J. L., Simard, M., Paquette, D., Parent, S., Vitaro, F., Pihl, R. O., & Séguin, J. R. (2010). Rough-and-tumble play and the development of physical aggression and emotion regulation: A five-year follow-up study. *Journal of Family Violence, 25*(4), 357–367.

Gee, J. P. (2003). What video games have to teach us about learning and literacy. *Computers in Entertainment (CIE), 1*(1), 20–20.

Gilbert, R., & Gilbert, P. (1998). *Masculinity Goes to School.* Florence, KY: Routledge.

Gleason, P., & Dynarski, M. (2002). Do we know whom to serve? Issues in using risk factors to identify dropouts. *Journal of Education for Students Placed at Risk, 7*(1), 25–41.

James, D. W., & Jurich, S. (1999). *More Things that Do Make a Difference for Youth: A compendium of evaluations of youth programs and practices* (Volume II). Washington, DC: American Youth Policy Forum.

Jordan, E. (1995). Fighting boys and fantasy play: The construction of masculinity in the early years of school. *Gender and Education, 7*(1), 69–86.

Kang-Brown, J., Trone, J., Fratello, J., & Daftary-Kapur, T. (2013). A generation later: what we've learned about zero tolerance in schools. New York (NY): Vera Institute of Justice.

Kimmel, M. S., & Davis, T. (2011). Mapping guyland in college. *Masculinities in Higher Education: Theoretical and practical considerations* (pp. 3–15). New York, NY: Routledge.

Kelley, B. T., Loeber, R., Keenan, K., & DeLamatre, M. (1997). Developmental pathways in boys' disruptive delinquent behavior. *Juvenile Justice Bulletin.*

Kindlon, D., & Thompson, M. (2009). *Raising Cain: Protecting the emotional life of boys.* New York, NY: Ballantine Books.

Klinger, L. J., Hamilton, J. A., & Cantrell, P. J. (2001). Children's perceptions of aggressive and gender-specific content in toy commercials. *Social Behavior and Personality, 29*(1), 11–20.

Lawry, J., Upitis, R., Klawe, M., Anderson, A., Inkpen, K., Ndunda, M., & Sedighian, K. (1995). Exploring common conceptions about boys and electronic games. *Journal of Computers in Mathematics and Science Teaching*, *14*, 439–460.

Lenhart, A., Kahne, J., Middaugh, E., Macgill, A. R., Evans, C., & Vitak, J. (2008). Teens, video games, and civics: teens' gaming experiences are diverse and include significant social interaction and civic engagement. *Pew Internet & American Life Project*.

Logue, M. E., & Harvey, H. (2009). Preschool teachers' views of active play. *Journal of Research in Childhood Education*, *24*(1), 32–49.

Martin, C. L., Ruble, D. N., & Szkrybalo, J. (2002). Cognitive theories of early gender development. *Psychological Bulletin*, *128*(6), 903.

National Governors Association (NGA) & Council of Chief State School Officers (CCSSO) (2015). Common Core State Standards Initiative. Retrieved from: http://www.corestandards.org

Newkirk, T. (2002). *Misreading masculinity: Boys, literacy, and popular culture*. Portsmouth, NH: Heinemann.

Olson, C. K., Kutner, L. A., & Warner, D. E. (2008). The role of violent video game content in adolescent development boys' perspectives. *Journal of Adolescent Research*, *23*(1), 55–75.

Pellegrini, A. D. (1988). Elementary-school children's rough-and-tumble play and social competence. *Developmental Psychology*, *24*(6), 802.

Pellis, S. M., & Pellis, V. C. (2007). Rough-and-tumble play and the development of the social brain. *Current Directions in Psychological Science*, *16*(2), 95–98.

Prensky, M. (2005). Listen to the natives. *Educational Leadership*, *63*(4), 8–13.

Rubin, K. H. (1980). Fantasy play: Its role in the development of social skills and social cognition. *New Directions for Child and Adolescent Development*, (9), 69–84.

Sawchuk, P. H., & Stetsenko, A. (2008). Sociological understandings of conduct for a noncanonical activity theory: Exploring intersections and complementarities. *Mind, Culture, and Activity*, 15, 339–360.

Sax, L. (2007). *Why Gender Matters: What parents and teachers need to know about the emerging science of sex differences*. Danvers, MA: Harmony.

Shaffer, D. W., Halverson, R., Squire, K. R., & Gee, J. P. (2005). Video games and the future of learning. WCER Working Paper No. 2005–4. *Wisconsin Center for Education Research (NJ1)*.

Singh, I. (2003). Boys will be boys: Fathers' perspectives on ADHD symptoms, diagnosis, and drug treatment. *Harvard Review of Psychiatry*, *11*(6), 308–316.

Skiba, R., & Peterson, R. (1999). The dark side of zero tolerance: Can punishment lead to safe schools? *The Phi Delta Kappan*, *80*(5), 372–382.

Sommers, C. H. (2013). *The War against Boys: How misguided policies are harming our young men*. New York, NY: Simon and Schuster.

Spelke, E. S. (2005). Sex differences in intrinsic aptitude for mathematics and science?: A critical review. *American Psychologist*, *60*(9), 950.

Squire, K. (2003). Video games in education. *International Journal of Intelligent Simulations and Gaming*, *2*(1), 49–62.

Squire, K. (2008). Video-game literacy: A literacy of expertise. *Handbook of Research in New Literacies*, New York, NY: Lawrence Erlbaum Associate.

Squire, K. (2011). *Video Games and Learning: Teaching and participatory culture in the digital age. technology, education—connections (The TEC Series)*. New York, NY: Teachers College Press.

Steinberg, S. R., Kehler, M., & Cornish, L. (Eds.). (2010). *Boy Culture: An Encyclopedia*. Santa Barbara, CA: ABC-CLIO.
Steinkuehler, C. A. (2005). *Cognition and Learning in Massively Multiplayer Online Games: A critical approach*. Madison, WT: University of Wisconsin.
Steinkuehler, C., & King, E. (2009). Digital literacies for the disengaged: Creating after school contexts to support boys' game-based literacy skills. *On the Horizon, 17*(1), 47–59.
Vygotsky, L. S. (1980). *Mind in Society: The development of higher psychological processes*. Cambridge, MA: Harvard University Press.
Weaver-Hightower, M. (2003). The "boy turn" in research on gender and education. *Review of Educational Research, 73*(4), 471–498.
Weick, K. E., Sutcliffe, K. M., & Obstfeld, D. (2005). Organizing and the process of sensemaking. *Organization Science, 16*(4), 409–421.
Yee, N. (2006). Motivations for play in online games. *Cyber Psychology & Behavior, 9*(6), 772–775.

12
EXPLORING CHINESE INTERNATIONAL STUDENTS' ACCEPTANCE OF MOBILE LEARNING

Zhetao Guo and Angela D. Benson

This chapter presents a summary of the findings of a study that investigated Chinese international students' use of mobile technologies for learning. The rapid growth of mobile technology and the increased use of mobile devices with Internet access by higher education students have opened additional avenues of communication, providing greater opportunities for collaboration and expanding access to traditional learning and information resources (Donaldson, 2010). According to the report by EDUCAUSE, mobile device ownership among undergraduate students increased about 60% in 2012 compared to the previous year. Moreover, nearly twice as many students in 2012 (67%) reported using smartphones for academic purpose than in 2011 (37%), with tablet or e-reader usage accounting for 67% and 47%, respectively (Dahlstrom, 2012), and Rossing, Miller, Cecil, and Stamper (2012, p. 1) comment that "Mobile technology figures prominently in the future of higher education, particularly in its integration into teaching and learning". Motivated by this trend, many colleges and universities plan to incorporate, or have started to explore, the use of mobile technology in academics. According to Akour (2010), "In higher education, the success of mobile learning depends upon student acceptance of the technology; therefore, student acceptance should be a key concern for administrators considering the implementation of mobile learning" (p. 9).

Statement of the Problem

The number of the international students, especially Chinese international students, in American universities has been increasing dramatically. According to the annual "Open Doors" report from the Institute of International Education, more international students attended American colleges and universities in the

2011–12 school year than ever before, making it the sixth consecutive year in which international student enrollment has increased. There were 764,495 international students enrolled at colleges and universities in the United States in the 2011–12 academic year. China continues to lead the way as the No. 1 country of origin, with 194,029 students in 2011–12, a 23.1% increase from the previous year (Abrams, 2012). Chinese international students make up about a quarter of the international student population in American colleges. On the one hand, like American students, Chinese international students are inevitably influenced by mobile technology. On the other hand, as minorities in American universities, Chinese international students may have different personal, academic, and cultural backgrounds than their American peers. A review of the literature provided very limited research on international students' use of mobile learning, especially of Chinese international students. Additionally, there is a lack of research on whether Chinese international students plan to use or are currently using mobile devices to facilitate their learning. More research is needed to determine the factors that affect Chinese international students' acceptance of mobile learning. This study seeks to address those needs.

Framework

The Unified Theory of Acceptance and Use of Technology (UTAUT) provided the conceptual framework for this study. UTAUT (Venkatesh, Morris, Davis & Davis, 2003) aims to explain user intentions to use a technology and their subsequent usage behavior. Behavioral intention to use a technology is defined as a person's subjective probability that he or she will use a technology (as cited in Konerding, 1999). Use behavior is the actual behaviors of using a technology by a user. For this study, behavioral intention to use mobile learning means a Chinese student's subjective probability that he or she will use mobile technology for learning. Use behavior means the actual behaviors of using mobile technology for learning by a Chinese student.

Venkatesh et al. (2003) called the main factors affecting the acceptance of Information and Communications Technology (ICT) determinants. The four determinants are performance expectancy, effort expectancy, social influence, and facilitating conditions. Age, gender, experience, and voluntariness of use are the four moderating factors. Moderating factors affect the strength of the relationship between the four determinants and behavioral intention, as well as the relationship between the four determinants and use behavior.

Methods

Data were collected through an online cross-sectional survey. The UTAUT survey instrument and Donaldson (2010)'s survey instrument were adopted for this study and modified to make the questions relevant to the context of mobile learning and the Chinese participant population. For example, the word "system" was replaced with "mobile devices" or "mobile device for school-related activities," and the word "job" was changed to "school-related activities." The resulting 33-item survey included one item regarding voluntariness of use, four demographic questions, one item regarding mobile learning experience, seven items regarding mobile device ownership adopted from 2013 ECAR Study of Undergraduate Students and Technology survey, four items regarding usage and 16 items assessing the ten UTAUT constructs: performance expectancy, effort expectancy, social influence, facilitating conditions, age, gender, experience, voluntariness of use, behavioral intention, and use behavior. Likert scales ranging from strongly disagree to strongly agree were used for each UTAUT-related item. Venkatesh et al. (2003) measured the reliability of the UTAUT instrument stating that "All internal consistency reliabilities (ICRs) were greater than .70" (p. 457). In the preliminary test of UTAUT, the reliability coefficient of the construct ranged from 0.83 to 0.94, while it ranged from 0.88 to 0.96 in the cross-validation test. Therefore, the reliability coefficient of the UTAUT instrument was strong.

Data Collection

The international office of the university sent two emails, each including the invitation letter and the URL of the online survey, to all 851 enrolled Chinese international students. The first invitation was distributed in March 2015. An additional email reminder was distributed two weeks later. However, the international office only committed to send the invitation email twice due to their concern of overwhelming of students with survey requests. Therefore, the researcher was not able to distribute the invitation email to Chinese international students again.

Sample

Sixty-six participants in total completed the survey, yielding a response rate of about 8%. Demographic information collected from each participant included gender, age, major, academic rank, and level of experience with using mobile devices for learning activities.

The participants consisted of 45% (n=29) male and 55% (n=37) female. The age range of the participants was 18–25 (n=41) and 26–33 (n=25). Participants' educational fields were reported as follows: 30% studied business, management, and marketing; 15% studied engineering and architecture; 11% studied physical sciences; 8% studied education; 6% studied social sciences; 5% studied communication and journalism; 5% studied biological or life science; 3% studied computer and information sciences; 2% studied fine and performing art; 2% studied health sciences; 2% studied liberal arts or general studies;

2% studied manufacturing, construction, repair or transportation; 2% studied public administration, legal, social and protective services; and 2% were undecided. Nine percent of the participants chose "other" and specified their education fields as statistics, public relations, math, social work and physical geography.

The participants represented all academic ranks from undergraduate to doctoral student. Nine percent were freshmen; 14% were sophomores; 18% were juniors; 5% were seniors; 14% were Master's or EdS students; 39% were doctoral students; 2% chose other.

Participants were asked about their experience with mobile learning. Eight percent of the participants used mobile devices for school-related activities one to three times a week; 48% used mobile devices for school-related activities once a day; 34% used mobile devices for school-related activities many times per day.

Research Question 1

What is Chinese international students' use of mobile leaning?

Mobile learning was popular among the participants. The majority of the participants owned mobile devices such as smartphones, tablets, iPads, MP3, or MP4 players. iPhones were the dominant smartphones these participants owned. Sixty-nine percent of the participants often used smartphones, tablets or iPads for school-related work. They used mobile devices to take notes (32%), check school-related emails (79%), and access course information such as assignments (70%), grades (62%), digital textbooks (52%), learning management system (38%), and class schedule (77%). They also used mobile devices to access academic services such as library resources (29%), grades (62%), registration (29%), campus events (36%), and financial aid information (13%). The survey results revealed that only 3% of the participants had not used mobile devices for school-related activities in the past four weeks; 8% had rarely used mobile devices for learning; 21% had used mobile devices for learning sometimes; 25% had often used mobile devices for learning; and 44% had used mobile devices for learning very often. A large majority of the participants had frequently used mobile devices for school-related activities. These results are consistent with Salisbury, Laincz, and Smith's (2015) findings that mobile devices have become widely common and popular, with a majority of respondents owning at least one small mobile device.

Research Question 2

Is there a significant difference between Chinese male students and female students on their behavioral intention to use mobile learning?

Behavioral intention to use mobile learning is a student's subjective probability that he or she will use mobile technology for learning. It is used to measure a student's acceptance of mobile learning. The t-test results revealed that there was no significant difference, $t(66) = -1.15$, $p > 0.05$, between Chinese male students ($M=3.57$, $SD=0.93$) and Chinese female students ($M=3.83$, $SD=0.86$), on their behavioral intention to use mobile learning. In other words, Chinese male students and female students had the same subjective probability that he or she would use mobile technology for learning. This finding supports the claim that there were no significant differences between males and females and intended use of mobile learning (Donaldson, 2010; Wu, Yu, & Weng, 2012; Willams, 2009). Some prior studies focused on examining the moderating effect of gender on user's behavioral intention. According to Wang, Wu, and Wang (2009), gender differences moderated the effects of self- management on users' behavioral intention to use mobile learning. There were significant gender differences in terms of the effects of the determinants on behavioral intention to use mobile Internet. For example, effort expectancy was a stronger determinant for women than for men (Wang & Wang, 2010). However, this study only investigated the gender differences on Chinese international students' behavioral intention to use mobile devices for learning, not the moderating effect of gender.

Research Question 3

Is there a significant difference between the participants' ages and their intention to use mobile learning?

The participants were categorized into two age groups: 18–25 (63%), and 26–33 (37%). The t-test results indicated that there was no significant difference, $t(65) = -1.30$, $p > 0.05$, between the 18–25 age group ($M=3.62$, $SD=0.94$) and the 26–33 age group ($M=3.92$, $SD=0.81$), on their behavioral intention to use mobile learning. In other words, age did not affect Chinese international students' subjective probability that they would use mobile devices for learning. This finding is consistent with Donaldson's (2010) finding that age did not have a relationship with the behavioral intention to use mobile learning. Besides mobile learning, a prior study also inferred that there was no significant difference between the age groups and their intention to use an electronic ticket system in Taiwan (Wu, You, & Weng, 2012).

Meanwhile, some prior research studied the moderating effect of age on the determinants on behavioral intention to use mobile learning and other types of technologies. It was found that age differences moderated the effect of effort expectancy and social influence on an individual's behavioral intention to use mobile devices for learning (Wang et al., 2009). This study only examined the age difference between the Chinese international students on their behavioral intention to use mobile learning, not the moderating effect of age on behavioral intention.

Research Question 4

Is there a significant difference between participants' levels of experience and their intention to use mobile learning?

The participants were categorized into three groups of level of experience with mobile learnings: novice, intermediate, and advanced. Since the experience level group sizes were very unequal (12, 32, 22, respectively), the weighted mean for each group was calculated in order to make the groups equally represented. The resulting one-way ANOVA results indicated that no significant difference existed between participants' level of experience and their behavioral intention to use mobile learning, $F(2, 62) = 1.28$, $p = .29$. In other words, Chinese international students with different levels of experience had the same subjective probability that they would use mobile technology for learning.

When implementing mobile learning, universities may not need to consider Chinese international students' experiences with mobile learning, since experiences will not affect their behavioral intention. This finding is consistent with Wu et al.'s (2012) study, which revealed that there was no significant difference in behavioral intention to use an electronic ticket system among respondents having different experiences. However, the majority of the previous studies mainly focused on investigating the moderating effects of users' experience on the determinants for behavioral intention. For example, mobile devices experience did moderate the effect of the determinants on behavioral intention (Liew, Kang, Yoo, & You, 2013). Moreover, experience was a significant moderating factor for social influence on behavioral intention to use electronic-government services (Awuah, 2012). Some other studies obtained different results. According to Barnes (2013), experience did not have the effect on any of the independent variables that affected the acceptance of information technology among laboratory science students. The effort expectancy-behavioral intentions relationship, social influence-behavioral intention relationship, and the facilitation conditions-user behavior relationship were not significantly moderated by experience with the technology system (Keeton, 2008). However, this study only probed into the differences between participants' levels of experience and their behavioral intention to use mobile learning, not the moderating effect of experience on behavioral intention.

Research Question 5

Is there a significant difference between the following two groups on their behavioral intention to use mobile learning: Chinese international students who feel that using mobile learning is voluntary, Chinese international students who feel that using mobile learning is required by professors?

The independent samples t-test results revealed no significant difference, $t(66) = 0.59$, $p > 0.05$, between Chinese international students who felt that using mobile learning was voluntary (*M*=3.75, *SD*=0.88) and Chinese international students who felt that using mobile learning was required by professors (*M*=3.58, *SD*=1.01), on their behavioral intention to use mobile learning. In other words, Chinese international students had the same subjective probability that they would use mobile technology for learning, no matter if it was required by their professors or not.

When universities decide policies for mobile learning, it may be unnecessary to make it mandatory for students. This finding is different from Donaldson's (2010) study, which suggested that voluntariness was a significant negative predictor of behavioral intention to use mobile learning: the less instructors require students to use mobile learning, the less students use mobile devices for learning. This difference may be due to the small sample size of this research. In addition, the majority of the participants (83%) in the present study were not required by their professors to use mobile devices for learning, which might affect the test results as well. Meanwhile, some prior studies examined the moderating effect of voluntariness of use on behavioral intention. Respondents who voluntarily used a technology were more concerned about performance expectancy than those who were required to use this technology (Wu et al., 2012). Voluntariness of use also moderated the effect of social influence on behavioral intention to use mobile devices for learning (Williams, 2009). However, this current study only examined the differences between these two groups and their behavioral intention to use mobile learning, not the moderating effect of voluntariness of use on behavioral intention.

Research Question 6

Are the following independent variables significant predictors of Chinese international students' behavioral intention to use mobile learning: performance expectancy, effort expectancy, social influence, and facilitating conditions?

A standard multiple regression was conducted to address this research question. The linear combination of performance expectancy, effort expectancy, social influence, and facilitating conditions was significantly related to participants' behavioral intention to use mobile learning, $F(4, 60) = 29.75$, $p <0.001$. The multiple correlation coefficient was 0.815, indicating that 66.5% of the variance in the behavioral intention to use mobile learning can be accounted for by the linear combination of performance expectancy, effort expectancy, social influence, and facilitating conditions. The coefficients indicate effort expectancy and facilitating conditions were significant predictors of participants' behavioral intention to use mobile learning. However, performance expectancy and social influence were not significant predictors.

Performance expectancy is "the degree to which an individual believes that using the system will help him or her to attain gains in job" (Venkatesh et al.,

2003, p. 447). For this study, it means the degree to which a student believes that using mobile devices for learning will help him or her to improve academic outcomes. The composite mean for the performance expectancy construct was 3.58. This indicates that the participants' attitudes about whether using mobile devices for learning can or cannot improve their academic performances fell between neutral and positive. The results obtained from this study suggest that performance expectancy was not a significant predictor of behavioral intention to use mobile learning. In other words, the degree to which the participants believed that using mobile devices for learning would help them to improve their academic performance did not affect their behavioral intention. This finding is different from the previous studies, which revealed performance expectancy to be significant predictor of college students' behavioral intention to use mobile learning (Wang et al., 2009; Liew et al., 2013; Abu-Al-Aish & Love, 2013; Donaldson, 2010). However, this study's finding is consistent with the studies that examined users' acceptance of other types of technologies. According to Tibenderana, Ogao, Ikoja-Odongo, and Wokadala (2011), performance expectancy did not have an impact on acceptance and use of e-library services. Vanneste, Vermeulen, and Declercq (2013) also found performance expectancy did not have significant influence on behavioral intention to use a web application by health professionals in Belgium.

Effort expectancy is "the degree of ease associated with the use of the system" (Venkatesh et al., 2003, p. 450). For this study, it means the degree of ease associated with the use of mobile devices for learning. The composite mean for the effort expectancy construct was 3.81. This means that the participants' attitudes fell between neutral and positive toward the ease associated with the use of mobile devices for learning activities. The results obtained from this study indicated that effort expectancy was a significant predictor of behavioral intention to use mobile learning. Therefore, the degree of ease associated with the use of mobile devices for learning influenced participants' behavioral intention to use mobile devices for learning. This finding is supported by the prior studies conducted by Wang et al. (2009), Abu-Al-Aish & Love (2013), Barnes (2013), Serben (2014), and Mandal and McQueen (2012), which found that effort expectancy had a positive influence on user's behavioral intention to use a technology. This implies that Chinese international students who perceive a high degree of ease with using mobile devices for learning will have a high intention to use mobile devices for learning.

Social influence is "the degree to which an individual perceives that important others believe he or she should use the new system" (Venkatesh et al., 2003, p. 451). For this study, it means the degree to which a student perceives that important others believe he or she should use mobile devices for learning. The composite mean for the social influence construct was 3.12. This means the participants held almost neutral attitudes toward the importance of whether or not others who are important to them believed they should use mobile devices for learning. The literature suggested that social influence had a positive influence on behavioral intention (Keller, 2009; Tibenderana et al., 2010; Foon & Fah, 2011; Donaldson, 2010; Martins, Oliveira, & Popovic, 2014). The more students think faculty, university, peers, and individuals important to them believe they should use mobile learning, the more likely they will engage in mobile learning (Donaldson, 2010). In contrast, the results from the present study suggested that social influence was not a significant predictor of behavioral intention. In other words, the degree to which Chinese international students perceived that important others believed they should use mobile devices for learning did not affect their behavioral intention. This finding is consistent with the studies conducted by Anderson, Schwager, and Kerns (2006), Barnes (2013), and Mandal and McQueen's (2012), which suggested that social influence had no significant relationships with behavioral intention. In this study, almost half of the participants took a neutral stance when they were asked for their opinions on the influence of their professors as well as the individuals important to them on their intention to use mobile learning. This could have affected the predictive power of social influence.

Facilitating conditions is "the degree to which an individual believes that an organizational and technical infrastructure exists to support use of the system" (Venkatesh et al., 2003, p. 453). For this study, it means the degree to which a student believes an organizational and technical infrastructure exists to support the use of the mobile devices for learning. The composite mean for the facilitating conditions construct was 3.34. The participants' attitudes fell between neutral and positive toward whether an organizational and technical infrastructure existed to support the use of the mobile devices for learning. The results obtained from this study indicated that facilitating conditions was a significant predictor of the behavioral intention to use mobile learning. In other words, the degree to which the participants believed an organizational and technical infrastructure exists to support their use of the mobile devices for learning influenced their behavioral intention. This finding is supported by the literature on the acceptance of mobile learning (Donaldson, 2010; Jairak, Praneetpolgrang, and Mekhabunchakij, 2009; Williams, 2009). This finding is also consistent with the literature on the acceptance of other types of technologies (Keeton, 2008; Serben, 2014). For example, Serben (2014) found that there was a positive relationship between facilitating conditions and users' behavioral intention to use social media by African American small business owners. The more students perceive an organizational and technical infrastructure is provided to support their use of the mobile devices for learning, the more likely they will engage in mobile learning (Donaldson, 2010).

Research Question 7

Are Chinese international students' behavioral intention to use mobile learning and facilitating conditions significant predictors of Chinese international students' use behavior?

A standard multiple regression was conducted to determine how behavioral intention to use mobile learning and facilitating conditions predict use behavior. Prior studies suggested that facilitating conditions had a significant relationship with use behavior (Barnes, 2013; Keeton, 2008; Serben, 2014). The initial UTAUT study also claimed that facilitating conditions and behavioral intention were two direct determinants of use behavior (Venkatesh et al., 2003). In contrast to the previous studies, the results from the present study revealed that facilitating conditions and behavioral intention were not significant predictors of use behavior, but there was slight interaction between these two variables. Therefore, neither facilitating conditions nor behavioral intention can determine Chinese international students' use behavior. In other words, the degree to which Chinese international students believed that an organizational and technical infrastructure existed to support their use of mobile learning, or the subjective probability that they would use mobile learning, did not affect their use behaviors.

Limitations of the Study

The key limitation of this study is the small sample size. A large sample size coupled with considerable statistical power and effect size usually yields more statistically significant results (Awuah, 2012). Because of the small sample size, this study may have missed important differences that actually existed. Moreover, the small sample size could affect the generalization of this study to a larger sample population. Therefore, the findings obtained from this study may not be generalizable.

Additionally, this study is geographically limited to the southeast region of the United States. The participants of this study are all from one public university. Thus, the findings may not be generalized to other public universities in other regions.

Lastly, since the main purpose of this study was to examine whether the UTAUT determinants (performance expectancy, effort expectancy, social influence, and facilitating conditions) affect Chinese international students' behavioral intention to use mobile devices for learning, the impacts of the moderators (experience, gender, age, and voluntariness) were not included in the test.

Conclusions

Acceptance of a technology can be crucial to its use and success. Understanding students' acceptance of mobile learning is essential to the successful delivery of academic, organizational, and instructional information (Donaldson, 2010). Many researchers have started to apply the UTAUT model to their research on students' acceptance of mobile learning. Because of the increasing enrollment of Chinese international students in American universities, the group of Chinese international students has gradually become a more significant part in American universities. However, most of the previous studies have only focused on

American students' or college students' acceptance of mobile learning in general. There remains a lack of research on Chinese international students' acceptance of mobile learning. Therefore, this study fills the gap in studying minority students', specifically Chinese international students', acceptance of mobile learning. Seven conclusions can be drawn from the study's findings.

Chinese international students are already using mobile devices for learning. The results of this study revealed that the majority of the respondents owned mobile devices such as smartphones, tablets, iPads, MP3, or MP4 players. iPhones were the dominant smartphones they owned. Most of the respondents frequently used these mobile devices for a wide variety of school-related activities, such as taking notes, checking school-related emails, accessing course information, and academic services.

Both the male respondents and female respondents intend to use mobile devices for learning in the near future. The results of this study indicated that there was no significant difference between the male respondents and female respondents on their behavioral intention to use mobile learning. Moreover, the findings indicated that there was no significant difference in the respondents' behavioral intention to use mobile learning based on age. Therefore, respondents of different ages have the same subjective possibility that they will use mobile devices for learning.

Respondents plan to use mobile devices for learning in the near future even if they are not required to do so by their instructors. The results indicated that voluntariness of use did not affect the respondents' behavioral intention to use mobile learning. No matter if mobile learning is required by the instructors or not, the respondents have the same subjective probability that they will use mobile devices for learning.

Respondents plan to use mobile devices for learning in the near future even if they are not experienced in it. The results revealed that experience did not have a relationship with the respondents' behavioral intention to use mobile learning. Respondents with different levels of experience have the same subjective probability that they will use mobile devices for learning.

Respondents who find mobile devices easy to use are more likely to use them for learning. The results indicated that effort expectancy was a significant predictor of the respondents' behavioral intention to use mobile learning. Respondents who perceive a high degree of ease in using mobile devices for learning will have a high intention to use mobile devices for learning.

Respondents are more likely to engage in mobile learning in the near future if they have the necessary organizational and technical support. The results revealed that facilitating conditions was a significant predictor of the respondents' behavioral intention to use mobile learning. The degree to which the respondents believe an organizational and technical infrastructure exists to support their use of the mobile devices for learning does affect their behavioral intention.

In addition, the UTAUT model is an effective tool for measuring the factors that affect the respondents' behavioral intention to use mobile learning. The results from this study indicated that the linear combination of the four UTAUT determinants—performance expectancy, effort expectancy, social influence, and facilitating conditions—was significantly related to the respondents' behavioral intention to use mobile learning. However, the results did not provide adequate support for all the relationships specified in this model. Only effort expectancy and facilitating conditions were found to be significant predictors.

Recommendations for Practice

The findings from this study provide university administrators and educators with information on Chinese international students' usage of mobile learning and the factors influencing their acceptance of mobile learning. This information will help administrators and educators make the best decisions and policies about the implementation of mobile learning. The results obtained from this study suggest the following:

1. Universities should utilize smartphones, tablets, and iPads when implementing mobile learning since Chinese international students already own and are using these devices. They should also develop or adopt mobile learning systems and mobile learning applications that are compatible with all of these mobile technologies;
2. When implementing mobile learning, universities may not need to consider Chinese international students' age or gender;
3. When administrators or educators decide policies for mobile learning, it may be unnecessary to make it mandatory for Chinese international students;
4. When implementing mobile learning, universities may not need to worry about the acceptance of mobile learning among the Chinese international students who have little or even no experience with it;
5. Administrators and educators should consider adopting mobile technologies, mobile learning systems, and mobile learning applications that are user-friendly and easy for Chinese international students to use. For example, universities can adopt a mobile learning application or a system that has Chinese language in the language settings. Before officially publishing a mobile learning system or application, universities may consider releasing a trial version to the Chinese international students so that they will have time to practice and become proficient in it. This will also provide universities an opportunity to collect feedback and make improvements on that system or application;
6. In order to encourage Chinese international students to engage in mobile learning, universities should provide the necessary organizational and technical support to Chinese international students, such as customized training,

workshops, technical support service, and any other helpful resources for mobile learning. Universities should consider recruiting trainers and technical support staff who can speak Chinese so they can provide Chinese international students with customized trainings, workshops, and resources delivered in Chinese; and
7. On the one hand, administrators should provide Chinese international students with convenient mobile applications to access the academic services, such as the mobile applications for utilizing library resources and learning management system. On the other hand, educators should identify ways in which mobile devices can be utilized to support classroom and online learning, and provide academic content and information on resources formatted for mobile devices (Donaldson, 2010).

Recommendations for Future Research

The following are the recommendations for future research on the acceptance of mobile learning:

1. To extend the generalizability of the findings, future research could duplicate the instrument of this study and randomly sample Chinese international students at public universities in the United States;
2. Instead of exploring the acceptance of mobile learning in general, future research could also investigate students' acceptance of using a specific mobile technology for learning, such as smartphones, tablets, or mobile apps;
3. This study focused solely on Chinese international students' acceptance of mobile learning at public universities in the United States. Future research could study the acceptance of mobile learning by the international students from other countries;
4. Besides public universities, future research could study international students' acceptance of mobile learning in private universities, community colleges, or other types of higher education institutions;
5. Future research could compare American students' and Chinese international students' acceptance of mobile learning, and examine whether there is significant difference between these two groups on their behavioral attention to use mobile devices for learning;
6. This study only utilized a quantitative approach. Future studies may use both qualitative and quantitative research in order to obtain more detailed results on Chinese international students' acceptance of mobile learning;
7. Further research is needed to validate the following four groups of relationships: performance expectancy and behavioral intention to use, social influence and behavioral intention to use, facilitating conditions and use behavior, behavioral intention to use and use behavior; and

8. This study did not examine the moderating effect of age, gender, experience, and voluntariness of use on behavioral intention. Future studies may further investigate the impacts of these four moderators in the UTAUT model.

Summary

Using UTAUT as the theoretical framework, this study gained an understanding of Chinese international students' acceptance of mobile learning. The descriptive data indicated that the majority of the Chinese international students owned mobile devices such as smartphones, tablets, iPads, MP3, or MP4 players. They used these mobile devices for all kinds of school-related activities, such as accessing library resources and learning management system, taking notes, checking assignments and grades, reading digital textbooks, and registering for courses. The findings showed that the mobile learning was popular among the Chinese international students.

The results obtained from this study further indicated that age, gender, and experience with using mobile devices for learning did not have significant influence on respondents' behavioral intention to use mobile learning. A multiple regression analysis was conducted to examine whether performance expectancy, effort expectancy, social influence, and facilitating conditions were significant predictors of Chinese international students' behavioral intention to use mobile devices for learning. The findings suggest that only effort expectancy and facilitating conditions were significant predictors. Facilitating conditions and behavioral intention were found to be non-significant predictors of use behavior. However, there was slight interaction between these two constructs. Overall, this study has significant implications on the implementation of mobile learning in universities. It also expands the existing body of knowledge in the fields of mobile learning and the UTAUT model.

References

Abrams, T. (2012, November 14). Chinese enrollment soars as more international students attend U.S. colleges. *The New York Times*. Retrieved from http://thechoice.blogs.nytimes.com/2012/11/14/open-doors-2012/

Abu-Al-Aish, A., & Love, S. (2013). Factors influencing students' acceptance of m-learning: An investigation in higher education. *The International Review of Research in Open and Distance Learning, 14*(5), 82–105.

Akour, H. (2010). *Determinants of mobile learning acceptance: An empirical investigation in higher education* (Doctoral dissertation). Retrieved from ProQuest Dissertations and Theses. (UMI3408682).

Anderson, J. E., Schwager, P. H., & Kerns, R. L. (2006). The drivers for acceptance of tablet PCs by faculty in a college of business. *Journal of Information Systems Education, 17*(4), 429–440.

Awuah, L. J. (2012). *An empirical analysis of citizens' acceptance decisions of electronic-government services: A modification of the unified theory of acceptance and use of technology (UTAUT)* model to include trust as a basis for investigation (Doctoral dissertation). Retrieved from ProQuest Dissertations and Theses. (UMI 3544016).

Barnes, B.C. (2013). *Use and acceptance of information and communication technology among laboratory science students* (Doctoral dissertation). Retrieved from ProQuest Dissertations & Theses Full Text. (1284766281).

Dahlstrom, E. (2012). *The ECAR study of undergraduate students and information technology, 2012.* Louisville, CO: EDUCAUSE Center for Applied Research. Retrieved from https://net.educause.edu/ir/library/pdf/ERS1208/ERS1208.pdf

Donaldson, R.L. (2010). *Student acceptance of mobile learning* (Doctoral dissertation). Retrieved from ProQuest Dissertations and Theses. (UMI 3483638).

Foon, Y.S., & Fah, B.C.Y. (2011). Internet banking adoption in Kuala Lumpur: An Application of UTAUT model. *International Journal of Business & Management, 6*(4), 161–167.

Jairak, K., Praneetpolgrang, P. & Mekhabunchakij, K. (2009). An acceptance of m-learning for higher education students in Thailand. *Special Issue of the International Journal of the Computer, the Internet and Management, 17* (SP3), 2009, 36.1–36.8.

Keeton, K.E. (2008)-UMI 3329917. *An extension of the UTAUT model: How organizational factors and individual differences influence technology acceptance* (Doctoral dissertation). Retrieved from ProQuest Dissertations & Theses Full Text. (304604450).

Keller, C. (2009). User acceptance of virtual learning environments: A case study from three Northern European universities. *Communications of the Association for Information Systems, 25*(1), 465–486.

Konerding, U. (1999). Formal models for predicting behavioral intentions in dichotomous choice situations. *Methods of Psychological Research Online, 4*(2), 1–32.

Liew, B.T., Kang, M., Yoo, E., & You, J. (2013, June). Investigating the determinants of mobile learning acceptance in Korea. *World Conference on Educational Multimedia, Hypermedia and Telecommunications, 1,* 1424–1430.

Mandal, D., & McQueen, R.J. (2012). Extending UTAUT to explain social media adoption by microbusinesses. *International Journal of Managing Information Technology, 4*(4), 1–11.

Martins, C., Oliveira, T., & Popovic, A. (2014). Understanding the Internet banking adoption: A unified theory of acceptance and use of technology and perceived risk application. *International Journal of Information Management, 34*(1), 1–13.

Rossing, J.P., Miller, W.M., Cecil, A.K., & Stamper, S.E. (2012). iLearning: The future of higher education? Student perceptions on learning with mobile tablets. *Journal of the Scholarship of Teaching and Learning, 12(2),* 1–26.

Salisbury, L., Laincz, J., & Smith, J.J. (2015). Undergraduate ownership of small mobile devices: Engagement and use in an academic environment. *Science & Technology Libraries, 34*(1), 91.

Serben, D.F. (2014). *The examination of factors influencing social media usage by African American small business owners using the UTAUT model* (Doctoral dissertation). Retrieved from ProQuestDissertations and Theses. (UMI 3613968).

Tibenderana, P., Ogao, P., Ikoja-Odongo, J., & Wokadala, J. (2010). Measuring levels of end-users' acceptance and use of hybrid library services. *International Journal of Education & Development Using Information & Communication Technology, 6*(2), 33–54.

Vanneste, D., Vermeulen, B., & Declercq, A. (2013). Healthcare professionals' acceptance of BelRAI, a web-based system enabling person-centred recording and data sharing across care settings with interRAI instruments: A UTAUT analysis. *BMC Medical Informatics and Decision Making, 13*(1), 1–14.

Venkatesh, V., Morris, M., Davis, G., & Davis, F. (2003). User acceptance of information technology: Toward a unified view. *MIS Quarterly: Management Information Systems, 27*(3), 425–478.

Wang, H.Y., & Wang, S.H. (2010). User acceptance of mobile internet based on the unified theory of acceptance and use of technology: Investigating the determinants and gender differences. *Social Behavior & Personality: An International Journal, 38*(3), 415–426.

Wang, Y., Wu, M., & Wang, H. (2009). Investigating the determinants and age and gender differences in the acceptance of mobile learning. *British Journal of Educational Technology, 40*(1), 92–118.

Williams, P.W. (2009)-UMI 3337432. *Assessing mobile learning effectiveness and acceptance* (Doctoral dissertation). Retrieved from ProQuest Dissertations & Theses Full Text. (304880387).

Wu, M.Y., Yu, P.Y., & Weng, Y.C. (2012). A study on user behavior for I Pass by UTAUT: Using Taiwan's MRT as an example. *Asia Pacific Management Review, 17*(1), 92–111.

13

STUDENTS MAKING SCIENCE GAMES

The Design Process of Students Incorporating Science Content into Video Games

Neda Khalili Blackburn and Kevin Clark

Introduction

Children love playing video games. A study from the PEW Internet and American Life Project found that 97% of American teenagers ages 12–17 play video games (Lenhart et al., 2008). Furthermore, this love of playing video games is shared amongst both boys and girls, with 99% and 94% playing respectively, and game play practices do not vary across racial and ethnicity groups or different socioeconomic levels. A survey of American students in grades K-12 found that, on average across the grades, students are playing video games 8–10 hours a week (Project Tomorrow, 2008). The entertainment industry can certainly back up this claim, as video game sales in the United States made over $15.4 billion in 2014 (Entertainment Software Association, 2015). This keen interest in video games has caused researchers and educators to examine how these games attract their audience and how this can be applicable for learning.

It is suggested that beyond the entertainment value, video games are becoming more complex and challenging, placing the player into rich learning environments where they are asked to think, problem solve and, often times, collaborate (Gee, 2003; 2012; Shaffer & Gee, 2012; Squire, 2011). Game players learn new game skills and strategies though a series of levels that increasingly become more difficult, asking the player to draw from knowledge gained from previous levels in order to advance (Lim, 2008; Prensky, 2007). The designers of these games must find a way to get the players to want to learn how to play and stay engaged throughout the challenges, a problem similar to that which a school teacher faces (Becker, 2007; Gee, 2003).

These aspects of video games where players learn and think while being engaged in the game have led to the development of educational games. It is apparent that designing games for learning is a big challenge for instructional designers (Becker, 2007). One of these challenges is that the games designed for learning simply turn out to be "boring," a side effect that Prensky (2007) says is a result of adults creating games without any input from the intended audience, kids. Druin (2002) states that children's input on designing technology allows the thinking to be moved away from traditional methods and can ultimately have an effect on the way the technology is used for teaching and learning. Indeed, research studies have looked at incorporating children of all ages during various stages of technology design processes (Druin, 2002; Flannery et al., 2013; Friedman & Saponara, 2008), including giving them the role of video game designers.

Before students were given the opportunity to be the creators of video games, they had to be given the opportunity to work with computers. In his 1980 book *Mindstorms*, Seymour Papert writes of children interacting with the computer and learning math through programming. This interaction was done by writing commands in LOGO to make a turtle object create geometric shapes on the computer screen. These children were taught methods on how to work with the turtle and the language and given the opportunity to explore the environment on their own. Papert looked at the "child as a builder." He builds on the theory of constructivism, learners creating their own knowledge through their experiences, and expands into *constructionism*, which relies on building knowledge structures while engaging in creating, or constructing, some kind of entity. According to constructionism, children creating an object like a square through LOGO commands are simultaneously building their understanding of a square through its creation.

The idea of children-as-designers with respect to learning and technology began with this research in the 1970s, but is even more relevant today. The advancement of technology has made electronics and software more readily affordable and accessible, with more sophisticated graphics and ease of usability. Game design programs such as *Game Maker*, *Scratch*, and *Storytelling Alice* take basic programming concepts and make them more understandable by incorporating icons and drag-and-drop moves for users to be able to create their own projects. Researchers who have introduced these programs to K-12 students have found that the students are motivated and engaged in creating their projects, collaborate with others, and learn valuable game design skills (Kafai & Peppler, 2012; Robertson & Nicholson, 2007; Sheridan, Clark, & Williams, 2013).

Culture and Computing

Building upon the educational qualities of game design programs, an informal education program, Game Design through Mentoring and Collaboration (GDMC), was established in the Washington, D.C. area to expose primarily African American students to aspects of game design through a peer-mentoring system (Clark & Sheridan, 2010). During the four years of this program, participants experienced a process where they began as new learners and cycled into peer mentors, helping newer students in the program, and later into instructors, where they led the lessons for the program. As the program evolved and students became more responsible for the design of its content, the program began to reflect a cultural background for an evolving community of learners (Sheridan et al., 2013). The students brought with them their individual backgrounds and interests and applied them to the design of the program, influencing both their own work and their peers' work. While GDMC did not start with a deliberate model of culturally relevant practices, it shares many qualities with this type of approach in that the assets of the participant take center stage in the design (Lee, 2003). As the students became mentors and even instructors, they were given more freedom to instruct the new students and shape the program, thereby using their own perspectives in what Lee (2003) would refer to as prior knowledge and cultural knowledge.

The Study

This study builds on the previous study (see Clark & Sheridan, 2010; Sheridan et al., 2013), which purposefully set out to provide technology-enriching experiences for a population that is traditionally underserved in areas of Science, Technology, Engineering, and Mathematics (STEM). This purpose is taken a step further in this study as the video game design workshop infuses the game ideas with science and the participants collaborate with a scientist.

The game design workshop was set in a computer lab for 3.5 weeks, meeting on weekdays during the summer. The day lasted for approximately six hours, with an hour break for lunch and socialization. Students collaborated with a scientist, who presented them with four topics in immunology: myelin sheath, neurotransmitters, signal transduction, and gene regulation. Students were prompted to select the topic that interested them the most. Fourteen of the 16 students selected their own topics; two students indicated they did not have a preference and were placed under a topic that only had three members. This created four groups with four members each. Students were then asked to design a video game to portray their understanding of the science topic.

The scientist met with each group once a week to help them understand their topics. Of the four meetings with the scientist, the first consisted of an introductory lecture to the entire group of students, followed by three more meetings with small groups, lasting from 30 minutes to an hour. In addition to these meetings, video game instructors gave presentations on how to work with the game design software throughout each week. Peer mentors were on hand to help the students on the technical aspects of their video games. At the end of the 3.5-week workshop, students had a workable artifact to be presented to the class and an audience of parents, which involved explaining both the science concept and the technical aspect of their video games.

Participants

Sixteen students participated in this study, ages 12–16, from both middle school and high school. There were 15 African American students and one Caucasian student, with the ratio of boys to girls being 7:1. In prior studies, there was a decrease in participation by girls. To address this situation, a deliberate effort was made to include more female mentors and instructors in the program. For this study, a female instructor led many of the lessons, and the scientist for the study was also female to ensure that the girls did not feel intimated in the workshop. Indeed, the girls interacted and got along well with all their peers; there were no indications that the girls did not feel comfortable during the program.

Eight male peer mentors, ages ranging from 15 to 20, assisted students with technical and programming issues in the workshop. The peer mentors were there (a) to allow students to feel comfortable in asking questions about their work from students close to their own age, and (b) to provide one-on-one instruction for students who fell behind or wanted to advance their work while the instructors continued their lessons without interruption (Clark & Sheridan, 2010; Sheridan et al., 2013).

There were three college-aged instructors available during the workshop; two male and one female. They led the students through an introductory lesson of the software, Game Maker, as well as specific lessons including adding multiple levels to the game, creating a starting page and ending credits, and building the documentation features of the game.

The subject matter expert was a scientist with a Ph.D. in biology, working with the Federation of American Scientists on incorporating technology with science learning. She had been the science coordinator for the educational science game Immune Attack (http://immuneattack.org), a game that allows students to explore immunology. The scientist also took part in the preliminary trial of this study of students creating their own science games (Khalili, Sheridan, Williams, Clark, & Stegman, 2011).

Data Collection and Analysis

Data were collected from observations and field notes, interviews with students, Game Design Journals that the students wrote in, and the artifacts the students created. Observations were made in the computer lab while students worked on their games and during the group meetings with the scientist. Interviews were done both informally—quick check-ins with students at their workstation—with all students and formally as semi-structured interviews with a representation of students from each of the four groups, 10 in total. The Game Design Journals were adapted from Harel's (1988) and Kafai's (1995) work with students creating video games with LOGO. They were found to be helpful to the students in terms of thinking through their ideas, and also helpful to the researcher in observing the progression of student ideas. The artifacts, or video games, the students created were monitored weekly, to view and record the progress students had made. At the end of the workshop, students played their games on a projected screen to an audience, explaining the science concept used in the game while doing so.

Analysis of the data occurred through coding and memo-writing (Corbin & Strauss, 2008), as well as artifact analysis. Coding involved multiple reviews of the interview, observation, game journal and memo data, and many revisions of the code. From that point, concentration was placed on finding patterns and making connections by going back through the notes with more focused coding (Creswell, 2008). Memo-writing occurred simultaneously with coding, for researcher reflection, note-taking, and to aid in making connections within the data. To address issues of validity, particularly the threat that researcher interpretations drawn from the data are not accurate with regard to what the students are doing, creating, and saying, a third-party coder was enlisted. She was provided with approximately 30% of the raw data and a codebook in order to code the data independently. The third-party coder did not find anything new in the data that differed from the researcher.

Artifact analysis was conducted to see how well students were able to convey their understanding of science through their games. The researcher and the scientist examined the completed games independently to establish categories of High, Medium, and Low with respect to (a) accuracy of the science content as explained by the students, and (b) the portrayal of the science topic in the game in itself. Only one game was ranked differently by the researcher and scientist and later reconciled through discussion. Guidance was taken from Yarnall and Kafai (1996), who in their study of students making games on oceanography, also looked across all the completed games to develop categories of rich, moderate, and minimal with regard to the science content incorporation in the games.

Findings

Students were immersed in a game design environment where they were able to design their own video games based on an unfamiliar science topic, and were provided with the support and tools necessary to express their understanding of the topic through their games. As they created their games, students were involved in the iterative process of design. This cycle includes time for reflecting on the game to be created, designing the game, testing the game, and having a period of discussion about the game, and indeed previous research confirms that students use some version of this process for design (Baytak, 2009; Flanagan, Howe, & Nissenbaum, 2005; Kolodner et al., 2003; Resnick, 2007; Robertson & Nicholson, 2007). Students in this study showed moments where they took time to think about their games in their journals, designed the game through sketches or the Game Maker software, tested it for technical issues or for others to see what they had made, and discussed their games with peers, mentors, or the scientist. They would take this information and apply it to another stage of the cycle, whether to think about a new idea or to jump right in and program another feature in the game. Robertson and Nicholson (2007) state that students do not necessarily visit the stages of the iterative design cycle in order.

Following the students in their design process, the following questions were asked: 1) What strategies do students as designers use in order to understand the science concepts? and 2) How do students exhibit their understanding of these science concepts? Five major findings were discovered during analysis.

Finding #1. The first finding showed that students create science video games based on games they already know. Twelve games in total were completed during this game design workshop, and 11 were based on well-known video game concepts. (The remaining game was based on a YouTube video.) When students were asked how they came up with their ideas, one student remarked, "Well, I kinda looked through the old games that I've done. Like one of the old Pac-Man games I did. I liked the way that was setup. So I went off the structure that it was, like the mazes and stuff." Another student said, "Well, when [the scientist] was here, I kinda automatically took an idea of what I wanted to do, and also I related it to other games I played. And how, yeah, it's like a search and find game, and those are the games I like."

By choosing to base their own games on games they had already played, students alleviated some of the problems of planning and designing a game from scratch. Indeed, prior research has also found that students have modeled game design on commercial games and films (Baytak, 2009; Robertson & Nicholson, 2007; Yarnall & Kafai, 1996). Using familiar games also introduced well-known game mechanics into the student-created games, from replacing shooting bad guys to shooting diseases with antibiotics, to traversing a maze like Pac-Man in order to turn genes on and off. For these games, the students are not giving an accurate or literal representation of the science topics. This approach to game design is referred to as an artistic or architectural design, as opposed to an engineering design (Kafai, 1995; Kafai & Ching, 2001).

Finding #2. The second finding of this study indicated that students gather information about unfamiliar science topics through the personal Game Design Journals, web searches, and discussions with a scientist. Students were provided with multiple tools and resources to help them understand their science topic, including personal Game Design Journals for note-taking and drawing sketches, and a website with instructional videos, a list of resources, and a tool for emailing among the students and with the scientist. Students most prominently used their Game Design Journals (to take notes and plan and sketch out their ideas) and web searches (to gather information about their topics). These journals provided a way for students to think about their topics and their games before starting programming and worrying about technical issues. Giving the students the Game Design Journals and time to write down ideas and sketches was a way to effectively prompt their reflection process. Davis (2003) notes that prompting for reflection can help students focus on their own thinking (metacognition) or on the content (sense-making).

All students met in small groups with the scientist weekly, and would show her ideas they had recorded in their journals and found through their searches. Many times they would come to her with a concept or image to explore further. Together, the students and the scientist would review the websites that were too difficult for the students to decipher on their own. Students would also gather information during these meetings through questions that other students asked. For example, Michael believed he found in his online searching of resources that the drug methamphetamine destroys neurotransmitters. Instead, the scientist explained that methamphetamines actually mimic neurotransmitters and try to bind to neurotransmitter receptor sites. This caused Michael to change his idea, but Ethan, another student, used the concept of methamphetamines mimicking neurotransmitters for his game.

Much of the initial information gathered from web searches was collected through sites such as Wikipedia. The scientist instructed that Wikipedia would be fine for the initial search, but all that information had to be verified through trusted sources. These trusted sources proved to be difficult for the students to understand without help. Therefore, the first meetings with the scientist consisted of ideas and questions based on initial notes from the introductory lecture and web searches. Students led the group discussions in the meetings; this gave the scientist insight to where the individual students were heading and what issues they had with their topics. It allowed her to scaffold her advice on the specific information a particular student needed in order to continue on with his or her game. These meetings were ideal for the scientist to support the learning process, and allowed students to once again take the initiative in creating their own games. For a constructivist learning environment, this constant support is crucial (Jonassen, 1991).

Finding #3. The third finding in this study showed that students create video games through collaborative interactions. The interactions between students working together and influencing each other's games are referred to as collaborative interactions. There were three styles of collaboration apparent: collaborative interactions with students in the classroom, within groups that came together to make games, and with peer mentors. Although most students made their own individual game, two groups were formed because students had started talking together about their ideas, and decided to create a game together. Those that made individual games would usually have a group around their computer while they played out their games on screen. Students would comment on suggestions to make the games more interesting, help each other with programming code, and even to point out if the science topic in the game made sense or not. The peer mentors also offered suggestions, reminding students to balance making the game with adding in the science.

The traditional methods of collaboration include a group of members involved in a social engagement and negotiation to share knowledge and ideas while working together toward one project. In the case of game-making in this study, however, most students were working on individual projects with similar topics and the same goals. Some studies describe collaboration as students sharing ideas and offering suggestions for games even while working on separate projects (Baytak, 2009; Robertson & Howells, 2008). Yet because in this study, these sessions between students are informal and rely more on helpful suggestions rather than working together to provide a solution, it deems it necessary to distinguish these episodes from traditional collaboration. Kafai and Harel (1991) describe the setting of an open computer lab where students created instructional software as a place where students could work together for periods of time or work alone. In this environment, students engaged in social interaction where ideas and knowledge "floated" between the computers. They referred to this as "collaboration through the air," a term for the social and helpful interactions of students working alongside each other. Students in this game design workshop participated in collaborative interactions similar to the ones described by Kafai and Harel (1991) when working with other students in the classroom, most prevalently through sharing code, playing each other's games, and giving helpful advice about the technical aspects of the games.

Finding #4. The fourth finding of this study was that students' games changed as their understanding of the science topic evolved. In other words, as students' understanding of their science topics grew, they made changes to their games to reflect their new understanding. This phenomenon was discovered by noting changes to student games at three different evaluation points during the design workshop (at Weeks 2, 3, and 4), and by looking at supporting information from interviews, observations of group meetings with the scientist, and field notes. It was found that 10 out of 12 games created had some element of redesign in relation to the science concept in the game by the first evaluation point.

As an example, Wanda, although she picked a game topic about gene regulation, began sketching ideas for a game that focused on destroying sexually transmitted diseases within the first few days. The scientist encouraged her interest and Wanda decided on a shooting game in order to "get rid" of the diseases. The discussions she had with the scientist led Wanda to think about what the body starts doing when it is infected with the disease. During Week 2, she concentrated on the diseases AIDS and syphilis. Her main weapons against these diseases were the T-cells. After talking with the scientist, Wanda realized the way syphilis and AIDS infect the body and the way they are treated would be quite different. She went back to the computer lab to do more research about diseases in the body and removed AIDS from her game, replacing it with chlamydia. This introduced questions about how to destroy the new disease. Her subsequent discussions with the scientist centered on the methods by which chlamydia and syphilis are treated in the body and how the treatment process could be translated to being "destroyed" in her game. During Week 3, Wanda's shooting mechanism then turned into shooting antibiotics in order to get rid of the diseases. Her new understanding about these diseases gave her game a specific and more accurate focus, and this is reflected in the many changes her game took on at these two evaluation points. By the third evaluation point, her game had been well established.

As the students created their video games, they entered an iterative process of design, as discussed earlier. It is interesting that the students' understanding of the science topic also went through a similar iterative cycle. In considering the technical aspects of the game, the *discuss* stage of the design process was driven by peer mentors, instructors, and fellow students. However, with regard to the science topic, this phase of the *discuss* stage was driven by the weekly meetings with the scientist. Here, the data shows that students were asking questions about their topic and leaving the meeting with some new information to enter the *reflect* stage, which would then be featured in their game. The continued iterations of the design cycle that were fueled by the scientist meetings were observed to have happened through student-led initiatives; that is, students were not instructed to change their games after the meetings. The scientist offered them suggestions and guided them toward the answers they had inquired about. This kind of scaffolding helped students reflect upon the new information and drove the elements of change in the game content, as well as elements of change for understanding the science topic itself. The iterative cycle of design for both the game and the game content, although distinguished here separately for discussion purposes, occurred simultaneously, as students could not separate their thinking of design from the content (Kafai & Ching, 2001).

Finding #5. The fifth finding of this study was the process of making video games that helped students articulate their understanding of the science topic. Students were introduced to the four science topics on the second day of the workshop. From that moment, the topic of conversation within the computer lab, between the students and the scientist, and inside their game took on a very specific focus of science. Evidence of their growth in understanding their topic was found from observations of the way they talked about their games in the classroom, during small group meetings with the scientist, and at the end of the workshop when they presented their science games to an audience.

To follow the progression of one student, Michael started his game on the topic of neurotransmitters, but he was still very unsure about the topic and did not know the definition of a neurotransmitter. He did research on his own before he met with the scientist for their first meeting. He created a game prototype but was uncertain about a virus being responsible for "chasing" the neurotransmitters. Michael believed that he found the answer that methamphetamines destroy neurotransmitters and brought this up before the scientist during the first meeting, where the true role of methamphetamines was revealed. This discussion caused him to remove methamphetamines from his game. At one point, the scientist drew a diagram on the board of the neuron, labeling the axon and the neurotransmitters.

Scientist:	How do they get there in the first place? Do you know where they are?
Michael:	Channels?
Scientist:	Uh-huh, we talked about channels, but they're doing something else.
Michael:	The receptors.
Scientist:	Where are the receptors? This is the neuron, this is the body of the neuron, and this is the axon. Where are the receptors of the neurotransmitters?
Michael:	On the body of the cell.
Scientist:	Yeah, that's right, there are the receptors. So how did the neurotransmitters get into the synapse?
Michael:	They're released from the axon.
S-SME:	That's right, that's right. So they're hanging out in these vesicles over here.

Although still uncertain in some areas, Michael was able to hold a conversation with the scientist about neurotransmitters while adding to the dialogue, a vast improvement over the first days when he could not accurately give a definition of a neurotransmitter. Indeed, he initiated this conversation, understanding that there were gaps in his own knowledge that he could not identify. In Week 3, Michael asked the scientist about neurotransmitters levels, prompting a discussion between the two of them. This feature made it into the new version of his video game, which he presented in front of an audience. The scientist found his game and his articulation of the topic to be accurate and that Michael was very confident during his discussion.

Michael:	A neurotransmitter is a brain chemical that sends information throughout your brain and body. They're responsible for affecting your health . . . your mood, your concentration, basically anything that's hooked up to your nerves, whatever. And they have to be balanced; they can't be too high or too low. Things that affect the diet are, like, poor diet, stress, lack of exercise, lack of sleep, and drugs.

During his presentation, an audience member asked Michael what happens when the adverse elements in his game hit the neurons.

Michael:	It alters the levels—well in the game, it makes your health go down, which is basically the level of your neurotransmitters. In real life, it alters it and that can result in, like, you acting differently, and not really responding to your senses correctly.

Michael went from not understanding what a neurotransmitter was to being able to articulate how these chemicals in the brain can become imbalanced and how that may affect one's body, a process that can be followed through his own words and the design process of making the video game.

As students articulated their understanding of the science topics, it revealed the conceptual changes that were occurring with respect to their topics from week to week. Conceptual change refers to how students build their knowledge based in new ideas while situated in the context of the old ideas (diSessa, 2005). Posner, Strike, Hewson, and Gertzog (1982) assert that there are four conditions for the accommodation of conceptual change: dissatisfaction, intelligibility, plausibility, and fruitfulness. In dissatisfaction, the learner must find that there is something wrong with the current way of thinking that does not fit to help to solve the current problem. Intelligibility refers to the learner being able to make sense of the new concept, and perhaps this is made clear to the learner through example and analogies. Plausibility must show to the learner that the new concept is able to solve the current problem better than the old concept. Fruitfulness refers to the new concept opening up new avenues of inquiry for the learner. These four conditions can be found throughout the iterative processes of designing games and thinking about the science content. When meeting with the scientist, students would bring questions that had brought them to a state of dissatisfaction with their current understanding of the concept. In Michael's example, he came into the meeting wanting to have an enemy for his neurotransmitter game, but realized that this did not make sense for neurotransmitters. The state of dissatisfaction was revealed when students realized the gaps in their own knowledge, that what they currently knew about the science topic was not adequate—gaps that were sometimes revealed when they tried to articulate their understanding, and found they could not. The condition of intelligibility came about during and after meetings, through discussions provided by the scientist, as well as after the meeting, when students had to make sense of the new information. Plausibility occurred when students realized new information helped them understand the topic better and incorporated this into their game. Fruitfulness came about when students began to use their new foundations of the science topic to continue to think in new avenues, such as the students in the group who worked on a myelin sheath game and decided to discover what causes the deterioration of the myelin.

Although the students of nine out of 12 games were shown to have been able to successfully articulate their understanding of their science topic by the end of the game design workshop, not all students in this study were able to do this well. The students who created the three games in the Low group had the most trouble with understanding—and communicating this understanding of—their topics. James, who created a game about the myelin sheath, was driven more by making an exciting game than staying true to the topic, although he showed an improved understanding of the myelin sheath over the first weeks of the program. Anthony created a game about gene regulation, but he was more interested in bacteria and ultimately incorrectly made connections between the role of bacteria and viruses with respect to his topic. For these two students, conflicting ideas they had could not be reconciled with their topic to make a cohesive game. The group of four students who created the last game in the Low group had a different dilemma. The group had issues collaborating together in order to create the game, which led to missed opportunities to engage with their science topic. Interestingly, this group consisted of strong learners, each with specific interests in programming, art, and research skills. However, they had not been able to agree on their roles within the group before focusing on their individual goals. After multiple discussions with the scientist, they seemed to have an idea to work with in the very final week of design, but it was too late in the program to make a coherent game.

Implications for Using Game Design for Science Learning

The iterative process of game design lent itself well to thinking about science within the context of making a game. It provided opportunities for students to engage with the science content by thinking and reflecting about the topic, designing the content into the game, testing the game, and through discussions with the scientist when they were gaining new information to take back to reflect upon, ready to start the cycle again. In this way, the students were thinking about the science in an iterative cycle alongside designing the physical game, and their understanding of the topic was being shaped through the iterations. Not only did the thinking and creating process get shaped by this iterative cycle, it provided an opportunity for students to question their own understanding and identify gaps in their knowledge. The period between testing and discussing with the scientist allowed an opportunity for students to explain their work, to articulate their understanding of the science up to that point, or as Sawyer (2005) indicates, a way for them to think out loud. It becomes an invaluable tool not only for the students to think about science, but also for educators to follow the progression of their thinking.

With respect to the resources students used to supplement their knowledge, students gathered information by conducting web searches. Students were given the approval to use websites like Wikipedia as a starting point for research, but were encouraged to use trusted websites that were provided to verify the information. As this proved difficult to do on their own, students brought their findings to the scientist to validate, or else they could verify them together. This highlights the need for proper support for students gathering information on the Internet in any setting, whether for making games or for writing reports. Having the scientist for student support was very important, to both search for the information and to discuss the findings. Therefore it would be essential to scaffold students on their research processes, and to allow for engaged dialogue with an expert on the topic.

Another component of the design process that helped students with their games was the collaborative processes they experienced in the game design workshop. Although most students in this study chose to create a game individually, they were still interacting with their peers in the computer lab. To continue the spirit of collaboration among students, it would be beneficial to encourage student testing of each other's games, and to allow for time for students to present and share their games to their peers at regular intervals during the game design workshop, or class. In this workshop, students presented their work only at the end, which was a great way to share knowledge and receive feedback from the crowd, something students would have undoubtedly benefited from if it had happened more frequently throughout the program.

Summary

The game design environment used in this study allowed students to be put in charge of designing their own games based on science topics. As supported by Papert's (1980) notion that learners can build knowledge through artifact creation, students were able to construct and build upon their understanding of immunology science topics through game design. This study showed that students were able to model their games on video games upon familiar games, gather information through design journals, web queries, and discussions with a science expert, work collaboratively, be involved in changing their understanding of the topics, including identifying what they needed to know and understanding that they did not know enough, and articulate their understanding of the science topic.

Future studies should continue to allow students to be exposed to the content, to collaborate with experts in the field, and to help shape their learning through their own design, giving them multiple opportunities to create with science and technology and to help fuel their interests and future career choices. It has become a national initiative to encourage youth interest in STEM fields, with the acknowledgement that certain populations such as African Americans are substantially underrepresented in these fields (see Federal Science, Technology, Engineering, and Mathematics (STEM) Education 5-Year Strategic Plan, 2013). Creating culturally relevant programs aimed at helping underserved populations develop their interests in STEM fields not only provides exposure to the content and the careers available, but can allow students to use their own talents and backgrounds to enrich their learning experience and help them make a meaningful connection to the design process.

Based on the findings of this research, deliberate efforts should be made to recruit and retain female participants, mentors, and instructors. This may help to increase and sustain the number of girls in the program. Additionally, similar efforts should be made to recruit and retain instructors of color as a way modeling participation the STEM careers and disciplines. Because students tended to base their designs on games they had experience with, exposing students to a wide range of video game formats and approaches may lead to more innovative video game design solutions.

Putting students in charge of creating their own video games based on unfamiliar science topics provided a window into the design process students undertook when placed in a constructivist and constructionist learning environment with available tools and support to complete their games. The findings of this work highlight student strategies during the design process which include modeling their games on video games with which they were already familiar, gathering information through design journals, web queries, and discussions with a science expert, and working collaboratively. These activities provide guidance to students as they learn what is needed to create their video games, as well as providing instructors and program developers with the types of skills and practices students need to accomplish these activities.

References

Baytak, A. (2009). *An investigation of the artifacts, outcomes, and processes of constructing computer games about environmental science in a fifth grade classroom* (Doctoral dissertation). Available from ProQuest Dissertations and Theses database (UMI No. 3399626).

Becker, K. (2007). Pedagogy in commercial video games. In D. Gibson, C. Aldrich, & M. Prensky (Eds.), *Games and simulations in online learning: Research and development frameworks* (pp. 21–48). Hershey, PA: Information Science Publishing. doi:10.4018/978-1-59904-304-3.ch002

Clark, K., & Sheridan, K. (2010). Game design through mentoring and collaboration. *Journal of Educational Multimedia and Hypermedia, 19*(2), 125–145.

Corbin, J., & Strauss, A. (2008). *Basics of qualitative research: Techniques and procedures for developing grounded theory* (3rd ed.). Los Angeles, CA: Sage Publications. doi:10.4135/9781452230153

Creswell, J. W. (2008). *Educational research: Planning, conducting, and evaluating quantitative and qualitative research*. Upper Saddle River, NJ: Pearson.

Davis, E. A. (2003). Prompting middle school science students for productive reflection: Generic and directed prompts. *Journal of the Learning Sciences, 12*(1), 91–142. doi:10.1207/S15327809JLS1201_4

diSessa, A. A. (2005). A history of conceptual change research: Threads and fault lines. In R. K. Sawyer (Ed.), *Cambridge handbook of the learning sciences*. New York, NY: Cambridge University Press. doi: 10.1017/CBO9780511816833.017

Druin, A. (2002). The role of children in the design of new technology. *Behaviour and Information Technology, 21*(1), 1–25. doi:10.1080/01449290110108659

Entertainment Software Association (2015). *2015 essential facts about the computer and video game industry*. Retrieved from http://www.theesa.com/wp-content/uploads/2015/04/ESA-Essential-Facts-2015.pdf

Flannagan, M., Howe, D.C., & Nissenbaum, H. (2005). Values at play: Design tradeoffs in socially-oriented game design. *Proceedings of CHI* (pp. 751–760).

Flannery, L., Kazakoff, E., Bonta, P., Silverman, B., Bers, M., & Resnick, M. (2013). Designing ScratchJr: Support for early childhood learning through computer programming. *Proceedings of the 2013 Interaction Design and Children (IDC) Conference* (pp. 1–10). New York, NY: ACM. doi: doi:10.1145/2485760.2485785

Friedman, R., & Saponara, A. (2008). The design, implementation, and effectiveness of educational software: Developing technology and geography skills through participatory design. *Journal of Interactive Learning Research, 19*(2), 271–292.

Gee, J. P. (2003). *What video games have to teach us about learning and literacy.* New York, NY: Palgrave MacMillan.

Gee, J. P. (2012). Digital games and libraries. *Knowledge Quest, 41*(1), 60–64.

Harel, I. (1988). *Software design for learning: Children's construction of meaning for fractions and LOGO programming.* Boston, MA: MIT.

Jonassen, D. H. (1991). Objectivism versus constructivism: Do we need a new philosophical paradigm? *Educational Technology Research and Development, 39*, 5–14. doi:10.1007/BF02296434

Kafai, Y. B. (1995). *Minds in play.* Hillsdale, NJ: Lawrence Erlbaum Associates.

Kafai, Y. B., & Ching, C. C. (2001). Affordances of collaborative software design planning for elementary students' science talk. *Journal of the Learning Sciences, 10*(3), 323–363. doi:10.1207/S15327809JLS1003_4

Kafai, Y. B., & Harel, I. (1991). *Learning through design and teaching: Exploring social and collaborative aspects of constructionism.* In I. Harel & S. Papert (Eds.), *Constructionism* (pp. 85–110). Norwood, NJ: Ablex Publishing Corporation.

Kafai, Y. B., & Peppler, K. A. (2012). Developing gaming fluencies with Scratch: Realizing game design as an artistic process. In C. Steinkuehler, K. Squire, & S. Barab (Eds.), *Games, learning, and society: Learning and meaning in the digital age* (pp. 355–380). New York, NY: Cambridge University Press. doi:10.1017/CBO9781139031127.026

Khalili, N., Sheridan, K., Williams, A., Clark, K., & Stegman, M. (2011). Students designing video games about immunology: Insights for science learning. *Computers in the Schools, 28*(3), 228–240. doi:10.1080/07380569.2011.594988

Kolodner, J., Camp, P., Crismond, D., Fasse, B., Gray, J., Holbrook, J., Puntambekar, S., & Ryan, M. (2003). Problem-based learning meets case-based reasoning in the middle-school science classroom: Putting learning by design into practice. *Journal of the Learning Sciences, 12*(4), 495–497. doi:10.1207/S15327809JLS1204_2

Lee, C. D. (2003). Toward a framework for culturally responsive design in multimedia computer environments: Cultural modeling as a case. *Mind, Culture, and Activity, 10*(1), 42–61. doi: 10.1207/S15327884MCA1001_05

Lenhart, A., Kahne, J., Middaugh, E., Macgill, A., Evans, C., & Vitak, J. (2008). *Teens, video games and civics.* Retrieved from http://www.pewinternet.org/2008/09/16/teens-video-games-and-civics/

Lim, C. P. (2008). Spirit of the game: Empowering students as designers in schools? *British Journal of Educational Technology, 39*(6), 996–1003. doi:10.1111/j.1467-8535.2008.00823_1.x

National Science and Technology Council, Committee on STEM Education. (2013). *Federal science, technology, engineering, and mathematics (STEM) education 5-year strategic plan.* Retrieved from https://www.whitehouse.gov/sites/default/files/microsites/ostp/stem_stratplan_2013.pdf

Papert, S. (1980). *Mindstorms.* New York, NY: Basic Books, Inc.

Posner, G. J., Strike, K. A., Hewson, P. W., & Gertzog, W. A. (1982). Accommodation of a scientific conception: Toward a theory of conceptual change. *Science Education, 66*(2), 211–227. doi: 10.1002/sce.3730660207

Prensky, M. (2007). *Digital game-based learning.* St. Paul, MN: Paragon House.

Project Tomorrow. (2008). *21st-century students deserve a 21st-century education.* Retrieved from http://www.tomorrow.org/docs/National%20Findings%20Speak%20Up%202007.pdf

Resnick, M. (2007). Showing the seeds for more creative society. *Learning and Leading with Technology.* Retrieved from http://web.media.mit.edu/~mres/papers/Learning-Leading-final.pdf

Robertson, J., & Howells, C. (2008). Computer games design: Opportunities for successful learning. *Computers & Education, 50*(2), 559–578. doi:10.1016/j.compedu.2007.09.020

Robertson, J., & Nicholson K. (2007). Adventure Author: A learning environment to support creative design. *Proceedings of the 6th International Conference on Interaction Design and Children—IDC '07.* doi:10.1145/1297277.1297285

Sawyer, R. K. (2005). Introduction: The new science of learning. In R. K. Sawyer (Ed.), *The Cambridge handbook of the learning sciences* (pp. 1–16). New York, NY: Cambridge University Press. doi:10.1017/CBO9780511816833.002

Shaffer, D. W., & Gee, J. P. (2012). The right kind of GATE: Computer games and the future of assessment. In M. Mayrath, D. Robinson, & J. Clarke (Eds.), *Games, learning, and society: Learning and meaning in the digital age* (pp. 403–433). Cambridge, UK: Cambridge University Press. doi:10.1017/CBO9781139031127.028

Sheridan, K., Clark, K., & Williams, A. (2013). Designing games, designing roles: A study of youth agency in an urban informal education program. *Urban Education, 48*(3), 45–57. doi:10.1177/0042085913491220

Squire, K. (2011). *Video games and learning.* New York, NY: Teacher's College Press.

Yarnall, L., & Kafai, Y. (1996). *Issues in project-based science activities: Children's constructions of ocean software games.* Paper presented at the Annual Meeting of the American Educational Research Association, New York, NY.

14
HOW THE CULTURAL CLASH OF ESSENTIALISM AND PROGRESSIVISM SHAPED TECHNOLOGY ADOPTION

A Case Study of Culture, Learning, and Technology

Steven Watkins and Mansureh Kebritchi

Introduction

Since the establishment and implementation of the national American public school system process in the mid- to late nineteenth century (Schutz, 2011), outside forces (social, cultural, political) have vied to influence, correct, manipulate, and guide educational content and conveyance in the public primary and secondary schools. Since the late twentieth and early twenty-first centuries, two notable educational theories have attempted to shape public education in this country; essentialist educational theory and its proponents and progressive educational theory and its proponents (Kessinger, 2011; Schutz, 2011). In education, essentialism is evidenced in initiatives like the National Defense Education Act of 1958, Elementary and Secondary Act of 1965, The National Assessment of Educational Progress, A Nation at Risk report, America 2000, Goals 2000, and the Elementary and Secondary Act of 2001, otherwise known as "No Child Left Behind;" progressivism is reflected in "pedagogies designed to nurture the individual voice within egalitarian classrooms" (Schutz, 2011, p.1). For example, under John Dewey's direction, specific instructional strategies such as cooperative learning, where students learned to work together in small groups on similar learning tasks in order to coordinate their efforts and learn to rely on each other for help. Progressives also emphasized such instructional strategies as problem-based learning, where students are presented with authentic and meaningful situations that serve as a basis for inquiry and investigation (Instructional Strategies, p. 12). The differences in the initiatives based in these theories are indicative of a cultural clash with potential impact on learning and technological practices.

Progressive and essentialist educational theories resonate with cultural clashes going on in all aspects of human life in the twenty-first century, often portrayed as traditionalist versus progress or conservative versus liberal. A starting point for this examination is a working definition given by Sorin and Dinu (2014) who state that culture usually consists of life experiences derived from more or less organized, learned created images and codes from the effort of individuals of a population and that are transmitted from generation to generation. Further, Sorin and Dinu (2014) suggest that culture and education possess a very direct and intimate relationship, and that in the past "traditional culture was preserved, transmitted due to the educational process." In the late twentieth and early twenty-first century, such an intimate relationship has been challenged by such forces as globalization; according to Sorin and Dinu (2014), such forces as globalization are promoting and heightening regional and global encounters/clashes between tradition and change. Huntington (1997) reinforces this idea by stating that cultures are clashing with values annunciated by such forces as globalization; this clash between tradition and change is demonstrated through all kinds of human endeavors, particularly education. Essentialist educational theory associates with tradition and competency and progressivism associates with change and challenge. Today, cultural clashes are attempts by people through the different permutations of culture (politics, social, religious, ethnic) to influence human activities (education, politics, religion, etc.) to a favorable status in regards to that person's or group's situation in society. Since education is such an intimate aspect of how culture passes on its ideas, values, and concepts to future generations, it is only fitting to examine how this process affects it.

Literature Review

Essentialist educational theory focuses on developing a competent and skilled person, with focus on teaching reading, writing, and arithmetic, liberal arts and science, and other academic disciplines (Hirsch, 2009; Kessinger, 2011). The essence of essentialism is dealing with "factual knowledge." Essentialism focuses on instructional strategies such as direct instruction, where the teacher and efforts can be directed imparting knowledge in a goal-directed, teacher-controlled environment (Instructional Strategies, pp. 5–6). Essentialists believe in a teaching environment where there are defined learning outcomes, transmitted new information, and skill demonstration and guided practice (Instructional Strategies, p. 6). Particularly since the mid-twentieth century, this potential conflict pits accentuating the basics; that is content, skills, and disciplines found in the context of education versus "recreating the democratic process," influenced by the thoughts and ideas of John Dewey (Giroux, 2012; Kessinger, 2011; Price, Duffy & Giordani, 2013; Schutz; 2011).

Progressivism, primarily under the influence of John Dewey, viewed the constant conflict between labor and management in the late nineteenth and early twentieth century with thoughtful reflection; Dewey and his associates examined this violent process as the unions, on one hand, being too focused on conflict and mass solidarity and, on the other hand, the rich as driven by too much greed and lack of social compassion (Schutz, 2011). Schutz (2011) noted how progressives focused on students' learning social skills such as learning to cooperate with each other on tasks and engaging in group thought to solve problems. Even today, it is noted that even in the era of "basic skills achievement era of No Child Left Behind" (Larabee, 2004, p. 142), most educators remain intellectually and emotionally committed to the one of the main ideas of progressive educational theory, that being "the school as a model democratic community," using the idea of educational reform to reform society around the principles of social justice and democratic equality.

The cultural/political conflict over educational policy and practice between proponents of essentialist educational theory and progressive educational theory continues today with long-standing beliefs and ideas. One area of definable conflict is over the issue of standards and accountability—a setting of what a student should minimally know and how the educational system should be evaluated in terms of meeting those standards (Schutz, 2011). Essentialist educational theory proponents have introduced the concept of accountability in evaluating how effective and efficient the public educational system is in teaching public school students (primary and secondary); to wit, progressives have resisted such attempts. E.D. Hirsch, a strong essentialist educational theorist, (2009) stated that progressives, or as he termed them, "the anti-curriculum movement," have slandered essentialists by the use of "effective, polarizing slogans that have been erected over the years, a propaganda effort that continues to preserve the anti-curriculum doctrine in the face of failure and decline" (p. 53). Hirsch continued in his discussion of how this opposition to an established core curriculum (the heart and soul of essentialism) had been strengthened since the early twentieth century. He complains that progressives have labeled essentialism as a certain academic approach that is anti-liberal, authoritarian, elitist, and right-wing, an effective rhetorical maneuver against it (p. 53). Other scholars concur with Hirsch on his position about the obstructionist ideas of progressive educational theorists and that public education cannot be continued in the old way as before in its progressive influenced practice (Kessinger, 2011; and to some degree, Peterson, 2003). Peterson (2003) pointed out that the seminal idea of defining the inadequacy of the public educational system under progressivism was that students could not count, read, or think out basic problems, skills needed to function in society. Peterson emphasized how the National Commission on Excellence in Education's famed 1983 study, *America at Risk*, highlighted how the country's educational institutions, under progressive influence, lost sight of the basic purposes of education on all levels of public education (Peterson, 2003, p. xvii). The value of the report was its emphasis on the threat of mediocrity, a threat which has not gone away and is still on the rise, stifling the need for intellectual and moral strength to stop it. Peterson (2003) pointed out that far from stemming the rising tide, the recommendations of the commission were only selectively adopted, providing reform more symbolic than substantive.

In contrast, progressive educators feel that the issue "of accountability," one of the primary goals of essentialist educational theorists, is really a mask for destroying public education and one of its main principals, that of teaching egalitarianism (Giroux, 2012). Diane Ravitch, a former official in the Department of Education during the George W. Bush presidency, who first believed that the proponents of this essentialism put forward a good idea. Ravitch (2010) argued that "in the decade following my stint in the federal government, I argued that certain managerial and structural changes—that is choice, charters, merit pay, and accountability—would help to reform our schools" (p. 8). With such changes, teachers and schools would be judged by their performance; this was a basic principle in the business world. Towards the end of the first decade of the twenty-first century, Ravitch (2010) experienced a change of heart; she noted that while sounding appealing, the one fatal flaw in this thinking was that a person could supposedly ignore traditional and established educational theory and practice. Ravitch further elaborated that "the lure of the market is the idea that freedom from government regulation was a complete solution all by itself. While appealing on the surface, such an idea did not stand up to scrutiny, especially when so many seemingly well-planned school reforms have failed to deliver on their promise" (p. 11). In a sharp contrast to her earlier support, Ravitch stated the new corporate reformers exhibited a strong ignorance of what education is all about when they attempt to adapt it to a business-type model (p. 11). Giroux (2012) echoed support for her analysis when he stated that when not functioning as a business or a lucrative for-profit investment, public schools have become containment centers. Schools become holding centers for punishing young people marginalized by class and race and Giroux holds the belief that profit is the main motive of "educational reformers" and thus is suspicious of its motives. The whole point of the contrast between essentialist educational theory and progressive educational theory is that they are being used to assert control over the public educational process for certain gains and are the context in which a contest for influencing public education is happening (Hirsch, 2009; Giroux, 2012). Giroux (2012), Price, Duffy, and Giordani (2013) strongly defended public education from what they call the obsession of venture capitalist types, focusing on managing public educational entities based on business principles. Price, Duffy and Giordani (2013) made clear that he and his colleagues were publishing news articles, academic journal articles and joining with students, parents, teachers, and union leaders in the Midwest to fight on behalf of public education. Giroux made clear his progressive spirit when he compared the present environment affecting public schools with a customized quote from Charles Dickens that "this is the worst of times for all kinds of public education in that their mission is viewed as primarily a business that should be focused on customer satisfaction and efficiency;" to Giroux the whole point of educational reform is to make a few dollars in profit at the expense of public education (Giroux, 2012, p. iv).

Today, that cultural clash between essentialists, perhaps more familiar to people as the school reform movement, and progressives (the anti-test movement) continues across the United States, in different public educational situations in various manifestations. In many parts of the United States, these two opposing educational theory viewpoints are influencing how public education students learn content.

Schutz (2011) opines about how many educators feel today about the public educational process; he suggests that many progressive educators still hope that the idea of "the school as a democratic community" (p. 1) can still be a means to reforming society around the principles of social justice and democratic equality. He points to a theory of power that explains how decisions are made in an actual societal setting, based on the ideas of Saul Alinsky (1971), as expressed in his writings and the development of his institution—the Industrial Areas Foundation. Through the coordination of two of his disciples, Richard Harmon and Edward Chambers, who codirected and coworked with Alinsky, these ideas provided insight into how the political process influenced education. Harmon (Schutz, 2011) and Chambers and Cowan (2003) developed their ideas about the political process on American society and refined the training and organizing methods in this institution that were needed in order to be an effective advocate for their political ideas.

Professional educators, in this emerging century, perform their task in an environment replete with potentially influential forces generated by this cultural conflict, one of which is political, and must recognize that condition. They cannot conduct or pretend to do teaching vis-à-vis adopted technological practices under the assumption of the education situation being an insular environment; the political forces unleashed by this cultural conflict examined here are political forces with unknown and unclear, yet potential and influential consequences in these educators' professional situation. Through the template provided by the ideas of Alinsky (1971), realizing certain principles developed by Harmon (Schutz, 2011) and Chambers and Cowan (2003), it is hoped that an initial awareness of such an influence, without judging its potential, can be culled from discussion with the literature, educational professionals (politicians, administrators, teachers), and associated personnel and entities.

One of the insights that individuals associated with the public education process in the United States must recognize is that politics are a part of this cultural conflict. Chambers and Cowan (2003) and Schutz (2011) note that teaching in a political context must be understood by progressive educators in the world of human experience, of which education is part and parcel, and that is understanding the tension of the world in terms of how it functions in human existence. Chambers and Cowan (2003) observes that in the world as it should be, democracy means participation in public decisions in which all are included because of the dignity of being "created equal" (p. 14). In the real world, democracy is dominated by the interests of a few wealthy and powerful institutions. He notes that one must accept two conditions of the world in which human beings exist; first, we are born into a world of needs and necessities, opportunities and limitations, and we cannot ignore this world of needs and necessities and the practices human beings will engage in in order to satisfy that situation, what he calls the "real world" (p. 14). Secondly, Chambers and Cowan (2003) points out that human beings have dreams and expectations, yearnings and values, a sense that there is an ideal, a greater good that matters, and if we do not attempt to reach that ideal, then we know that we have not fulfilled ourselves.

Chambers and Cowan (2003), Harmon (Schutz, 2011), and Schutz (2011) insisted academics must realize that learning and technological practices do not exist in a vacuum. Cultural forces, such as politics, exert a strong and clear influence on the learning process and how it is communicated to public school students. Lareau (2003) and Collins (1990) insisted that this lack of awareness came from the middle-class practices of children of professionals who were asked for their opinions, participate in dialogues about issues, lived in a world of negotiations, existed with uncertainty, not established traditions and mores.

Case Study

A school system in a southwestern state provided an example of the cultural conflict between essentialist theory and progressive theory in education and its impact on technology adoption in public schools. The essentialist perspective is represented by political proponents of the school reform movement (hereafter referred to as the Essentialist Movement) while the progressive perspective is represented by the anti-test movement who have pressured state government to reduce the number of state-mandated testing for public school students (hereafter referred to as the progressive movement). The ethnic makeup of the district was 76% Hispanic, 20% White, and 7% Black.

Two questions guided the exploration of this cultural clash:

Research Question 1: What is/was the influence of the cultural clash of essentialism and progressivism on the adoption of a system-wide technology innovation, Educational Curriculum Management System (ECMS)?

Research Question 2: How do ECMS stakeholders (professional educators, administrators, educational-related entities, and political individuals) perceive the cultural clash of essentialism and progressivism now and for future learning content and technological practices?

To answer these questions, a purposeful sampling of educational professionals, associated entity organizational staff, university scholars, and political observers and activists involved in the public educational process (primary and secondary) in a school district in a southwestern state (hereafter, Southwestern State School

District) were studied using a qualitative case study research design. A sampling size of ten educational professionals and related individuals were recruited to focus on the perception of this situation as a positive or negative social change. In an attempt to be fair-minded about including all perceptions about the potential cultural clash growing out of the expanding influence of the Essentialist Movement in this southwestern state's public education, we attempted to reach out to individuals in this district who might represent a different point of view. Most of the individuals interviewed possessed progressive ideas with a realization of the need for essentialism; we reached out to a number of essentialists, but they declined to participate in the study.

The individuals recruited for this study were:

1) Arthur, local newspaper journalist familiar with this problem;
2) Jack, an essentialist and a member of this state's Board of Education, whose father helped write the modern version of the state's educational policy 32 years ago;
3) Louise, an essentialist and a former trustee of this school board;
4) Fred, a progressive and an African-American trustee from another local school board familiar with the situation;
5) Hector, a progressive and the local leader of a teachers' union;
6) Ralph, a non-aligned local professor/scholar of politics in this state;
7) Edward, a non-aligned high-placed administrator in a local school district;
8) Taylor, a progressive and a writer for a statewide political organization;
9) Tom, a progressive and a local organizer for a community group that specializes in quality of life issues;
10) Mary, a progressive and teacher with the affected school district;
11) Louise, a progressive and teacher with the affected school district;
12) Henry, an essentialist and recently elected school board member.

These 12 individuals responded to my interviews for the study. Other educational personnel, essentialist and progressive, were invited to participate in the study; some educators declined for fear of retribution. If they talked to me, they might be sued for violating a non-disclosure act they had signed with the school district.

Background

In this state in 2013, people aligned with the Essentialist Movement and philosophy, and flexed their ideological and intentional influence over a statewide electronic curriculum management system (Floyd, 2013; Selk, 2013). ECMS offered Web-based lesson plans and exams for teachers to use in their classroom lessons; it was developed "to help teachers adhere to state educational requirements" (Dallas News, 2013, p. 2). In this school district, ECMS emerged as a potential way to help the school district with student achievement on the annual standardized tests that gauged student competency. Selk (2013) mentioned that up until May 2013, the Southwestern State School District had integrated ECMS into its educational year; he noted that there had been some hiccups such as bogging teachers down in paperwork, failing to prepare students for state tests, and inflexibility for teachers to use optional material, but the school district leadership felt comfortable with the potential essentialist benefits. It had emerged as a popular program, being used in 857 school districts—70% of the school districts in this southwestern state. To Essentialist Movement activists involved in the political process in this school district, the biggest problem was the perception of how such instructional strategies like problem-based instruction (based on progressivism) was developing scenarios and incorporating them into the ECMS-generated lesson plans that favored acceptance of Islam and Socialism. Selk (2013) pointed out that Essentialist Movement-oriented school board trustees complained that ECMS-generated lesson plans indoctrinated students into Islam and Socialism. At the last minute, in the 2013–2014 school year, once Essentialist Movement-oriented trustees assumed control, Southwestern State School District had its learning content and technological adoption of this program altered significantly, eliminating ECMS and its attendant technological adoption. In this cultural clash, the participants, both essentialists and progressives, felt that their approach to learning and technological conveyance practices were in the interest of the children and youth of this district.

Results/Discussion

Research Question 1

What is/was the influence of the cultural clash of essentialism and progressivism on the adoption/implementation of ECMS?

The first observable influence coming out of this cultural clash is any type of learning content, and instructional technological adoption not in alignment with the goals and objectives of the essentialist (school reform movement) is not acceptable and will not be implemented. As Louise, the former trustee in this affected school district said, "the point of using ECMS was essentialist in nature. She noted that the trustees, administrative, lead teachers, and other key personnel thought ECMS would help struggling students on statewide mandated tests, particularly minority students, who made up the majority of students in that district; the ethnic makeup of the district was 76% Hispanic, 20% White, and 7% Black. Once Essentialist Movement-backed trustees ascended into domination on this school board, the use of the teacher-developed ECMS curriculum was immediately terminated. And these trustees did not stop there; they attempted to eliminate the bilingual program with a focus on total immersion in English.

According to this former trustee, the reason that the bilingual program was not gutted more was because of Federal and State regulations. The practice of dual language acquisition skills was frowned upon by Essentialist Movement-led trustees, even though the ethnic makeup of the school district was 76% Hispanic, 20% White, and 7% Black.

A second observable influence growing out of this situation is the lack of interest in providing any learning content and instructional technology resource. The newly appointed Essentialist Movement-led trustees displayed an ideological influenced lack of interest in discussing, planning, and implementing a school bond program for infrastructural needs. In this southwestern state, school bond elections are used for upgrading a school district's infrastructural needs such as buildings, either directly or indirectly associated with the district's educational mission. In addition, and usually included in a school bond election, are technologically enhancing necessities such as upgrading Internet speed and capability in order to increase bandwidth accessibility to access various computer programming and technological resources and applications. According to Louise, the former trustee involved in such planning for this district, the Essentialist Movement-leaning school board members "exhibited no desire to engage any effort on such issues." Louise declared that such "an empathy for smallness is part of the Essentialist Movement ideology on education, nurtured by the essentialist movement."

Ralph, a history professor familiar with culture and politics in this southwestern state noted the attitude of Essentialist Movement members towards public education; he observed that many individuals and organizations associated with the Essentialist Movement, "considered public education nothing more than a vast bureaucracy bent on socializing and manipulating society." In response to the question, "how do you perceive the Essentialist Movement and its ideology shaping and influencing the way government policy and procedure is done in the next few years, particularly as it relates to learning and instructional technological policies and practices?," his response was that "this southwestern state's legislature would be loath to fund public education to the levels envisioned by educational professionals because it would be influenced by Essentialist Movement sympathizers who believe any governmental apparatus needs to be small." He further added that Essentialist Movement believers and their influenced politicians would be interested in such public education funding approaches such as vouchers, charter schools (both online and onground), funding access for private and religious schools that they felt could teach students cheaper and better than public school entities. He emphatically stated that Essentialist Movement ideologues and sympathizers focused on the accountability aspect of public education in terms other than of monetary funding and supplemental support. Henry, an essentialist elected trustee of Southwestern State school district's was given the opportunity to respond to this question, but declined to do so for this report.

Research Question 2

How do ECMS stakeholders (professional educators, administrators, educational-related entities, and political individuals) perceive the cultural clash of essentialism and progressivism now and for future learning and technological adoption and practices?

First, according to the individuals interviewed for this study, political influence, arising out of the cultural clash between essentialism and progressivism, is going to influence learning and instructional technology adoption and practice on a broader scale and that the event with ECMS was just the forerunner of events to come.

Fred, an African-American trustee, involved in the governance of a large urban school district that was targeted by essentialist-motivated activists to become a large charter school district not regulated by state law, responded to this developing cultural clash by stating that "the essentialist movement with its attendant alliances was developing an intentional and ideological effort to control public education content and instructional technology adoption in this state," and in his opinion, the Essentialist Movement political effort was part of the overall essentialist effort. This individual strongly opined that in this southwestern state the purpose of public education is no longer about education; "it is the new Jim Crow law designed to slight and stymie minority students' education."

Secondly, in this developing cultural conflict, the attitude of ECMS stakeholders involves three approaches. First, in the affected school district, professional educators Mary and Louise cited the attitude of passive acceptance in that the educational administrator or classroom professional accepts or ignores the political situation as the reality and adjusts their decision making approaches to educational content and technological adoption and practices accordingly. Mary, an educator in the school district stated that "everyone was made to feel that they should march to the new orders in order to keep their jobs." Louise stated that many educators who felt hindered by the new approach "accepted payouts, if they were close to retirement, with the stipulation that they sign non-disclosure agreements." My efforts in trying to gather additional information for this study, particularly from other educational professionals in this school district, were stymied because many were loath to discuss or express their views on the issue, even when guaranteed anonymity. For example, Jackie, another educator in the district, complimented my comments over the blog, but would never respond when I sent her an email for further comment. Oliver, the school district public information officer, would not return the three to four phone calls and emails requesting comment from him.

The second approach was the approach of active antagonism, in that the individuals would work through their local teacher, administrator, or school board association to thwart a perceived essentialist agenda. In interviewing Hector, the local leader of the teachers' union that was politically active in an urban school district, he stated that "the union's efforts helped in a decisive school district's school board trustee election situation." He believed that the effort paid off in electing a trustee that opposed establishing a charter for the school district, an obscure educational option promoted by Essentialist Movement activists that would make that school district a private entity, thus freeing it from state regulation. Fred, the African-American trustee, stated that "it seemed that this movement's main focus was to scuttle public education through any means possible." In this school district, Hector and the union members felt that active antagonism, in such efforts like going door to door encouraging people to vote, using phone banks, doing mass mailings, and engaging in social media worked to their advantage politically.

The third approach was trying to actively engage the developing situation and seek to work, neutralize, or co-opt it. This third approach proved very interesting to examine as a reaction to political influence and activity. An example of this third approach to the developing cultural clash between essentialism and progressivism occurred when a top-ranking administrator for another local school district discussed the influence of the Essentialist Movement on learning content and instructional technological conveyance in that individual's school district. Edward, a highly placed administrator, stated that "the top administrators in his school district saw the changing educational environment and chose to be proactive and work with the developing situation instead of reacting to it." One of the things that his school district did was to set up agreements with local charter schools for transferring of credit, create specialized focused academies for students to attend; for example, if a student wanted to specialize in math, an academy was set up to address that student's need. Edward mentioned that in response to "the growing need for Information Technology specialists, skilled machinists in local industries, and other non-degreed career needs, the local school district set up a specialized high school for that purpose." Edward felt that by being aware and proactive, this school district was able to minimize such political influence and activity's potential disruption and maintain its educational focus. Tom, the local organizer for the community group, applauded such an approach; he believed that this school district "realistically understood the political process is going to be governed by someone; for an activity such as public education, political control and influence cannot be treated as an event to be ignored in the public education environment." Such awareness appeared to pay off for this school district, because stakeholders on this developing educational situation (essentialists and progressives) praised their efforts.

Conclusion

Pertinent insights on culture, learning, and technological practices can be extracted from this case study. First, if one is to develop authentic and competent learning and technological practices, then that individual (educator, lead educator, administration, politician, etc.) needs to realize that culture influences such practices. This process does not exist in a vacuum. Secondly, manifestations arising out of that cultural atmosphere, conflict, etc., are going to influence the learning and technological conveyance practices for that situation. Such manifestations as the Essentialist Movement, using many different approaches, impact the learning aspect by prohibiting certain types of content material, but sometimes more so the technological adoption aspect of the situation when such political influence pursues withholding necessary funding to public schools who need technological upgrades in order to use more technically advanced computer hardware. A case in point is the lawsuit brought by over 70% of the school districts in this southwestern state against the legislature for not providing sufficient funding for educating public school students. Thirdly, such impediments will only grow in the atmosphere arising from the essentialist/progressive conflict over public education; the incident with ECMS is merely a forerunner of similar cultural clashes to come over education practices. In this cultural clash, the participants, both essentialists and progressives, feel their approach to learning and technological practices are in the interest of the children and youth of this district. If this situation is the context in which primary and secondary educators, administrators, related organizations, politicians, and activists must function, then it is necessary to perceive how such a context affects them. One fact is noteworthy: other problems with the learning process augmented by technological practices will arise and people associated with the public education process must understand that reality in today's cultural environment.

References

Alinsky, S. (1971). *Rules for Radicals*. New York: Vintage.
Chambers, E. & M. Cowan. (2003) *Roots for Radicals: Organizing for Power, Action, and Justice*. New York: Continuum.
Collins, P. (1990). *Black Feminist Thought: Knowledge, Consciousness, and the Politics of Empowerment*. New York: Allen and Unwin.
Dallas News (January 31, 2013). Under the dome. *DallasNews.com.*, p. 1.
Floyd, J. (September 15, 2013). Why can't Texas evolve beyond anti-science foolishness? *Dallas News.com*, p. 6.
Giroux, H. (2012) *Education and the Crisis of Public Values*. New York: Peter Lang.
Hirsch, E.D. (2009) *Making of America*. New Haven and London: Yale University Press.
Huntington, S. (1997) *Ciocnirea civilizatilor si refacerea ordinii mondiale*. Filipestii de Targ, Prahova, Romania: Editura Antet.
Instructional Strategies- History, nature, and categories of instructional strategies, instructional strategies and learner outcomes. Retrieved from http://educational.stateuniversity.com/pages/2099/Instructional-Strategies.html.
Larabee, D. (2004) *The Trouble With Ed Schools*. New Haven: Yale University Press.
Lareau, A. (2003) *Unequal Childhoods: Class, Race, and Family Life*. Berkeley: University of California Press.
Kessinger, T. (2011). Efforts toward educational reform in the United States since 1958: A review of seven major initiatives. *American Educational History Journal, 38*(1/2), pp. 263–276.

Peterson, P. (Ed). (2003) *Our Schools and Our Future*. Stanford: Hoover Institution Press.

Price, T., J. Duffy, & T. Giordani (2013) *Defending Public Education from Corporate Takeover*. New York: University Press of America.

Ravitch, D. (2010) *The Life and Death of the Great American School System: How Testing and Choice are Undermining Education*. New York: Basic Books.

Schutz, A. (2011). Power and trust in the public realm: John Dewey, Saul Alinsky, and the limits of progressive democratic education. *Educational Theory*, *61*(4), pp. 491–512.

Selk, A. (March 10, 2013) Third-party curriculum could soon be gone from Irving school district. *Dallas News.com*, p.1.

Topor, S., & Dinu, M.-S. (2014). Culture and e-learning–global challenges and perspectives. The 10th International Scientific Conference eLearning and software for Education, Bucharest, April 24–25. 10. 12753/2066-026X-14-308

CONTRIBUTORS

Bodi Anderson is an Assistant Professor of Educational Technology at Indian River State College. He spent eight years teaching at university and high school level in Japan. He received his Doctorate from Northern Arizona University in Curriculum and Instruction with a focus on Educational Technology, as well as his M.A. in applied linguistics with a focus on Computer Assisted Language Learning (CALL). His research agenda lies in cultural influences on online learning, game-based and virtual worlds learning, and inquiry into the online mini-mester.

Angela D. Benson is Associate Professor of Instructional Technology at the University of Alabama. Her research addresses the socio-cultural impact of learning technologies and technology-related teacher professional development. She has published in a variety of academic publications and is a frequent presenter at academic conferences. She holds a Ph.D. in Instructional Technology from the University of Georgia, an M.S. in Human Resource Development from Georgia State University, an M.S. in Operations Research and B.S. in Industrial Engineering from Georgia Tech, and a B.A. in Mathematics from Spelman College. She currently serves as President of the Culture, Learning, and Technology Division of the Association for Educational Communications and Technology (AECT).

Amy C. Bradshaw is Associate Professor of Instructional Psychology and Technology at the University of Oklahoma. Her scholarly interests include social and cultural implications of instructional technologies; visuals for learning and instruction; scaffolding higher order and critical thinking; and educational philosophy. Her teaching practice reflects commitment to integrating equity and social justice with instructional technology. In 2012, she received the University of Oklahoma's Jeannine Rainbolt College of Education Teaching and Advising Award. She has also received awards for outstanding publications and professional service. She currently serves as a Board Member at Large in AECT's Culture, Learning, and Technology Division.

Lequisha Brown-Joseph currently serves as an Associate Faculty Member for the University of Phoenix and for Walden University facilitating Bachelors and Masters level courses in the College of Education. She also works in the School of Advanced Studies as a dissertation chair and committee member. For more than 18 years, she has specialized in science education for grades 4–12. She holds a Ph.D. in Education, an M.A. in Urban Education and Multicultural Education, and a B.S. in Science Education.

Erik J. Byker is an Assistant Professor in the Department of Reading and Elementary Education at the University of North Carolina at Charlotte. Erik has conducted field studies in Cuba, England, Germany, India, South Korea, and the United States. His research surrounds the meanings and uses of educational technology among elementary school teachers and students.

Alison Carr-Chellman is the Dean of the College of Education at the University of Idaho and a Professor of Learning, Design, and Technology. She conducts research focused on systemic change, radical school reform, and disengaged learners. Her work includes potential innovations such as cyber charter schools and video gaming. She teaches courses in research method, diffusion of innovations, gaming to learn, instructional design for teachers, and teaching online in K-12 settings.

Kevin Clark is a Professor in the Division of Learning Technologies and the Founding Director of the Center for Digital Media Innovation and Diversity in the College of Education and Human Development at George Mason University. His research focuses on the role of interactive and digital media in education, broadening participation in STEM careers and disciplines, and issues of diversity in children's media. He has more than 20 years' experience as a designer, advisor, and consultant to informal learning and media organizations, and currently serves as the Strategic Advisor for Diversity in Children's Content Production to the Corporation for Public Broadcasting (CPB). He holds both a B.S. and M.S. in computer science from North Carolina State University and a Ph.D. in Instructional Systems from Pennsylvania State University.

James Diamond, Ph.D., is Senior Research Associate, at Educational Development Center, Inc.|Center for Children & Technology. He previously served as the lead evaluator on the NSF iDesign project and is currently the principal investigator for the NSF DRK-12-funded *Playing with the Data*, a project to learn how teachers use data from video games for formative assessment. His previous research and evaluation experiences include work on the Corporation for Public Broadcasting's American History and Civics Initiative, a multiyear evaluation of several game-based history and civics programs for middle schools; and the *Possible Worlds* project, a U.S. Department of Education project to develop handheld games to help students overcome misconceptions in science.

Zhetao Guo is an Instructional Designer in the Division of eLearning and Professional Studies at the University of Alabama at Birmingham. She provides instructional design support for UAB faculty and staff developing academic and continuing education online courses. She also provides faculty training and consulting for academic technologies. She earned her Ph.D. in Instructional Technology in 2015 at UAB. Prior to joining the doctoral program at Alabama, she worked at the University of Kansas where she taught Chinese language courses online and served as lead instructor for STARTALK national language learning program. Her research interests are in the areas of online and mobile learning.

Jason A. Engerman studies learning ecosystems towards student agency in creating educational pathways. Particularly, his research focuses on marginalized populations and the utility of indigenous knowledge. He has worked to unpack the cultural meanings, values, and social practices between boys and video games for the past four years.

Leshell Hatley is a passionate computer engineer, educator, and researcher who continuously combines these three attributes to create innovative approaches to teaching STEM concepts to students between the ages of 3 and 73. She is an Assistant Professor of Computer Science at Coppin State University and is the Founder and Executive Director of Uplift, Inc., a nonprofit organization whose mission embodies her passion. Over the past several years, Uplift's trailblazing work with students in the areas of robotics, mobile app development, and culturally relevant learning technology has provided inspiration, insight, and guidance to similar organization's across the globe.

Keith Heggart is an Organizer for the IEU NSW/ACT. He was a senior leader in independent, Catholic systemic and public schools in Australia and the UK. He is a Google Certified Teacher and an Apple Distinguished Educator. He is a doctoral student in education at the University of Technology, Sydney.

Akesha M. Horton, Ph.D., is an Instructor at Michigan State University in the College of Education. She is a Fulbright Scholar and NSF/AECT Early Career

Fellow. Her primary research interests explore the intersections between learning, technology, and culture for youth and young adults.

Roberto Joseph is an Associate Professor in the Department of Teaching, Learning and Technology, and is the Graduate Director of the Educational Technology program. His primary research interest centers on understanding how the combination of culture and instructional technology can improve student learning. He is a Gates Millennium Scholar and the Director for Project Promise, Teacher Opportunity Corps (TOC), a program funded by the New York State Education Department's Office of K-16 Initiatives and Access, which is designed to increase the number of historically underrepresented and economically disadvantaged individuals in teaching careers. He is also PI of the iDesign project, funded by NSF, to prepare middle schoolteachers to implement a culturally relevant curriculum in game design.

Mansureh Kebritchi is the Research Director of the Center for Educational and Instructional Technology Research; she holds a Ph.D. in Education, Instructional Technology. She has a wealth of experience in teaching, mentoring doctoral students to complete their dissertations, conducting research, and publishing and presenting the results in the field of instructional technology. She is interested in studying innovative ways to improve quality of teaching and learning in K-12, higher education, and corporate settings in online and face-to-face formats.

Neda Khalili Blackburn holds a Ph.D. in Instructional Technology from George Mason University and an M.S. in Computer Science from Johns Hopkins University. She has been involved in programs to encourage females towards the field of computer science and has worked on NSF-funded research projects in mathematics and cryptography. Most recently, she has worked on the NSF-funded project, Game Design through Mentoring and Collaboration, at George Mason University. Her research interests include encouraging youth towards STEM fields and creating educational programs focused on technology and computer programming.

Joi L. Moore is a Professor in the School of Information Science and Learning Technologies at the University of Missouri. In addition, she is a Core Faculty member in the MU Informatics Institute and an Affiliated Faculty in the Black Studies Department. She received her B.S. in Computer Science and M.S. in Management from North Carolina State University, both focusing on a minor in Management Information Systems. She earned her Ph.D. in Instructional Technology from the University of Georgia—with a cognate area of Management Information Systems. Her research areas include Human Computer Interaction, Usability Engineering, and Pedagogical Usability.

Yelim Mun is a Ph.D. student of Cognitive Psychology and Ergonomics at the University of Twente in the Netherlands. Yelim Mun currently conducts research on serious gaming for learning and training adaptability. Her previous research at Pennsylvania State University focused on video gaming for male students and knowledge structure validation for L1L2 setting.

Sandra G. Nunn, DM, MBA, is a Management Consultant, Executive, Board Member, and former diplomat with more than 30 years of experience in government and private industry. In addition, she serves as a Research Fellow with the Center for Educational and Instructional Technology Research at University of Phoenix where she focuses on research concerning leadership ethics, education, and technology. She also serves as an Associate Faculty member for the School of Advanced Studies at University of Phoenix. She holds a Doctor of Management in Organizational Leadership, an M.B.A. in Global Management, and a B.S. in Electronics Engineering Technology.

Gina M. Paige is co-founder of African-Ancestry, Inc., and a pioneer in tracing African lineages using genetics. She has worked with and revealed the roots of the world's leading icons, including Oprah Winfrey, John Legend, Spike Lee, Condoleezza Rice, and The King Family. Her work has been featured in hundreds of media outlets including *Time Magazine*, *USA Today*, *60 Minutes*, *NewsOne Now* with Roland Martin, *FOX Business News*, *Reuters*, *New York Times*, *Black Enterprise*, and NPR. She holds a degree in Economics from Stanford University, an M.B.A. from the University of Michigan Ross School of Business, and an Honorary Doctorate of Philosophy from Global Oved Dei Seminary University.

Deepak Prem Subramony is Associate Professor of Educational Technology in the Department of Curriculum and Instruction at Kansas State University. He holds a Ph.D. in Instructional Systems Technology from Indiana University Bloomington, and taught at Utah State University and Grand Valley State University before arriving at K-State in 2015. A past President of Minorities in Media, his scholarly interests include exploring issues related to equitable access to educational technology, the impact of educational technology on minority and non-Western learners, and the culturally cognizant practice of educational technology.

Michelle Susberry Hill, Ed.D, is an online facilitator for the University of Phoenix. She teaches Models and Theories of Education and is a Dissertation Chair for students working on their Doctorates. Her interests are in the advancement of education with the use of technology and social media. She holds a Doctorate in Curriculum and Instruction, a Masters Degree in the Teaching of Reading, and an undergraduate degree in Economics.

Joseph (Joe) M. Terantino (Ph.D., University of South Florida; Second Language Acquisition & Instructional Technology) is Director of the Language Resource Center at Brown University. His expertise lies in teaching methodology, second language acquisition, and computer-assisted language learning. He is a passionate user and researcher of instructional technology and social media who enjoys the challenge of tinkering with new technologies. In particular, his research interests relate to computer-assisted language learning, foreign language education, and the integration of technology in teaching.

Michael K. Thomas is a member of the faculty in the Department of Educational Psychology at the University of Illinois at Chicago. His research focuses on the philosophical and cultural dimensions of instructional design and technology.

Steven Watkins is a Research Fellow in the Center for Educational and Instructional Technology Research. He has been associated with the center for two years and has taught at the University of Phoenix for over 11 years. He is a Senior Humanities Professor with the university; he holds a Ph.D. in Comparative Literature from the University of Texas at Arlington. He has written a book on the relationship between the short story writer Flannery O'Connor and the philosopher Teilhard de Chardin. He has written articles on technology, religion, writing, philosophy, and other fields of study in the humanities.

Cynthia E. Winston-Proctor is Professor of Psychology and Principal Investigator of the Identity and Success Research Laboratory at Howard University. Also, she is Principal of Winston Synergy L.L.C., a psychology consulting firm. Her research and practice work focus on the psychology of success within the lives of women and African Americans. With her collaborators, she has designed culturally responsive behavioral cybersecurity and computational thinking STEM education models. She is President of the Society of STEM Women of Color and Co-Principal Investigator of HU ADVANCE-IT. She earned a B.S. from Howard University and Ph.D. from the University of Michigan.

Shulong Yan is a Ph.D. student of Learning, Design, and Technology at the Pennsylvania State University. She holds a Masters Degree in Childhood Education & TESOL. Her research interests include design thinking, games and learning, computer-supported collaborative learning, and the design of learning environments. Currently, she is working on developing an informal collaborative design environment for K-12 children.

INDEX

Note: italic page numbers indicate tables and figures; numbers in brackets preceded by *n* are chapter endnote numbers.

Abe, D. 62
Abu-Al-Aish, A. 187
accountability 214–215
ACTFL (American Council on Teaching Foreign Languages) 76
ADHD (Attention Deficit Hyperactivity Disorder) 165
Adorno, T.W. 46, 48
adult education 31, 52
AECT (Association of Educational Communications and Technology) 1; Culture, Learning and Technology (CLT) Division 1, 32–34, 35, 39; *Handbook of Research on Educational Communications and Technology* 36; inattention to cultural diversity by 35–36; journal of *see ETR&D*; revised definition of IT by (2007) 30–31
African-American scholars 31
African-American students 5; and game design 197–198; and genetic technology/ancestry 118, 120–121; learning styles/culture of (afro-cultural ethos) 112–113, *see also* computational thinking
Akour, H. 180
Akyol, Z. 92, 104
Alcoff, L.M. 21
Alessio, J. 62

Alinsky, S. 216
Altman, D.G. 99
America 2049 (game) 152
American Council on Teaching Foreign Languages (ACTFL) 76
Anakwe, U.P. 96
Anderson, J.E. 188
Anderson, T. 136, 139, 140, *141*
Andrzejewski, J. 62
anti-test movement 216
Aoki, K. 97–98, 100
Appiah, Kwame 60–61
Apple iPhone 30
Apple, M.W. 47, 51–52
Archer, W. 93, 136, 139, 140, *141*
Arroyo-González, R. 127
Asia 32, 91, 94, 95, 96, *see also* Japan
Asia Society 61
Association of Educational Communications and Technology *see* AECT
Attention Deficit Hyperactivity Disorder (ADHD) 165
audio visual technology *18*
Australia, hip-hop in *see* hip-hop culture
authenticity 11, 13–14
authoritarian models of education 11, 12

Bandura, A. 133
banking model of education 14, *15*

Barbour, M.K. 52
Barnes, B.C. 185, 187, 188
Bauman, Z. 44, 45
BBS (Bulletin Board Systems) 129
Bennett, M.J. 75, 76–77, 85
bilingual education 219–220
Black Cultural Ethos (BCE) 116, 120, *121*
blogs 65, 66, 129
Blum, L. 130
Bonk, C. 95, 98, 99
Bourdieu, P. 136, 137, 140, *141*
Bowers, C.A. 29, 33
Boykin, A.W. 112–113, 120
boys 165–176; and ADHD 165; crisis in education for 6, 165–166, 174, 175; culture of 166–170, 175, 176; and feminine ethos of schools 168, 169, 175; and identity formation 166, 167, 169, 170, 171; and incompatibility of school system 166, 168–170, 175; and literacy 170, 172; and male role models 166–167, 168; and peer relationships 166, 167; and *rough and tumble* play 166, 167–168, 169, 170, 175; and social norms 167, 170, 171; and teacher assessment/No Child Left Behind policy 169–170; underperformance of 6, 165–166; and Zero Tolerance policies 168, 169
boys and video games 6, 168, 170–176; and agency 171; as autonomous environment 174; and collaborative/competitive environment 171, 173–174; and emotional literacy 173; and English language Arts Literacy Standards 172; implications for schools of 174–176; learning potential of 172, 175, 176; and peer interaction/teamwork 171, 174; as positive tool of engagement 171; and simulated aggressive play 173, 174; and situated learning spaces/opportunities 171–173; and violence 170–171
Bradshaw, A. 37
brainstorming *122*, *123*, 129, 154
Bray, E. 97–98, 100
Brennan, K. 156
Bridges, T. 63
Brush, T. 93
Buckingham, D. 47
bulletin boards 129
Bullock, M. 136
bullying *161*
business 52, 53, 128, 131, 132, 138, 215

camera phones 30
Caribbean 31
Chambers, E. 216–217
Chernoff, J.M. 59
China 94
Chinese international students 180, 181, 189, see also mobile learning and Chinese international students
Cho, M.O. 76
Christensen, E.W. 96
citizenship 12; active 71; global see global citizenship
civil rights movement 130
Clark, K.A. 31, 32
CMC (Computer-Mediated Communication) 92, 93, 102
co-creation of knowledge 9, 11, 13, 14
cognitive development 14, *15*, 133–134
cognitive presence 139
collaborative constructionist approach 93
collaborative learning 5, 92–93, 97, 98, 100; defined 2; fact-/skill-oriented 172; formal/informal 2–3; intentional/incidental 3; meaningful, characteristics of 3; and social media/cultural competency 133–134, 136, 138, 140, *141*; and video games 168, 171, 173–174, 196, 202–203, 208
collective liberation 22
collectivist cultures 94, 95–96, 99, 104
Collins, P. 217
communalism 113, 120, *121*
communication context 93, 94, 95, 96, 97, 100, 102, 103, 104
communication skills 122, 153, see also cross-cultural communication
Community of Inquiry, Model of 136, 139, 140, *141*
computational thinking (CT) 5, 109–123, 156; and CRP 112, 113, 115, 116, 120–121; and CRT 111–112, 113, 115–116, 120; and cultural modeling design principles 113–116, *114*, 120; described/history of 110; and empowerment *114*, 116, 120, 121; pilot study on see CS2; socio-cultural approach to 109, 111, 112–113, 115, 119; and students of color 109, 110–111, 112–113; theoretical framework for 113
computer programming skills 5, 109, 111, 121–122, 153, 156, 197, see also iDesign
Computer-Mediated Communication (CMC) 92, 93, 102

constructivism 5, 6, 44, 197, 202; critical 16, *18*
constructivist/constructionist learning environment 6, 162
Cooke, S. 154
Cooper, H. 132
Cowan, M. 216–217
Creswell, J.W. 78
critical consciousness 9–10, 11, 12, 17, 60, 70, 155–156
Critical Cosmopolitan Theory 4–5, 58, 60–62, *61*, 69–71
critical pedagogy 4, 8–25; and CLT 8–9, 20, 24; and co-creation of knowledge 9, 11, 13, 14; and critical consciousness 9–10, 11, 12, 17; and cultural competence 20, 21, 24, 25; and dialogue/trust/critical humility/radical love 11–12; and educational technology *see* critical pedagogy and educational technology; and empowerment 9, 10, 12, 14, *15*, 16, *18*, 19, *19*, 21, 25; and equity 9, 16–17, 19–25; and ethics 8, 9, 17; and freedom 13–14, 23; and inclusion 8, 14, 17, 19–25; issues encompassed by, overview of 9; key concepts/themes in 9–15; and myth of neutrality 12; as political 12–13, *18*, 24; and praxis *see* praxis; and social justice 9, 12, *15*, 16–17, *18*, *19*, 22, 23; and transformation 14–15, *15*, *19*
critical pedagogy and educational technology 8, 15–25; and critical reflection 21–24; and naming/further learning 20–21; philosophical orientations of 15, 16, *18*; priorities of 15, 16–17, *18*; reconciling the fields of 19–25; stances regarding core concerns 15, 17–19; tensions/resonances in 15–19, *18*–*19*; and transformation 22, 24–25
critical scholars 39–40(*n*3)
critical theory 9, *18*, 48, 53–55, *54*, 55
Cross, T. 155–156
Cross-Cultural Collaborations 137, 139, 140, *141*
cross-cultural communication 127, 130, 131, 132, 138–139, *141*, 144
CRP *see* Culturally Relevant Pedagogy
CRP (Culturally Relevant Pedagogy) 112, 113, 115, 116, 120–121, *153*, 163; defined 152, 155
CRT (Critical Race Theory) 55

CRT (culturally responsive teaching) 5, 111–112, 113, 115–116, 120
CS2 (computational thinking pilot study) 111, 116–121; and BCE 116, 120, *121*; communalism in 120; CRC goals in 115, 119; CRT in 120; curriculum 118, *118*–*119*, 122; data collection in 117; empowerment/self-pride in 116, 120, 121; genetic technology/African ancestry in 118, 119, 120–121; instructional strategies in *122*; learner activities in 122–123, *123*; overview of 116–117; problem-solving in 121–122; psychological tests in 119; results/conclusions of 120–123, *122*–*123*; and Scratch programming environment 116, 117, *117*, 119, 123
CSEd (Computer Science Education) 109, 115–116, 123
CSTA (Computer Science Teachers Association) 110
CT *see* computational thinking
Cuban, L. 29, 48
Cultural Capital Theory 136, 137, 140, *141*
cultural clashes 212–213, *see also* essentialist–progressivist clash in education
cultural competency 5, 130–131, 155; benefits of 138; and critical pedagogy 20, 21, 24, 25; defined/described 130; manifestations/strategies of 130; and social media *see* social media and cultural competency; theories 135–137, 140, *141*, 142
cultural dimensions model 93–94
cultural diversity 1, 20–21, 52, 113, 120, 130, 131, 136, 139; deficit perceptions of 36–37, 39; defined 39(*n*1); inattention to *see* instructional technology (IT) community and cultural diversity
cultural identity 77, 116, 123
cultural knowledge 112, 131, 136, 137, *141*, 142, 198
cultural modeling design principles 113–116, *114*, 120
cultural scaffolding 111, 113
culture: and computational thinking *see* computational thinking; defined 2, 39(*n*1), 93–95, 113, 130; and educational technology 8, 20, 29, 48–49; pop- *see* hip-hop music; and technology adoption/usage 6

culture dimensions model 93
cultures of silence 12, 21
Cultures-of-Use Theory 136, 137, 140, *141*
curricula, hidden/null 21
Curtis, D.D. 98–99

Davies, I. 66
Davis, E.A. 201–202
Davis, N. 76
de Mooij, M. 128
democracy 9, 11, 12, 51, 214, 216–217
Designing Effective Instruction (Morrison/Rose/Kemp) 36–37
Detroit 70, 71
development 45, 49–50
Dewey, J. 62, 172, 175, 212, 213–214
dialectical engagement 11, 14, 22
Dickson-Deane, C. 33
Diffusion of Innovations Theory 30, 136, 138, 140, *141*
Digital Divide 29, 30
Dinu, M.-S. 213
DiPietro, J.A. 167
discourse analysis 81, 98–99
discrimination 13, *161*
distance learning 51–52, 91–105; and CMC 92, 93, 102; collaborative 92–93, 97, 98, 100, 103–104; and communication context 93, 94, 95, 96, 97, 100, 102, 103, 104; and cultural dimensions model 93–97, 99, 100, 104–105; defined 92; and individualism–collectivism context 93, 94, 95–96, 97, 99, 100, 101, 102, 103, 104; in Japan 97–98; and power distance 93, 94–95, 96, 97, 99, 100, 101, 102, 103, 104; social constructivist-based models of 5, 91–92, 93, 97, 99, 104–105; and social interaction 92, 98, 102, 103, *103*; studies on, review of 95–97; study, data analysis in 99–100; study, implications/recommendations from 104–105; study, limitations of 104; study, methodology of 98–99; study, participants in 94, 97, 98; study, results 100–103, *102–103*; in U.S. 94, 95, 96, 97, 104
Dlugosh, L. 97–98, 100
Donaldson, R.L. 182, 184
Druin, A. 197
Duffy, J. 215
Duncan-Andrade, J.M.R. 62
Durkheim, E. 136
Dynamic Social Impact Theory 135

ECAR Study of Undergraduate Students (2013) 182
education: and critical consciousness 60; privatization/commodification of *19*, 52; purpose of *19*
educational and communications technologies (ECT) 29–32; and AECT's CLT Division 32–34; and AECT's journal *see ETR&D*; in AECT's revised definition 30–31; culturally cognizant products/initiatives 32; and democratization of knowledge 33; and Minorities in Media 31–32; sociocultural impact of 29, 32, 39; ubiquity/affordability in 30; and Young's Culture Based Model 32
Educational Curriculum Management System (ECMS) 217, 218–220, 221
educational technology implementation 47, 48; performative 52–54, *53*, 54, 55
Educational Technology (journal) 28, 32, 36, 38
Edwards, K. 144
egalitarianism 212, 215
ElectroCity (game) 152
emotional intelligence 119, *119*, *122*, 123, 167
empowerment: and computational thinking *114*, 116, 120, 121; and critical pedagogy 9, 10, 12, 14, *15*, 16, *18*, 19, *19*, 21, 25; and cultural diversity 31, 38
English language Arts Literacy Standards 172
epistemology 16; of ignorance 21
Epstein, D. 168
equity/equitable access 1, 29, 30, 40(*n*4); and critical pedagogy 9, 16–17, 19–25; and literacy 22, *see also* instructional technology (IT) community and cultural diversity
essentialism 6, *18*, 23, 212; and "factual knowledge" 213; and school reform movement 216, 217, 218, 219–222, 223
Essentialist Movement 216, 217, 218, 219–222, 223
essentialist–progressivist clash in education 212–223; and bilingual program 219–220; and business model 215; case study 217–222; case study, background to 218–219; case study, participants in 218; case study, research questions 217; case study, results/discussion 219–222; and cultural clashes in society 212–213,

222–223; and ECMS 217, 218–220, 221; literature review 213–217; and politics/"real world" 216–217; and school infrastructure 220; and school reform/anti-test movements 216; and standards/accountability 214–215; and technological adoption 221–222
ethnic diversity 113, 120
ethnocentrism 36, 77, 83, *83*, 84, *84*, 86
ETR&D (Educational Technology Research and Development, AECT's journal) 34, 35; inattention to cultural diversity in 35–36
Evans, J.M. 62
Expectation States Theory 135

Facebook 33, 129, 144, 152
fairness 9, 19, 40, 50–51, *see also* equity/equitable access
Fang, L. 97
Feenberg, A. 48
foreign language learning *see* online cultural learning modules
formal learning 2–3, 14
free market/trade 50–51
freedom 13–14, 50; negative 13, 23–24
Freire, Paolo 10–12, 14, 19, 60, 61, 70
Friedman, T.L. 30, 36
futurism 49–50
fuzzy sets 2

GAFE (Google Apps for Education) 64
Gallegos, J.S./Gallegos, S.A. 130, 136, 142
Game Maker 197, 199, 200
game-based learning 5, 6, 152, *see also* iDesign
Gamestar Mechanic (game/online community) 153, 154, *155*, 160
Garrett-Rucks, P. 78, 81, 82, 88
Garrison, D.R. 92, 93, 104, 136, 139, 140, *141*
Gay, G. 113, 116, 120, 152
GDMC (Game Design through Mentoring and Collaboration) 197–198
gender 20; and academic achievement 165–166; and mobile learning 183–184
genetic technology 118, 120–121
Gilbert, R./Gilbert, P. 166–167
Giordani, T. 215
Giroux, H.A. 9–10, 215
global citizenship 33, 58, 59, 60, 61, 62, 63, 65; plural/parallel allegiances in 66
global competency 60, 61; defined 76; and intercultural sensitivity 76–77

Global Kids, Inc. 152, 158
globalization 4, 28, 30, 38, 44–55, 63, 213; and culture 48–49, 75; and development/progress 45–46; and educational technology 44, 45–46, 48, 54, 55; and empowerment/disempowerment 44–45; and state/corporate interests 45; and virtual schools 51–52
Goodrich, K. 128
GPS (Global Positioning System) 156
Greene, M. 13
group identities 21, 120
Gun-Free Schools Act (1994) 169
Gunawardena, C.N. 96

Habermas, J. 46–47, 48
Haenlein, M. 129
Hagenson, L. 76
Hall, E.T. 93, 95, 100
handheld devices *see* mobile technologies
Hanson, C. 135
Harel, I. 199, 203
Harmon, R. 216, 217
Harton, H.C. 136
Harvey, D. 50
Hawthorne effect 88
hegemony 10, 13, 35, 38
Heidegger, M. 45–46, 48
Heilman, E.E. 66, 68
hidden/null curricula 21
hierarchies 12–13
Hill, D. 51
hip-hop culture 4–5, 58–71; compassion in 65, 66–67; course in (*Hip-Hop for Global Justice*) 5, 63–71; creativity in 65, 68–69; and critical consciousness 60, 61, 62, 69, 70–71; and Critical Cosmopolitan Theory 58, 60–62, *61*, 69–71; defined 58–60; five elements of 59; future research on 71; and global citizenship 58, 59, 60, 61, 62, 63, 65, 66; and global competency 60, 61; and ill-literacy 69; and indigenous communities 64, 65; literature review of 62–63; and marginalized communities/social justice 59–60, 71; multimodal media in 63; and pedagogy 62, 63; research gaps in 62; research on, data collection/analysis 64–65; research on, findings 65–69; research on, methods 63–65; research on, questions in 63; and rewriting the world 60, 61, 62, 70–71; as second

orality 62; and social/political change 62, 66, 68, 69, 70; and technology 58, 63, 65, 71
Hirsch, E.D. 214
Hispanic students 110, 219–220
Hofstede, G. 93–94, 99, 113; Cultural Dimensions Theory of 136, 138, 140, 141
hooks, b. 13, 14
Horkheimer, M. 46, 48, 55
Howland, J. 3
Huang, W.D. 143
humility, critical 11
Hung, H.T. 144
Hunt-Gómez, C.I. 127
Huntington, S. 213

Ibrahim, A. 62
iDesign 5, 151–163; computational thinking in 156, 157, 158; constructionist principles in 162; and critical consciousness 155–156; and CRP 152, 153, 155, 163; and cultural competency 155; culturally relevant themes/activates in 155–156; game design principles in 154–155, 154; and *Gamestar Mechanic* 153, 154, 155, 160; and Maker Movement 162–163; model/curriculum 152–157, 153, 156, 157; overview 151–152; results of 158–160, 159; and Scratch interface 153, 156, 157, 160; student-designed game ideas in 160–162, 161; and Tic-Tac-Toe/Rock, Paper, Scissors 154, 158–160
ignorance, epistemologies of 21
ill-literacy 69
Immune Attack (science game) 199
inclusion/inclusivity 1, 5; and critical pedagogy 8, 14, 17, 19–25
indigenous communities 64
individualism–collectivism dimension 93, 94, 95–96, 97, 99, 100, 101, 102, 103, 104
Industrial Areas Foundation 216
informal learning 2, 5, 109
information exchange/sharing 5, 33, 128, 140
information technology 137, 152, 181, 222; teaching 5
innovation 14, 30; and globalization 45, 47; and performative implementation 4, 52–53

Institute of International Education 180–181
Institute of Play 154
Instruction, Merrill's First Principles of 5
instructional design 1, 3; and critical theory 48
instructional strategies 3
instructional technology (IT) community and cultural diversity 4, 28–39; and AECT's CLT Division 32–34; and AECT's journal see *ETR&D*; in AECT'S revised definition 30–31; continuing issues with 34–37; and *Designing Effective Instruction* 36–37; and Digital Divide/inequitable access 29, 30; and ECT see educational and communications technologies; and ethical practice/appropriate solutions 31; and ethnocentric bias 36; future for 37–39; and globalized/"flat" world 30, 36; and graduate programs 37, 39; and ISTE's 14 Essential Conditions 38; and K–12 courses 31, 33, 38; and Minorities in Media (MIM) 31–32, 39; overview of papers on 28; products/initiatives 32; and reformist scholars 28, 33, 34, 38
intercultural sensitivity 5, 75–89; description/model of 77, 77, 78, 81, 85; developing 78, 85–86; Developmental Model of 77, 77, 78, 81, 85; and ethnocentrism/ethnorelativism 77, 83–85, 83, 84, 86; and global competency 76–77; and native speaker perspectives 75, 82, 87–88; study, data analysis in 81–82, 82; study, data collection in 81; study, evaluation of 88–89; study, implications for future of 89; study, limitations of 88; study, online cultural module in 75–76, 77, 79–80, 79, 86–87; study, overview of 78–80; study, participants in 81; study, post-module statements in 84–85; study, pre-module statements in 82–84; study, results of 82–88
International Society for Technology in Education (ISTE) 38, 40(n7)
international students 91, 180–181, see also mobile learning and Chinese international students
Internet 131, 154, 156, 220; and cultural diversity 30, 33–34; lesson plans/exams on 218, see also social media; Web 2.0

intersectionality 13, 22
IT (information technology) 137, 152, 181, 222
IT (instructional technology) *see* instructional technology (IT) community and cultural diversity

Jackson, A. 61
Jamison, P.K. 29
Januszewski, A. 8, 31
Japan 5, 71, 92, 94, 97–105
Jonassen, D.H. 3
Joseph, R. 32, 38
Journal of Negro Education 31–32
Jung, I. 97, 102

Kafai, Y. 154, 199, 203
Kaplan, A.M. 129
Karahanna, E. 138
Kim, K. 95, 98, 99
Kindlon, D. 167, 169, 173
knowledge: and citizenship 71; co-creation 9, 11, 13, 14; construction 3, *15*, 92, 93, 134; cultural 112, 131, 136, 140, *141*, 198; democratization of 33; prior 114–115, *114*, 198; traditional/local 51
Koch, G.G. 99
Kramsch, C. 76
Ku, H. 96
Kvasny, L. 137
K–12 education 3, 31, 33, 38, 52, 152; and boys 165, 169; and computational thinking 110, 111; and video games 196, 197

L-Fresh (hip-hop artist) 54
Ladson-Billings, Gloria 112, 115, 155
Laincz, J. 183
Landis, J.R. 99
laptops/tablets 30
Lareau, A. 217
Lawson, M.J. 98–99
Lea, M. 136, 137, 140, *141*
learning management systems 3, 98, 183, 192, 193
learning technology *see* technology, educational/instructional
Lee, C.D. 113–114, *114*, 115, 120, 198
Lekhanya, L.M. 138
Liang, A. 96
liberation ethics 9, *18*

Lifelong Kindergarten (MIT Media Lab) 156
linguaculture/languaculture 76
LinkedIn 33
Listserv 129
literacy 51, 170, 172; emotional 173; new/ill- 58, 63, 69; technological 5, 152
Livingstone, D.W. 2
Loflin, J.H. 62
LOGO 197, 199
love, radical 1–12
Love, S. 187

McBride, K. 78
Macedo, D. 11–12
McJulien, W.J. 31, 33
McQueen, R.J. 96, 187, 188
Malaysia 49, 53
Malone, C. 59
Mandal, D. 187, 188
Mansilla, V.B. 61
Marcuse, H. 46, 48
market forces 50–51
Marra, R.M. 3
Martinez Jr, G. 59
Martinez, S.L. 163
mathematics teaching *see* STEM education
Matusky, R. 129
Merriam, S.B. 64
Merrill, M.D. 5, 79
Messick, S. 53
Mexico 96
Middle East 91
Minorities in Media (MIM) 31–32, 39; and AECT's CLT Division 32–33
MIT (Massachusetts Institute of Technology) 154, 156
Mitchell, K. 137–138
Mitchell, T. 60
mobile learning and Chinese international students 6, 180–193; and age 184, 193; and behavioral intention/use behavior 188–189, 193; data collection in study 181, 182; and effort expectancy 187, 190, 193; and experience level 185, 190, 193; and facilitating conditions 188, 190, 193; and gender 183–184, 190, 193; limitations of study 189; methods in study 181–182; participants in study 182–183; and performance expectancy 186–187, 193; recommendations for future 192–193;

recommendations for practice 191–192; research gap for 181, 189–190; and social influence 187–188, 193; use of mobile devices 183; UTAUT framework for study 181–182, 189, 191, 193; and voluntary/required use 185–186, 190
mobile technologies 30, 78, 129, 180, 181
modernity 49
Moldenda, M. 8, 31
Moody, M. 144
Moore, J.L. 3, 31
Morino, M. 29
Morrell, E. 62
MUD (Multiuser Dungeon) 129
multicultural awareness 138, 140, *141*, 142
multiculturalism 64, 130

Nakane, I. 100
Nat Turner, K.C. 63
National Science Foundation (NSF) 151, 158
Native American students 110–111, 113
native speakers 75, 82, 87–88
neoliberalism 4, 50–51, 52, *53*, 54, 55
neutrality, myth of 12, 21, 23
New York State After-School Network (NYSAN) 152
New York, urban youth project in *see* iDesign
Nicholson, K. 201
No Child Left Behind policy 40(*n*6), 169–170, 212, 214
Nolla, A.C. 96
NSF (National Science Foundation) 151, 158
NYSAN (New York State After-School Network) 152

online cultural learning modules 75–76, 77, 79–80, *79*, 86–87
online discussion boards 75, 78, 81, 99
online games *see* video games

Pac-Man 201
Papert, S. 197, 208
Partnership for 21st Century Schools 52, 53
peer mentoring 197–198, 199, 202, 294
Pellegrini, A.D. 168
Pennycook, A. 59, 60, 62

performance-based policies 215
performative implementation 4, 52–54, *53*, 54, 55
Peterson, P. 214
Pike, G. 66
Planned Behavior Theory 133, 134
podcasts 33
political pedagogy 12–13, *18*, 24
positivism 16, *18*, 25
Posner, G.K. 206
postmodernism 55
Powell, G.C. 28, 32, 36
power distance 93, 94–95, 96, 97, 99, 100, 101, 102, 103, 104
power structures 13, *18*, 23, 60, 62
praxis 10–11, 12, 17, 19–25; and critical reflection 21–24; and input/engagement/support 22; and naming/further learning 20–21; and reading lists 21–22; and self-reflection/-interrogation 22–24
Prensky, M. 197
Price, T. 215
primatology 168
prior knowledge 114–115, *114*, 198
privilege, unearned 13, 21, 22, 24
problem-solving 14, 79, 117, 121–122, 123, 212, 219; and gender 165; and video games 172, 196
process/product technologies 3
professional development 3, 22
progressive educational theory 6, 9–10, *18*, 212, 213–214; and essentialist theory *see* essentialist–progressivist clash in education
Puerto Rico 54, 76, 79, *79*, 80, *80*, 81, 83–84, *84*, *161*

race/racism 20–21, 22, 23, 60, 156
Ragan, T.J. 44
Ravitch, David 215
Reeves, T. 92
Reeves, T.C. 52
Reigeluth, C. 37–38
religion 70
Resnick, M. 154, 156
rewriting the world 60, 61, 62, 70–71
Risager, K. 76
Roaf, M. 29
Robertson, J. 201
Rodriguez, S. 127
Rogers, E.M. 30, 136, 138, 140, *141*
Rusk, N. 154

Salisbury, L. 183
Samy Alim, H. 59, 60, 62, 64, 69
Sawyer, R.K. 207
school reform movement (Essentialist Movement) 216, 217, 218, 219–222, 223
Schutz, A. 212, 214, 216, 217
science games *see* student-designed science games
science teaching *see* STEM education
Scott, K.A. 115
Scratch (programming environment) 116, 117, *117*, 119, 123, 197; and iDesign 153, 156, *157*, 160
self-assessment *119*, 131, 136, 156
self-awareness 11, 63
self-interrogation 9, 11, 22–24
Serben, D.F. 187, 188
Sernhede, O. 63
Shattuk, K. 91
SIDE model 136, 137, 140, *141*
Small, A.W. 172
Smart Schools project 53
Smith, J.J. 183
Smith, P.L. 44
So, H.J. 93
Social Capital Theory 136, 137, 140, *141*
social constructionism 5, 91–92, 93, 97, 99, 104–105; and social media 133, 134
social Darwinism 50–51
Social Identity Theory 135, 136–137, 140, *141*
Social Impact Theory 135
social interaction: and distance learning 92, 98, 102, 103, *103*
social justice 59–60, 71, 156, 214, 216; and critical pedagogy 9, 12, *15*, 16–17, *18*, *19*, 22, 23, 25; and educational technology 47, 51
Social Learning Theory 133
social media 58, 127–145, 188; and cultural diversity 30, 33–34; theories 133–136
social media and cultural competency 5, 127–144; background to 128–131; and communication gap 128; and cross-cultural communication 127, 130, 131, 132, 137–138, 138–139, *141*, 143; educational/business benefits of 127, 131, 132; integration, five elements of 131; literature review 131–144; literature review, contributions/implications of 144–145; literature review, data collection/analysis 132–133; literature review, methodology 132; literature review, overview 131–132; literature review, recommendations from 142–143; literature review, research questions 132, 140–142; literature review, theories of cultural competency 135–136, 142; literature review, theories of integration 136–139, 140, *141*; literature review, theories of social media 133–135
Social Presence Theory 133, 135
Social Systems Theory 135, 136
socio-cultural approach 109, 111, 115, 119, 156
sociopolitical educational approach 10, 155–156
Söderman, J. 63
Southwestern State School District 219–222, 223
Spanish language learning *see* online cultural learning modules
Spears, R. 136, 137, 140, *141*
Spelke, E.S. 165
Spencer-Oatey, H. 2
Srite, M. 138
Stager, G. 163
Stavrias, G. 64
STEM (science, technology, engineering, mathematics) education 11, 109, 110, 165; and African American students 208; and game design *see* student-designed science games; and iDesign 151, 152, 154, 158, 162, 163
storytelling 116
Storytelling Alice 197
student engagement 1, 11, 14, *see also* social media and cultural competency
student-centered learning 92, 97, 104
student-designed science games 196–209; and African American students 197–198, 199, 208; as constructivist learning environment 197, 202; and gender 199; and peer mentoring 197–198, 199, 202, 294; study, coding/memo-writing in 200; study, collaboration in 202–203, 208; study, conceptual change in 206; study, findings 200–207; study, Game Design Journals in 199–200, 201, 209; study, implications for science learning 207–208; study, information-gathering

in 201–202, 207, 209; study, iterative design cycle in 200–201, 204, 207; study, overview 198; study, participants 199; study, prior knowledge in 198, 201, 208–209; study, questions in 201; study, understanding of topic in 203–207; subject matter expert in 199, 202, 204, 205, 209
summer camps 109, 116–117
Suzuki, K. 97, 102
systems thinking 153, *153*, 154

Taiwan 49, 96
Tajfel, H. 136–137, 140, *141*
TaleBlazer (games platform) 153, 156, *157*
Tapscott, D. 29
teachers: and critical pedagogy 11–12; and gender 167; performance assessments for 169–170
teachers' union 221–222
teaching presence 139
technological adoption/usage 6
technological fluency 5, 152, 153, 154
technological literacy 5, 152
technological sublime 4, 49–50, 52, *53*, 54, 55
technology, educational/instructional 45–48; and business/competition 52, 53; and critical pedagogy *see* critical pedagogy and educational technology; critical theory of 48, 53–55, *54*, 55; and culture 8, 20, 29, 48–49, 52; defined 3–4, 8, 30–31; and diversity *see* instructional technology (IT) community and cultural diversity; and essentialist/progressive theories 6; and ethical responsibility 8; and globalization 44, 45–46, 48; implementation of 47, 48; instrumentalist/substantive view of 46–47, 49; and local knowledge/autonomy 51–52; and neoliberalism 50–51, 52, *53*, 54, 55; and pedagogical usability 4; and power 29; product/process 3; and virtual schools 51–52, *see also* computational thinking; instructional technology (IT) community; STEM education
Tempest in Crescent City (game) 152
Terkourafi, M. 62
Thompson, L. 96
Thompson, M. 167, 169, 173
Thorne, S.L. 137, 140, *141*
Tibenderana, P. 187
Tindall, C. 130

Tolkein, J.R.R. 46
transformative/transmissive education 14–15, *15*, *19*, 22, 24–25
Treux III, D. 137
trust 11, 12
Turkey 49
Turner, J.C. 136–137, 140, *141*
Twitter 33, 129, 144

university students *see* intercultural sensitivity; international students
urban youth development project *see* iDesign
Usenet 129
UTAUT (Unified Theory of Acceptance and Use of Technology) 6, 135, 181, 189, 191, 193

Vanneste, D. 187
Vasquez, M. 29
Venkatesh, V. 181, 182, 186–187, 188
video games 6, 129, 196–197; and boys *see* boys and video games; and collaborative learning 168, 171, 173–174, 196; and iterative design cycle 200–201, 204, 207; and literacy 172; and problem-solving 172, 196; students as designers of *see* student-designed science games; and violence 170–171, *see also* iDesign
virtual schools 51–52
Vygotsky, L.S. 92–93, 133–134, 136–137, 139, 140, *141*

Wang, H. 184
Wang, Y. 184, 187
Web 2.0 33–34, 78, 129, 138
Weber, M. 45
West, Kanye 68, 69
Wikipedia 202, 207
Wildner-Bassett, M. 78
Wing, Jeannette 110
Woo, Y. 92
workshops 22, 23
Wu, M.Y. 185

Yarnall, L. 200
Yoo, S.J. 143
Young, P.A. 32, 34, 48, 105
YouTube 64, 129, 144, 201
Yuen, S.C.Y. 144

Zero Tolerance policies 168, 169
Zone of Proximal Development model 92

CPSIA information can be obtained
at www.ICGtesting.com
Printed in the USA
LVHW051043130120
643366LV00008B/188/P